ELLEN GLASGOW

Centennial Essays

Edited by M. Thomas Inge

University Press of Virginia

Charlottesville

THE UNIVERSITY PRESS OF VIRGINIA
Copyright © 1976 by the Rector and Visitors
of the University of Virginia

First published 1976

The essays "Glasgow, Cabell, and Richmond," by Edgar E.
MacDonald, and "Glasgow and the Southern Renaissance" by
Dorothy Scura, first appeared in the *Mississippi Quarterly,* 27
(Fall 1974). Copyright by Mississippi State University. Reprinted
by permission of the editor. The essay by C. Hugh Holman first
appeared as "April in Queenborough: Ellen Glasgow's
Comedies of Manners" in the *Sewanee Review,* 82 (Spring
1974). Copyright by the University of the South. Reprinted
by permission of the editor. Portions of the bibliographical essay
by Edgar E. MacDonald first appeared as "Ellen Glasgow: An
Essay in Bibliography" and "Biographical Notes on Ellen
Glasgow," *Resources for American Literary Study,* 2
(Autumn 1972), and 3 (Autumn 1973). Copyright by
Resources for American Literary Study, Inc. Reprinted by
permission of the editors. Permission to quote from Ellen
Glasgow's published works has been granted by the
Richmond SPCA and Harcourt Brace Jovanovich, Inc.

Library of Congress Cataloging in Publication Data

Main entry under title:
Ellen Glasgow: centennial essays.

Nine essays, 6 of which were read at the centennial symposium held
at Mary Baldwin College on Oct. 19, 1973, and at the Richmond Public
Library on Oct. 20, 1973.
 Bibliography: p.
 Includes index.
 1. Glasgow, Ellen Anderson Gholson, 1873–1945—Addresses, essays,
lectures. I. Inge, M. Thomas. II. Mary Baldwin College, Staunton, Va.
PS3513.L34Z653 1975 813'.5'2 75-15976 ISBN 0-8139-0620-2

Printed in the United States of America

Contents

1874- 1945

Preface   vii

Introduction
    Louis D. Rubin, Jr.   1

Prologue
    Northern Exposure: Southern Style   7
    Howard Mumford Jones

The Woman
    Glasgow, Cabell, and Richmond   25
    Edgar E. MacDonald
    Glasgow and the Southern Renaissance   46
    Dorothy Scura

The Novels
    The Earliest Novels   67
    Howard Mumford Jones
    The Prewar Novels   82
    Frederick P. W. McDowell
    The Comedies of Manners   108
    C. Hugh Holman

The Ideas
    Ellen Glasgow's Civilized Men   131
    Blair Rouse
    Ellen Glasgow as Feminist   167
    Monique Parent Frazee

An Essay in Bibliography   191
    Edgar E. MacDonald

Index   227

Preface

Six of the essays in this volume, those by Howard Mumford Jones, Frederick P. W. McDowell, C. Hugh Holman, Blair Rouse, and Monique Parent Frazee, were read at the Centennial Symposium honoring Ellen Glasgow held at Mary Baldwin College in Staunton, Virginia, on October 19, 1973, and at the Richmond Public Library in Richmond, Virginia, on October 20, 1973. The symposium was made possible through a grant from the Robert G. Cabell III and Maude Morgan Cabell Foundation and sponsored by Mary Baldwin College, the Society for the Study of Southern Literature, the Friends of the Richmond Public Library, the Association for the Preservation of Virginia Antiquities, and the Humanities Center of the Richmond Public Schools. The biographical essays by Edgar E. MacDonald and Dorothy Scura were prepared for the Seminar in Southern American Literature held at the meeting of the Modern Language Association in Chicago on December 27, 1973, and chaired by this editor. The bibliographical essay by MacDonald contains material originally published in *Resources for American Literary Study* and revised for its appearance here. Without the generous assistance of the individuals and institutions listed here, and especially the services of William W. Kelly and Louis D. Rubin, Jr., this volume of essays could not have been offered as a centennial tribute to the achievement of Ellen Glasgow.

M. Thomas Inge

Virginia Commonwealth University

Ellen Glasgow
Centennial Essays

Introduction

Louis D. Rubin, Jr.

THE year 1973 was the 100th anniversary of the birth of Ellen Glasgow—until late in her life she had thought she was born in April, 1874, but then she discovered that the family Bible gave the date as 1873. She was born in Richmond less than a decade after it had served as the embattled capital of the Confederate States of America, and at a time when the issues and loyalties of the Civil War were still white-hot. When she died in November, 1945, the United States of America had just finished winning a second world war, and the history of the Confederacy was a field of antiquarian inquiry.

The leading Virginia novelist in the year of her birth was John Esten Cooke, whose *Virginia Comedians* (1854) epitomized the antebellum romance. In the year that she died, Malcolm Cowley published the reevaluation of the Yoknapatawpha saga of William Faulkner that helped rescue his fiction from popular and critical neglect and make him our most noted twentieth-century author. When Ellen Glasgow published her own first novel in 1897, Thomas Nelson Page was topmost among Virginia writers of fiction. The year 1941, when the last work of Ellen Glasgow's to be published in her lifetime, *In This Our Life*, won the Pulitzer Prize, was also the year that saw publication of Carson McCullers's second novel and Eudora Welty's first collection of stories.

I cite these facts in order to suggest just how immense were the changes that took place in American life and in Southern American literature during Ellen Glasgow's lifetime; they may also help to suggest something of what her own role in that process was, and why, in the history of Southern literature, she occupies the remarkable position that she does. In 1897 *The Descendant*, published anonymously, was held to be a shocking, even sordid novel; she once quoted the remark of an elderly relative, "But it is incredible that a well brought-up Southern girl should even know what a bastard is." By the 1930s and 1940s, her own application of that "blood and irony" she had prescribed as a cure for the feebleness of Southern literature was considered a bit tame. Faulkner, Caldwell, Wolfe, and others had carried social frankness to lengths that were shocking even to *her,* so that, in her own words, "realism had so often degenerated into literary ruffianism. . . ." The rebel had become the conservator; it is a familiar story. The young critics who were championing the novels of Faulkner and his contemporaries had taken to disparaging Ellen Glasgow's fiction for what seemed to them its inadequate grounding in actuality, while critics of her own generation who were appalled by the barnyard crudities of the newer novelists made use of her work as a weapon for clubbing at what they did not like or understand about her successors. All this tended, and still tends, to make it difficult to arrive at any real consensus as to the nature, the worth, and the importance of Ellen Glasgow's work.

Yet after all, it has been more than thirty years since *In This Our Life* was published, and more than seventy-five since *The Descendant*, and many of the Southern writers of Faulkner's generation have now in their own turn felt the reversal of fortune that attends the change of a literary guard. So it ought to be possible at last to read Ellen Glasgow's work not simply as being a rebellion against Southern-style Victorianism or primarily as a way station en route to Yoknapatawpha County, but in its own right, for what it sets out to do, and whether or not and to what extent it succeeds in doing it. To that end, in any event, the symposium that resulted in the present volume was directed. A group of scholars, all of them convinced that Ellen Glasgow's fiction *was* important and needed reassessment, were asked, in the summer of the centenary of the author's birth, to examine and write about various aspects of her life and work. To those essays several more have been added in order to round out the presentation.

I am afraid that the story of how the centenary symposium came into being does not do especial honor to the Commonwealth that Ellen Glasgow lived in, chronicled, and so loved. But it is part of the story and should be recorded. Truth to tell, the way that it happened bears out all too aptly the continuing accuracy of Ellen Glasgow's estimate of the cultural and literary zeal of her native state. She and her fellow Richmond novelist James Branch Cabell spent much time chuckling wryly over the obstinate refusal of

Richmonders to consider books as useful objects or to look upon those who wrote them as being other than somewhat socially suspect.

To get to the point, it was not until the midsummer of the 100th anniversary of her birth that any public notice whatever was taken of it by anyone in Virginia. Neither in Richmond nor at the University of Virginia in Charlottesville, where her papers are housed, were commemorative activities planned. Not until Professor Edgar MacDonald, of the faculty of Randolph-Macon College in Ashland, wrote an article for the Richmond *Times-Dispatch* calling attention to the centennial did anything happen. Then, President William W. Kelly of Mary Baldwin College, himself a noted Ellen Glasgow scholar, saw the article and was chagrined at the failure of the state of Virginia to commemorate so noteworthy a birthday; the upshot was that, with the help of the Robert G. Cabell III and Maude Morgan Cabell Foundation of Richmond, a symposium was hastily arranged for that fall. Fortunately, some distinguished scholars from elsewhere in the nation and even from France, mindful of what the fiction of Ellen Glasgow signified for American literature, were willing to drop what they were working on and prepare papers upon no more than two months' notice. The symposium was held at Mary Baldwin College in Staunton, and there was an additional session the next day in Richmond, sponsored by the Friends of the Richmond Public Library.

All this was in sharp contrast to what was going on in Nebraska during the same year. There, the centenary of another Virginia-born woman author,,Willa Cather, who had spent her formative years in Nebraska, was being commemorated by an extensive, year-long festival, involving concerts, dramatic readings, dedication of parks, exhibits at museums, lectures, symposia, and publication of a series of commemorative volumes. Indeed, the political representatives of that state to the U.S. Congress even arranged to have a commemorative postage stamp issued in Miss Cather's honor. (I doubt that many of the Virginia congressional delegation had ever even so much as read a line of Ellen Glasgow's fiction.) Especially considering Ellen Glasgow's known attitude toward the merits of Willa Cather, it was all very ironic and amusing—and a little sad.

Yet however much these things may vex—and as a longtime resident of Virginia I confess that it still makes my blood boil every time I get to thinking about it; the Old Dominion may be the Mother of Presidents, but she is certainly the Stepmother of Authors—they are not finally important. What is important is the shelfload of books that Ellen Glasgow wrote, works which are still being read and enjoyed. Her novels vary in quality, and different persons care more for different aspects of her work. I tend to hold with C. Hugh Holman that it was in the comedies of manners of the late 1920s and early 1930s that her art was at its finest. But whatever the differences in individual tastes, this much seems certain: together with the books of her friend James Branch Cabell, there exists no more distinguished, more lasting, or more admirable a monument to what was best and most important about life in the Commonwealth of Virginia during the twentieth century than these works of the artistic imagination. They will very likely outlast the memory of all the politicos and athletes and financial and business tycoons. When future historians wish to know what went on in Virginia society in the late nineteenth and early twentieth centuries, this is where they will look for the answers.

In the history of Southern literature Ellen Glasgow's place is assured. She was, simply, the first really modern Southern novelist, the pioneer who opened up for fictional imagination a whole spectrum of her region's experience that hitherto had been considered inappropriate for depiction in polite letters. From the very beginning she meant business, and she had no patience with those who would have literature be anything less or other than an honest portrait of human experience and human meaning. Decades before Faulkner, Wolfe, Warren, Caldwell, Welty, and the others, she did her best to write about Southern experience as she actually viewed it, not as her neighbors thought she ought to be seeing it. In the words of the historian C. Vann Woodward, "When eventually the bold moderns of the South arrested the reading and theatrical world with the tragic intensity of the inner life and social drama of the South, they could find scarcely a theme that Ellen Glasgow had wholly neglected. She had bridged the gap between the old and the new literary revival, between romanticism and realism."

The essays that follow are offered in tribute to the achievement of Ellen Glasgow. I like to think that if Miss Glasgow could have known that decades after her death a group of literary scholars would be meeting to study the lasting significance of her life and work, she would have been pleased.

Prologue

Northern Exposure: Southern Style

Howard Mumford Jones

I HAVE devoted all my professional life to the theory and practice
of humane scholarship, and now, looking back over half a century,
I find myself again puzzling over the wild variety of value judgments that I find in literary history. I begin to wonder also whether
historical considerations—or, more accurately, what historical
considerations—explain the curious changes I have witnessed in the
fame of a distinguished novelist named Ellen Glasgow. For I insist
that she is distinguished. I think her development as a stylist is one
of the wonderful events not merely in the literary history of the
South but in the literary history of the United States. I think she
represents a tradition of the literature of civility that I find virtually
extinguished in contemporary fiction; and if, as is sometimes said,
no great single personage emerges from her fiction (a possible
exception is Dorinda Oakley in *Barren Ground*), I would still insist
that a great personality is stamped upon her pages, a personality
that possesses something of the quicksilver appeal of Thomas
Jefferson. Jefferson's prose, wrote Carl Becker, is distinguished by
its haunting felicity. I think that Miss Glasgow's style is so distinguished.

Public history—records and interpretations of the actions of gods
and men and of the rise and fall of empires—is an ancient discipline
which runs continuously from Herodotus to the irony of Halberstam's treatment in our day of the best and the brightest. Over the
centuries that discipline has developed techniques for evaluating
evidence, and solid modes of research. As in most human enterprises there remains in public history a wide margin for the personal
equation. Indeed, by an odd paradox, the finest histories are in
greater or lesser degree reliable and in a lesser or greater degree
personal—Gibbon and Macaulay, Tacitus and Voltaire, Parkman
and Henry Adams are examples. One may protest that Macaulay
gives a thoroughly Whiggish, a thoroughly Victorian version of
British India, but one cannot say that Macaulay did not know his

materials about India. A history of India written from the point of view of Mrs. Gandhi, were she a historian, would differ markedly from Macaulay's account of British India, but neither writer would deny the importance of the Indian mutiny nor of the impact of British law and British education upon Indian civilization.

We reach an agreement about a good many things in literary history. We agree that Shakespeare is a fixed star and that Milton is a great poet—a prince of poets, wrote Byron, a little heavy but not less divine. On the other hand it is probable that Walter Savage Landor knew quite as much about British politics as Wordsworth did, but Wordsworth's political views get all the attention. It is canonical to give space to Browning, albeit with a sigh; it is not canonical to give space to John Masefield, though he once excited all the critics and all the classrooms.

Perhaps literary history is too young a learning to be certain what it is doing. I find the earliest specimen of British literary history—something more than a mere chronicle of names—is Thomas Warton's *History of English Poetry*, completed in 1781. The American candidate is apparently Samuel Knapp's *Lectures on American Literature* (1829), a book that is not imposing for two excellent reasons: there was not much literature to discuss and the discussions are not very good. The earliest mature example is presumably Moses Coit Tyler's majestic *History of American Literature, 1607-1765,* published in 1878 and still unsurpassed as a treatment of colonial writing.

Literary history is the product of scholarship, and scholarship is in theory supposed to be as objective as the frailty of human nature will permit. It cannot be argued that all literary historians should reach precisely the same conclusions; if they did, our English departments would fade away. On the other hand, after two centuries of this sort of writing, there should be, one thinks, some mild measure of agreement about importances, whatever one may wish to say about the idiosyncrasies of authors. But I find myself bemused by the vagaries of scholarly judgments. For example, the novels of Anthony Trollope, who made the mistake of publishing an honest autobiography, were formerly downgraded to about the level of *Lady Audley's Secret* or the mediocre prose of Hall Caine; now, Trollope is in there with Dickens and Thackeray, a Victorian giant. In 1900 Barrett Wendell, who had the misfortune to be a

Harvard don, published *A Literary History of America*, in which the total discussion of Herman Melville consists of one sentence that concludes: "he began a career of literary promise, which never came to fruition."[1] But a book entitled *The American Adam*—in that case who was Eve? Margaret Fuller?—devotes twenty-five pages to Melville, "the apotheosis of Adam."[2] An American literary history of 1908 tells me about Poe's mastery over dismal, superstitious, and waste places; a literary history published in 1913 tells me that Poe "with a taste for palaces and Edens, lived in sprawling cities."[3] In the *Cambridge History of American Literature* completed in 1918 a specialist writes that Poe's originality consisted "rather in combination and adaptation than in . . . inventive exercises of the fancy."[4] Another specialist writing in the now standard *Literary History of the United States* tells me thirty years later that although Poe claimed the world as the only proper stage for a writer, he betrays a provincialism arising out of his belief that, to prove he was a Virginian, he followed the tradition of John Marshall rather than that of Thomas Jefferson.[5] As Marshall and Jefferson were both Virginians, this leaves me a bit confused.

I freely grant that history is never written, it is always rewritten, and that judgments change. But the eccentricities of change in literary history are more confusing than is true of public history. Political history does not in one book dwell on George Washington as a brash young officer who got himself thoroughly whipped at Fort Necessity and then again on Long Island, and in another book raise him to the dizzy height of an American demigod. Political history does not on the whole describe William Jennings Bryan as the Prometheus of the people in one volume, and then turn him in

[1](New York: Charles Scribner's Sons, 1900), p. 229.

[2]R. W. B. Lewis, *The American Adam* (Chicago: University of Chicago Press, 1953), pp. 127–52.

[3]John Macy, *The Spirit of American Literature* (Garden City, N.Y.: Doubleday, Page & Co., 1913), p. 123.

[4]Killis Campbell, "Poe," in *The Cambridge History of American Literature*, ed. William Porterfield Trent et al. (New York: G. P. Putnam's Sons, 1918), II: 69.

[5]F. O. Matthiessen, "Edgar Allan Poe," in *Literary History of the United States*, ed. Robert E. Spiller, et al., 3d ed. (New York: Macmillan, 1963), p. 328.

another into a windy rhetorician crushed by Clarence Darrow at the Scopes trial. It tries to see Bryan as a great figure in the days of McKinley and influential in the days of Wilson; it tries to explicate him in terms of the age that produced him, the age that he influenced, and the age in which his influence declined.

It is of course true that all historical writing, though an author try to depersonalize his view—an aim that some historians, lamentably, fulfill—inevitably reflects local and temporal interests. The generation of Samuel Knapp, for example, was engaged in defying the attitude of patronage represented by Sydney Smith's famous slur: In the four quarters of the globe, who reads an American book? After the Civil War evolution and racial theory took over, and literary historians, among them Wendell, produced books in the spirit of a scholarship fund at Harvard which stipulates that after other eventualities have been exhausted, the money shall go to any worthy representative of that fine old Anglo-Saxon stock which went forth from New England to make our country what it is today. The generation of Parrington and the compilers of *The Literary History of the United States* went in for social significance, and meanwhile the Marxists and the Freudians demanded their days in court. Thus Ludwig Lewisohn in a book called *Expression in America* (1932) declared that the novels of William Dean Howells were acutely and negatively sex-conscious. Others, such as V. F. Calverton, offered salvation according to the gospel of St. Marx. Since that day we have had the New Criticism, which is now old hat, the formalists, who are essentially the art-for-art's-sake school in disguise, ready to die of a rose in aromatic pain, and a scattering of more civilized and cultured men with a cosmopolitan outlook, such as Alfred Kazin and Lionel Trilling. And lastly there are the neo-Jungians, inclined to discover racial myths in even the plainest prose. It may be objected that a critic like Lionel Trilling does not write literary history, but his point of view is historical, he benefits from formal histories, and his treatment of writers in such a book as *The Opposing Self* (1955) enriches our fund of historical knowledge.

Well, what have these not very original remarks to do with the repute of Ellen Glasgow? I have tried to find out. I went to our library shelves and pulled down at random some forty or fifty books concerned with either literary history or historical criticism—

that is, criticism not primarily formalistic or æsthetic but criticism that acknowledged the validity of Emerson's instruction: Every scripture should be read in the light of the circumstances that brought it forth. My random titles ran from 1913, the year Miss Glasgow published *Virginia*, to 1970, when all of her novels save *Barren Ground* were out of print. The books fell into two groups: those which did not mention her at all and those which gave her a bewildering variety of interpretations.

I begin with the negative ones. In 1913, John Macy published *The Spirit of American Literature*, a pioneering bit of iconoclasm dedicated to the proposition that in the United States each literary generation looks with a too Chinese reverence upon its ancestors. Miss Glasgow's treatment of the passing generation in Virginia was not precisely one of Chinese reverence, but Macy did not discuss her. The authoritative *Cambridge History of American Literature* (1921) omitted her. In 1927, one year after *The Romantic Comedians*, the collected essays of C. Alphonso Smith of Louisiana, North Carolina, and Virginia, the first Edgar Allan Poe professor of English at Charlottesville, were published. They ignored her. In 1928 Gorham B. Munson brought out his *Destinations: A Canvas of American Literature since 1900.* He gave space to Jean Toomer, characterized as a master of literary art; he omitted Miss Glasgow. Vernon L. Parrington's *Main Currents in American Literature* vigorously backed liberalism and vigorously excoriated conventional Southern literature. The third volume is entitled *The Beginnings of Critical Realism* (1930) and was posthumous. Miss Glasgow seems to most commentators closely associated with the beginnings of critical realism in the South; Parrington's book passed her over in silence, though it gave ten pages to James Branch Cabell. In 1933 Albert Parry published *Garrets and Pretenders*, a study of Bohemianism in this country, revised in 1960, and his book was followed by Emily Hahn's *Romantic Rebels* (1967), on the same theme. Neither author troubled to read *The Descendant* and *Phases of an Inferior Planet*, though both novels are set in New York's Bohemia. In his *Shock of Recognition* (1943), one year after Miss Glasgow received the Pulitzer Prize, Edmund Wilson suffered no shock from recognizing her or from noting that others had recognized her. A group of essays in 1950, *American Writers and the European Tradition*, said nothing about a novelist steeped in Flaubert,

Maupassant, Balzac, and Zola, an author who continually reread
Samuel Richardson. In 1957/58 Wright Morris explored *The Territory Ahead* in the light of the illumination behind. He found Tom
Wolfe and William Faulkner ahead of him, but not Ellen Glasgow,
though the theme of the essays is the relation between raw material
and technique. This is the theme of Miss Glasgow's collection of
prefaces in *A Certain Measure* (1943), and earlier available in the
Virginia edition. In 1959 seven lectures were published under the
title of *The Young Rebel in American Literature. The Descendant*,
upon its publication in 1897, was hailed with astonishment as the
work of the youngest literary rebel in her generation. She was
omitted. Nor did Richard Poirier find this remarkable stylist worth
including in *A World Elsewhere: The Place of Style in American
Literature* (1966). But in a philosophic sense is not a search for
meaning the very heart of the Glasgow canon? In 1968 Ray B.
West, in *The Writer in the Room*, compared an author to a man in
a disordered room, and his theme seemed to be the usefulness of
the stream-of-consciousness technique. This technique Miss Glasgow had employed with increasing effectiveness as she matured;
she is not discussed. Nor is she included in a survey of research,
Fifteen Modern American Authors (1968), which, however, gives
a good many pages to that extremely uncertain artist, Sherwood
Anderson. In 1969 John F. Lynen published *Design of the Present*,
the theme of which I take to be: "There is in American literature
a curious duality which its functional characters often illustrate."[6]
I am not altogether clear how one differentiates a functional character in a novel from a nonfunctional one, but Miss Glasgow had
been for years studying duality. She is not discussed. Nor did
Malcolm Cowley treat her in essays on American writers in 1970,
A Many-Windowed House. You will understand why I am a little
bewildered by the theory and practice of literary history among
scholars. Anybody has a right to accept or reject an author of name
value, but to have a leading writer rejected by so many persons
writing on phases of literary art in which the rejected writer excels
is on the whole disturbing.

  Let me now turn to the second group of my random samples,
books which have the immense advantage of recognizing Miss

_____

[6](New Haven: Yale University Press, 1969), p. 1.

Glasgow's existence. One of the earliest in date is Granville Hicks's *The Great Tradition* (1933), a Marxist literary history containing a rather superficial discussion of Miss Glasgow, somewhat vitiated in point of credibility by the assertion that in 1897 she had already begun her career with a determination faithfully to portray Virginia society. Books two, three, four, and five on the shelves were one-volume histories of American literature. The first (1929) says that Miss Glasgow has written novels which have both historical and provincial backgrounds but in which the treatment is from the national point of view—a literary stance the historian never defines. He does, however, offer as her characteristics: a profound sense of the interdependence between man and nature, ready humor, wit, ethical consciousness, breadth, vision, and a lucidly beautiful style— the first time mastery of style had been noticed in this clutch of studies. A book of 1934 says she is a realist and a thorough artist. Another volume of that year remarks that her intensely critical satire sometimes bites too sharply and her situations are sometimes strained, but that she is an accomplished writer of fiction and a finished stylist. A third history blithely remarks that Ellen Glasgow is "also a Virginia novelist" who "used the material she had at hand,"[7] a statement that, as Byron once said of another platitude, seems extremely true. In 1936 Walter Fuller Taylor bracketed her with Edith Wharton and Willa Cather. I did not find his discussion illuminating, but an extensive bibliography is part of his volume.

The parallel to Wendell's one-sentence discussion of Melville is in Ludwig Lewisohn's *Expression in America* (1932), where I read: "There is not enough quality in her work to justify discussing it."[8] And in 1943 Floyd Stovall, in a treatise on American idealism, noted that Miss Glasgow wrote many novels of character and social criticism, but he discussed only *Barren Ground*. I finally reached pay dirt in a book of studies honoring James Southall Wilson, which in 1951 contained Majl Ewing's fine essay, "The Civilized Uses of Irony." Mr. Ewing insists that Miss Glasgow's long career

---

[7] I have forgotten where I picked up this remarkable remark.

[8] This remark first appeared in *Expression in America* (1932) and was retained when the book was amplified as *The Story of American Literature* (New York: Random House, 1939). I have used the Modern Library edition, where on page 515 Miss Glasgow is coupled with Gertrude Atherton.

was devoted to studying the moral values of life and said that she could have been a sentimentalist but that common sense showed her the folly of luxuriating in feeling. In maturity, his argument runs, she came to understand the civilized uses of irony. This is shrewd commentary, the first I had come to.

In 1952 Van Wyck Brooks brought out *The Confident Years.* For him Ellen Glasgow confronts the social world with a strong, clear gaze, whatever that means, and is temperamentally on the side of the disinherited, a doubtful assumption which he backs up by asserting that she loved and admired the "white trash Governor Vetch" in *One Man in His Time.*[9] Well, *One Man in His Time* certainly concerns Governor Vetch, but the phrase Brooks quotes is found in a stream-of-consciousness passage in the mind of Stephen Culpepper. Brooks concludes his discussion by saying that Miss Glasgow was the first to take the South out of the South, a dark saying the reader is left to solve. He said nothing about her in his *The Writer in America* of 1953, though Miss Glasgow's correspondence is replete with letters to Brooks.

In Cyrille Arnavon's French *Histoire Littéraire des Etats-Unis* (1953) I found a compact but undistinguished paragraph, as I did in Marcus Cunliffe's British *The Literature of the United States* (1954). Robert Spiller's *Cycles of American Literature* (1955) yielded nothing important. In a book of essays honoring Richmond Croom Beatty, *Reality and Myth* (1964), John R. Welsh discussed *Barren Ground* in terms of its parallels to Egdon Heath in Hardy's *The Return of the Native.* Out of seventeen books I took down, only two others seemed to me adequate. One was Mr. Rubin's *The Curious Death of the Novel* (1967), and the other was a collection of essays of 1953 edited by Mr. Rubin and Mr. Jacobs, *Southern Renascence.* The absence of any mention of Miss Glasgow in the *Cambridge History of American Literature* is perhaps offset by a cogent analysis of her work by Henry Seidel Canby's chapter, "Fiction Sums Up a Century," in *The Literary History of the United States.* Canby—alack! who now remembers that gentle spirit?—placed Miss Glasgow in both the tradition of fiction and the tradition of the South, remarked that there is less irony and more discrimination in her than one expects, and concluded with

[9]*The Confident Years, 1885–1915* (New York: E. P. Dutton, 1952), p. 351.

a sensitive paragraph on her style, which, he thought, by its consciousness, summarized an era of American fiction soon to end.
He put her between the old guard and the new naturalists. I could
not follow him when he seemed to derive Miss Glasgow's style
from that of Thomas Hardy.

Let me go back for a minute to the books associated with Mr.
Rubin. Mr. Rubin holds, as I understand him, that Miss Glasgow
wrote best about the breakdown of the old society in Virginia and
that she is less convincing when she deals with an emergent society,
arguing, indeed, that her best work rises out of the collapse of the
old Southern tradition. This gets us a step onward, it seems to me,
for it locates one of the sources of all this ambiguity. Mr. John E.
Hardy, in his essay in *Southern Renascence*, asks other questions
we need to have answered. He thinks Miss Glasgow's work has
become more and more the property of the literary historians and
that few of her commentators have been able to get away from
historical considerations. He notes the ambiguity of the phrase
"social historian," too often applied to this novelist, and feels that
she seems important rather out of our feelings than out of our
convictions. He finds her estranged from the old, romantic tradition, represented, I take it, by someone like Mary Johnston, and
without liking for the new fiction of, I suppose, somebody like
Erskine Caldwell or Faulkner. He further argues that, though she
has been called realistic, she was essentially a sentimentalist and
that no book by her is without sentimentality. Her radicalism, says
he, is the sentimentalization of themes an elder generation had
romanticized, partly, I infer, because her characters suffer rather
than act. He also dislikes the dogs that wander through her books—
I have not, I confess, discovered an excessive canine population in
Miss Glasgow's prose—says that her fondness for ideas is superficial,
and declares that she never realized her best potentiality as an
artist.[10] I am not quite sure what this last means. Few of us realize
our full potentialities, and I dare say most of us want to be judged
by our attainments, not by our failures. If, on the other hand,
Mr. Hardy means that, like the poet Thomas Gray, Miss Glasgow

[10]"Ellen Glasgow," in *Southern Renascence: The Literature of the Modern South,*
ed. Louis D. Rubin, Jr., and Robert D. Jacobs (Baltimore: The Johns Hopkins Press,
1953), pp. 236–50.

never spoke out, I must utter a courteous, firm denial. Given the handicaps of her life, the astonishing thing is that she achieved so much, and that the curve of her artistry is, with some inevitable retrogressions, an ascending curve as she more and more firmly mastered the art of narrative.

I again insist that my samplings are random. They did not include some of the fine monographs on Miss Glasgow, some of them by scholars present here. It happens to omit the informed account of her by Maxwell Geismar in *Rebels and Ancestors* (1953). It also omits James W. Tuttleton's *The Novel of Manners in America* (1972), to which I turned expectantly only to discover that Mr. Tuttleton skips Miss Glasgow, Theodore Dreiser, and John Updike for reasons of space.

But my random exploration of this body of comment or lack of comment was nevertheless revealing. Miss Glasgow is so clearly one of the most distinguished writers the South has produced, she was in my lifetime so obviously a leading literary artist, and she remains so distinguished a figure that these conferences are being held to commemorate the centenary of her birth. Why, then, these discrepancies? Even given the vagrom nature of literary history, why do historians, who accept in some degree the validity of history, come up with such a variety of uncertainties in assessing her work?

I suggest a possible source for this confusion in the ambiguity of four or five literary terms or phrases that always appear in discussions of her novels. Mr. Hardy's essay puts us on their trail, and others suggest themselves. Among them let me select four for a brief analysis: *ideas, sentimentalism, realism,* and *novelist of social life in Virginia.*

Ideas or *idea* is like *romanticism,* one of those nouns the importance of which everyone concedes and the meaning of which nobody can give. I have been for some years a member of one of the boards charged with publishing *The Journal of the History of Ideas,* and I have seen the editors struggling with the puzzle of what the journal is supposed to do. If by *ideas* in the context of fiction one means a set of congruent notions about philosophy, science, religion, or aesthetics, it is clear that Miss Glasgow was keenly aware of ideas from her childhood, but a novelist of ideas in this sense is virtually a contradiction. The primary responsibility of the fiction writer is to narrative, however he may bungle it, and if he turns his drama into a debating society (possible perhaps on the stage), he ceases to be a novelist, though he may be a writer. A novelist is of course influenced by ideas, as who is not? But a novelist *of* ideas is another matter.

Take, next, *sentimentalism.* As a term in philosophy *sentimentalism* is in a way an idea, and we therefore speak of a philosophy of sentimentalism or sensibility in the eighteenth century. More broadly, I suppose, sentimentalism is vague and diffuse, indeed, but many resent it as Keats resented didacticism, because it has too palpable a design upon us. Augusta J. Evans Wilson is palpably a sentimental novelist, but is Miss Glasgow? All novelists try to convert the reader to a point of view by the manipulation of both intellectual and emotional appeals—what the trade calls "reader appeal"—and among the successful are Richardson, Fielding, Dickens, Thackeray, George Eliot, William Faulkner, and Ellen Glasgow. But at what point does proper use pass into improper use? The crux comes not so much in the work of the user as in the response of the used. It is proper nowadays to laugh at the death of Little Nell in *The Old Curiousity Shop;* from the villa of Walter Savage Landor in Florence to California mining camps, it once reduced strong men to silence or tears. Is Ellen Glasgow disproprotionately sentimental? I do not think so, but there are those who do, and I can but quote William Blake a propos of another difference of opinion:

> The vision of Christ that thou dost see
> Is my own vision's greatest enemy.

What is realism? I wish I knew. Back in 1837 Emerson, that radical, implored American writers to embrace the common, to explore and sit at the feet of the familiar, the low, and celebrate the meal in the firkin, the milk in the pan. Life, he said in that same address, life is our dictionary, and this brave utterance was supposed to mature the American muse. Later in that same century realism got entangled with biology, chemistry, determinism, Darwinism, sex, and psychology, and in its darker aspects was indistinguishable from naturalism, a doctrine that assumes the imbecility of man, though it grants him the curious capacity to understand why he is imbecile. Miss Glasgow was at one time attracted to this doctrine, as her earliest novels reveal, but she abandoned Herbert Spencer for Sophocles in later years, so that one has to face the insoluble riddle of all art: is biological or cosmic determinism the same thing as the older doctrine that character is fate?

Finally, one comes to the famous phrase about the social historian of Virginia. *Social* has been confused with *sociological,* the result being that Miss Glasgow, who thought she was writing the novel of manners in successive layers of time, has been found fault with for not doing what she had no intention of doing, namely, writing a history of sociology in Virginia. She was not Zola, she did not visit a tobacco factory, notebook in hand, as Zola once spent some hours in a Paris brothel in preparation for writing *Nana.* The novel of manners does not pretend to be a sociological treatise. It assumes that particular social groups have patterns of behavior revolving around status symbols, and that these patterns sometimes oppress the soul. This, I take it, is what Miss Glasgow mainly studied. In his more mocking phrases the historian of manners writes the comedy of manners after the fashion of George Meredith; in his more somber mood he tends toward Euripidean tragicomedy or Sophoclean irony. I suggest that most of Miss Glasgow's major novels fall into one or another of these several categories. It should be superfluous to add that the novelist of manners must himself belong to a group of some stability, a truth self-evident when one considers the abysmal failure of novels of manners written by authors wholly on the outside; for example, such gross caricatures as Lord Frederick Verisopht, whom Dickens wants us to accept as a true aristocrat in *Nicholas Nickleby.* One can scarcely expect James Fenimore Cooper to write about the nascent American industrial world in the Leatherstocking novels, for he knew little about that world. I suggest it is quite as unreasonable to complain that Miss Glasgow did not write about railroad yards, unskilled labor, slum clearance, housing for the blacks, and other sociological and economic headaches. Yet some of her commentators seem dejected because she is neither socialistic nor sociological. Neither was Jane Austen.

It may be that we are looking for the wrong things or in the wrong place for the governing quality of Miss Glasgow's art. Literary history, under the influence of the textbook world of New York, likes facile categories and falls too easily into the fallacy of the struggling sophomore who, asked why *Hamlet* is a tragedy, responded that this was because it was written in Shakespeare's tragic period. Whether Miss Glasgow was a realist or a sentimentalist, a social psychologist or a Southern writer—these are fallacies the textbook world likes to exploit. They neatly pigeonhole an author and can be returned to the paper-grader, unsoiled by thought, at the end of a course in American literature.

She was not unacquainted with ideas, not unacquainted with actuality, not unacquainted with sentiment, not unacquainted with the human heart, and not unacquainted with life in Virginia and in the United States, but above all she was an artist in humanity as Hawthorne, as Jane Austen, as Turgenev were artists in humanity. She blended innumerable ingredients into a shimmering pattern of values for which there is no other word than that good old ugly German noun, *Weltanschauung.* Out of her anguish and rebellion, out of her own feeling that her good conceit of herself should at least be occasionally recognized in the world, she strove to put down in elusive words, subtle and penetrating, her answer to the eternal question: "What is man that thou art mindful of him, or the son of man that thou regardest him?" How far is the will of any human being free? How far is it forever bounded by desire? Metaphysicians have debated for centuries; in this matter logic and sermons never convince, but only passionate experience.

She was wise enough to understand with Goethe and Schopenhauer that desire is not the creation of sex but that sex is the creation of desire, a double power forever exemplified by the opposition in *Faust* of Mephistopheles and Margarete. She understood, as our embattled radical women do not understand, the meaning, secret and profound, of the last lines in Goethe's great poem, a work which sums up so much and which we refuse to read:

> Das Ewig-Weibliche
> Treibt uns hinan—

not badly paraphrased by somebody: "The womanly in the womanly compels us forward." She understood that the tensions of sex were more often the tensions of physiology. All our vogue of topless waitresses does not negate the truth that sexual tension is more fully realized in *Dombey and Son*, though Mr. Dombey and Edith Skewton never enter a bedroom during the whole course of the novel, than it is in *Lolita* or *Portnoy's Complaint*, a matter, by the way, in which Faulkner sides with Dickens and not with *The Memoirs of Fanny Hill.*

Miss Glasgow's theme is not so much the decay of the Old South or the vulgarity of the modern city as it is the meaning of Janus, the two-faced god, who looks alike on contest and repose. Her insistence is that here is the riddle to which the human soul, lonely and apart, must find an answer by itself. She brought to this great theme, the theme of Sophocles and Goethe, Hawthorne and Dostoevsky, a richer learning than most novelists evince, but she knew that neither Hegel nor Darwin nor Spencer nor John Stuart Mill nor any other formal thinker, though he may penetrate human society, therefore penetrates the human soul. She seized upon variant forms of the novel, as her instinct told her, that might be apt for her purpose. That purpose was to illuminate, in Malraux's phrase, the human condition. From the poignancy of her own experience, her own deprivation through deafness of a fuller joy in the world of sound, she came more and more to realize how subtle, how baffling, how tragic, and how comic is human experience. "What is the motive," she asks in a letter of 1935, "that enables human beings to endure life on the earth?"[11] The answer? Fortitude. With increase in insight and in an inner profundity of vision, her style developed in range, richness, and subtlety till it became a superb instrument for exploring the human consciousness and transferring that consciousness, not into broken phrases from the psychoanalyst's couch, but into harmonious speech, into an orchestration of words beyond the capacity of most writers then and now.

But as the men and women she created had to live somewhere, she utilized the only place and time she really knew, the Virginia of her time and the Virginia of legend, or at least part of it. But she wrote rather of men and women living in Virginia than of Virginia local color. One has but to compare the abrupt shifts of scene, the melodrama of dying infants, radicals turned into priests, the self-conscious epigrams of the pseudo-intellectuals, and the contrived ending of *Phases of an Inferior Planet* with the great soliloquy of General Archbald in *The Sheltered Life* to see the

---

[11]Blair Rouse, ed., *The Letters of Ellen Glasgow* (New York: Harcourt, Brace & Co., 1958), p. 193.

gigantic change in her art in a mere thirty years. As with all artists blessed or cursed with the instinct for the right word in the right place, she sometimes fell below her highest level, but her life in art is marked by a ceaseless thirst for perfection in that most difficult of literary endeavors, the credible union of passion with intelligence, the fusion of experience with universals. She is, it seems to me, above all else the novelist of sweetness and austerity, of a stoicism fused out of inward suffering and human compassion that transcends the sound and fury of our time. If I were asked to choose an epigraph for a new edition of her books, I should be torn between saying with the Anglo-Saxon poet: "That was endured, this may be also," and citing Matthew Arnold:

> the world, which seems
> To lie before us like a land of dreams,
> So various, so beautiful, so new,
> Hath really neither joy, nor love, nor light,
> Nor certitude, nor peace, nor help for pain;
> And we are here as on a darkling plain,
> Swept with confused alarms of struggle and flight
> Where ignorant armies clash by night.

The Woman

Glasgow, Cabell, and Richmond

Edgar E. MacDonald

I

WHEN Henry James visited Richmond in the winter of 1906, he expected to find still vibrant in the air some of the tragic glamor that had been associated with the name of the capital of the Confederacy. He had envisioned a "ghost-haunted city," but to his dismay it appeared to him "simply blank and void." True there was ice on the streets so that the populace kept close to their grates and the sweet gardens lay symbolically dormant. For James, there were no "references" in the romantic tradition apparent; then he realized that "the large, sad poorness was in itself a reference." He surveyed the desolate scene and wrote mournfully of the low aesthetic level, antedating the sage of Baltimore by some years. As he wandered about the White House of the Confederacy, he mused on the sorry objects of veneration. "It was impossible . . . to imagine a community, of equal size, more disinherited of art or of letters. . . . The social revolution had begotten neither song nor story—only, for literature, two or three biographies of soldiers, written in other countries."[1] While James composed this dirge in the solid, Edwardian comfort of the Jefferson Hotel, he seemed remarkably unaware that scarcely more than a block away on Main Street a thirty-two-year-old Ellen Glasgow had already published six novels, three of which were to merit prefaces for later editions—prefaces, ironically enough, compared with his own for excellence. The social revolution that James in 1906 felt was neglected and therefore so unproductive of song and story was the very soul and theme of the six-year-old *The Voice of the People* and the two-year-old *The Deliverance*. If James was ignorant of these "social histories" and their author, Miss Glasgow was nevertheless aware of Henry James. In 1906, James was also unaware of the twenty-

---

[1]*The American Scene* (London: Chapman & Hall, 1907), pp. 386–87.

seven-year-old James Branch Cabell, who had enjoyed a modest success with his first attempt at a comedy of manners, *The Eagle's Shadow* (1904), and whose short stories were appearing in respectable magazines. While James's assessment of the cultural scene in Richmond appears unflattering to the two embryonic writers, they both echoed his judgment in their latter assessments.

After their attainments were recognized, both Ellen Glasgow and James Branch Cabell commented at some length on the absence of a great literature in the South prior to their day. In her preface to *The Miller of Old Church*, she cited the apology of John Esten Cooke in his "Virginia Literature in the Nineteenth Century": "It may be said of it with truth that it is notable for its respect for good morals and manners; that it is nowhere offensive to delicacy or piety; or endeavors to instill a belief in what ought not to be believed."[2] Ellen Glasgow more forthrightly suggested that the South, Virginia in particular, produced no great works because of its complacency, its blind contentment, its moral superstition, resulting in a literature of evasion. Inasmuch as the region produced great men, if not great writers, she went on to suggest "that the creative art of the South was not a substitute for experience but experience itself, circumscribed and intensified." In short, the art of life was in living, not in contemplation. In his turn, James Branch Cabell, in his "Mr. Ritchie of Richmond," cited Agnes M. Bondurant's *Poe's Richmond.* " 'It was not the planters'—that is, the landed aristocracy of Virginia—'but the professional and businessmen of Richmond who were responsible for the promotion of literary culture in the city. These were the people who showed enough appreciation for Dickens and Thackeray to give them pleasant receptions.' "[3] Mr. Thomas Ritchie was the toastmaster at the *petite souper* which some ninety of Richmond's merchants and tobacconists tendered Charles Dickens on his visit to the city. Mr. Ritchie admitted that he, a semiretired editor of the *Richmond Enquier*, was the only one present who might qualify as being literary. He explained that "the *forte* of the Old Dominion [was] to be found in the masculine production of her statesmen . . . who have never indulged in works of imagination, in the charms of

[2]Ellen Glasgow, *A Certain Measure* (New York: Harcourt, Brace, 1943), p. 131.

[3]James Branch Cabell, *Let Me Lie* (New York: Farrar, Straus, 1947), p. 120.

romance, or in the mere beauties of the *belles lettres.*"[4] Oratory, richly elegiac, served the literary hungers of most southerners. Cabell went on to reflect that even in his day the businessmen ran Virginia's colleges, its symphonies, its museum of fine arts, "while the culture of Virginia, as thus comfortably conducted, has proved to be sterile in every field of aesthetics—except only, as I have suggested elsewhere, in the superb and philanthropic romanticizing of Virginia history and in a free-spirited invention of priorities and relics."[5] Though Cabell made these observations over twenty-five years ago, today he could still observe that "throughout all Virginia, Mr. Thomas Ritchie, under one or another alias, is still talking."

If the literary tradition was oral, the great theme, infinitely embroidered during the early years of both writers, was the war. In "Almost Touching the Confederacy" and "As to Childish Matters of Long Ago," Cabell gives us two charming insights into the Richmond of his childhood. In the former essay, he marveled at the creation by his elders of the noble myth "of the Old South's perfection," of their "half-mythopoeic and half-critical frame of mind" which allowed them to talk one way upon a platform and another way "in your father's drugstore." Ellen Glasgow, in her preface to *The Battle-Ground,* also comments in some wonder on the "chanting chorus of male and female voices" which during her childhood recounted the heroic legends of the Lost Cause. A grimly realistic Ellen Glasgow would observe, "A War in which one had lost everything, even the right to own a doll with real hair, was not precisely my idea of romance." Much later, after she had written *Virginia,* Ellen Glasgow recounts the visit she received from the elderly widow who reproved her for not "writing about the War." " 'If only I had your gifts, I should devote them to proving to the world that the Confederacy was right. Of course, I know that even the best novelists are no longer so improving as they used to be; but I have always hoped that either you or Annie Cabell's son would write another *Surry of the Eagle's Nest.*' "[6] Significantly,

---

[4] Ibid., p. 123.

[5] Ibid, p. 135.

[6] *A Certain Measure,* p. 84.

while both authors eschewed the historical and sentimental romance that might have appealed to the tastes of Richmonders, it
was those same sentimentalists who served the two writers as the
basic model for their fictional "heroes."

II

In his treatise on *The American Novel and Its Tradition,* Richard
Chase sees the distinction between British and American as essentially the novel of manners versus the romance, the former realistic
and "staunchly middlebrow," the latter abstract, probing the
extreme ranges of experience. The history of the American novel
also marks the rise of realism, but Chase does not equate the
realistic novel with the novel of manners. The latter

is distinguished from the novel in general because it concentrates
so calculatedly on manners, because it focuses on a particular
social class or group of classes above the lower economic levels,
and because it has an affinity in tone and method with the high
comedy of the stage. Most important of all, such moral standards
as are advanced by the author are those of a society . . . or have, at
least, a concrete social sanction and utility.[7]

He goes on to add:

Only in Cooper's New York and Westchester, in old New England,
in the Old South, in Mrs. Wharton's New York, in Ellen Glasgow's
Richmond, and perhaps one or two other places, like G. W. Cable's
New Orleans, have there been momentarily settled social conditions
involving contrasting classes with contrasting manners.[8]

Ellen Glasgow's *Romantic Comedians* and *They Stooped to Tally*
are prime examples of the novel of manners in America, but even
her sociological studies of the rising lower and middle classes in
such early works as *The Voice of the People* and *One Man in His
Time* are predicated on a social structure that recognized class distinctions. While the Civil War destroyed a multiple class structure

[7](Garden City, N.Y.: Doubleday, 1957), pp. 157-58.

[8]Ibid., p. 159.

in the South—slave, free Negro, poor white, merchant, planter—
the fifty-year hiatus between that war and World War I was marked
by an accompanying economic stagnation that essentially prolonged black slavery and retarded the evolution of class structures
among the whites. In addition, Richmond as a symbol of the
defeated South, a city which had known the vicissitudes of war
including occupation, enjoyed its own heightened sense of fallen
grandeur. It was Troy, it was Rome. It was a mythic city along
with Charleston and New Orleans. In time, its myths became
salable products, like its antiques.

Georgian morality, Victorian prudery, and post–Civil War
neuroses combined to give Richmond its defined class structure
and its social attitudes, attitudes sharpened by the general poverty
of the Reconstruction period. Both Ellen Glasgow and James
Branch Cabell commented at various times on the strictures of the
accepted mores; they permeate the Glasgow opera and are reflected
in much of Cabell's work. Ellen Glasgow wrote, "Even in the Richmond of my childhood certain imponderables were more precious
than wealth," but went on to add that gradually "imponderables
might be respected, but possessions were envied."[9] Like most older
cities that did not change too rapidly, Richmond had its distinctive
criteria as to social rank, and the people whose names were known
fell into three general classifications: the old families, the old
citizens, and the old merchants.[10] The old families were those
whose ancestors had been prominent officeholders in colonial
times, whose forebears traced to the younger sons of the English
landed gentry and minor nobility. The old citizens were the respectable, pious yeomanry, whose antecedents had also been
landholders but on a smaller scale and who had not known the
glories of office. The old merchants included the Scottish tobac-

---

[9]*The Woman Within* (New York: Harcourt, Brace, 1954), pp. 217-18. As late as
1954, one of Richmond's self-appointed social arbiters confessed in print how puzzling
it was to her that Ellen Glasgow "would receive the ever-present social climbers"
although, the arbiter added ingenuously, "one of her brothers [Arthur Glasgow] had
married a charming lady from one of these so-called 'golden key' families [Branch]"
(Helena LeFroy Caperton, "Ellen Glasgow's 'Honest' Autobiography," *Richmond Times-
Dispatch*, Oct. 31, 1954).

[10]Outside Richmond, the distinction is made between "good families" and "good
people," as Ellen Glasgow makes clear in the opening pages of *Barren Ground.*

conists, the few but highly respected Jewish shopkeepers, and other German and Irish tradesmen, all of whom were addressed with respect. There was a rapport among these three "old" categories, a mutual observance of the distinctions very much like British acceptance of class.

An example of class-consciousness in Richmond, albeit one of democratic coloring, was occasioned by a visit to the city by the Prince of Wales, later Edward VII. When he visited in October 1860, as Lord Renfrew, he was accompanied around the city by a delegation of prominent citizens which included the leading merchants, among them a Mr. MacFarland, who owned a shoe store down on Main Street, and a Mr. Dooley, an Irish hatter, the proprietor of an establishment next to Mr. MacFarland's. The prince mentioned in the hearing of his civic hosts that he needed a pair of shoes, and all Mr. MacFarland's fellow citizens looked expectantly toward him. The gentleman said never a word, however, not about to divulge to royalty that he was in trade. A little later, the prince mentioned that he needed a hat, whereupon Mr. Dooley spoke up. "Your Grace, I have a little hat business and would be honored if you would accept whatever may be to your liking. It's down on Main Street, right next to Mr. MacFarland's shoe store."

While the older citizens of Richmond felt in accord with its social structure, new people, whatever their financial status, were received with reserve; they were on probation. But if you had ancestors, why there you were! Nobody could take ancestors away from you, no matter what you did. But if you had no known ancestry, what else could one judge except the conduct of the person? It was very simple and in no way snobbish; only new people who had to worry about their position were ever snobs. But careful social deportment, very public respect for the late Confederacy, commendable industry leading to wealth, these could mitigate social distrust of the new, and by judicious intermarriage with the daughters of the old families (everyone knew the flower of Southern manhood had perished in the War), one could acquire ancestry, or at least cousins who had it. Another way, after industry had proved worth, was to discover ancestors by means of genealogical research. Mrs. Archibald in Ellen Glasgow's *The Sheltered Life* does a delicious job of translating the family of her new brother-in-law, Joseph Crocker, a carpenter, from "plain people" to "quiet people" and finally, with the aid of a genealogist, to an "old family."

Ellen Glasgow both accepted Richmond and rejected it, refusing to take any of its inherited notions as the Gospel. Socially and financially, her family was as secure as any in Richmond. One of the younger children in a large family, her self-confessed "morbid sensitivity" made her side with a delicate mother exhausted from childbearing, frequently not rational in later life, a condition common in that era. A father who enjoyed remarkable bodily vigor, one who could reconcile his Calvinistic stoicism with his physical pleasures, would incur her defiance. Her mother would die when Ellen was twenty, a traumatic experience for the sensitive girl. Her father remained an enduring enigma until she was forty-three. Even then the gentleman required a tumble down the stone steps of 1 West Main at the age of eighty-seven before he could be sufficiently impaired physically to hasten him to his spiritual reward. In the disparity of parental temperaments, the resulting stress for Ellen Glasgow would give her the double vision of life which results in protest, in art. The code of chivalry as practiced in Virginia, more immediately in Richmond, would become the focus of her attack. The church, which upheld the code, would be the first institution openly rejected.

But Ellen Glasgow's hostility to the enslaving notions of her native culture in no way lessened her social standing in Richmond. Lila Meade Valentine, Mary Branch Munford, Mary Johnston, and other forward-looking Richmond ladies were enlightening the Southern male that his chivalrous pose was a subterfuge long overdue for public exposure. Ellen Glasgow's iconoclasm had resulted in a novel by a twenty-two-year-old young woman being published by a Northern press, and if the financial reward was not consideration enough, there was her considerable personal charm. Charm in Richmond was, as elsewhere, proof of breeding. Ellen Glasgow continued to enjoy close friendships with her childhood friends. Even in later life, she did not play the role of authoress for Richmonders that she played so successfully for visiting critics. Her closest personal friend was Carrie Coleman Duke, a vivacious woman whom many thought scatterbrained, even superficial, but one who told anecdotes well, who brought into Ellen Glasgow's life the easy laughter of one who lived on the surface. She was

Ellen Glasgow's ears for the hard-of-hearing writer, especially on
her flights from Richmond into the surrounding universe. James
Anderson, a faithful Glasgow house servant, observed of Mrs. Duke,
"Miss Carrie wears life like a loose garment." In the latter half of
her life, Ellen Glasgow's closest companion was her nurse-secretary,
Anne Virginia Bennett, who had been in attendance at the death
of two sisters and Glasgow père. Of her companion, Ellen Glasgow
wrote:

Few persons have ever felt less interest in, or respect for, the
profession of letters; and, as with the other inhabitants of Richmond, some of them almost as dear to me as Anne Virginia, she
has always looked with suspicion upon "the people who write."
But I have always done both my reading and my thinking alone.
I have known intimately, in the South at least, few persons really
interested in books more profound than "sweet stories." My oldest
and closest friends, with the exception of James Cabell, still read
as lightly as they speculate, and this description applies as accurately to the social order in which I was born. . . . Nevertheless, as
I had discovered in New York and in London, the social levels are
very much the same everywhere.[11]

   While Ellen Glasgow's two earliest works were set in New York,
her best work was inevitably of her native state. As she observed,
"I could write only of the scene I knew, and this scene had been
furnished, however inadequately, for the past three hundred
years."[12] When she came to write of Richmond specifically, she
"saw a shallow and aimless society of happiness-hunters, who lived
in a perpetual flight from reality, and grasped at any effort-saving
illusion of passion or pleasure."[13]
   In *A Certain Measure,* Ellen Glasgow confessed that at the
beginning of her career she was meticulous in describing real places
in setting the scenes of her novels; "my realistic conscience sternly
forbad me to turn a maple into a mulberry tree." Later, when her
artistic purpose was served, she did not hesitate "to make two
trees grow in my Queenborough where only one was planted

[11]*The Woman Within,* p. 216.

[12]*A Certain Measure,* p. 68.

[13]Ibid., p. 203

before me in Richmond." Richmond as a setting was used exten-
sively; its houses, parks, gardens, and streets serve exclusively as
background for seven of her novels, *The Romance of a Plain Man,*
The Builders, One Man in His Time, The Romantic Comedians,
They Stooped to Folly, The Sheltered Life, and *In This Our Life.*
Richmond also provides settings for *The Voice of the People, The*
Battle-Ground, The Deliverance, Life and Gabriella, and *Vein of*
Iron. In addition, characters in other novels make trips to Rich-
mond. Ellen Glasgow first utilized Richmond in *The Voice of the*
People, its Jeffersonian capitol and her own house at 1 West Main
are described. Eugenia Battle Webb, the heroine, rides down
Franklin Street; then "presently the carriage turned into Main
Street, halting abruptly while a trolly car shot past. 'Please be very
careful,' called Miss Chris, nervously gathering herself together as
they stopped before a big gray house that faced a gray church on
the opposite corner [Grace]."[14] In *The Sheltered Life,* a mature
Ellen Glasgow sat in her garden at 1 West Main and poured her
hard-won stoic philosophy into the mind of General Archbald.
Even today, over forty years later, the garden is much as she
described it, with its wall, its stone birdbath, its old sycamore. "In
the garden, which was reached by stone steps from the back porch,
splendor flickered over the tall purple iris that fringed the birdbath, and rippled like a bright veil over the grass walks and flower
beds. A small place, but it held beauty. Beauty, and that deep
stillness through which time seems to flow with a perpetual rhythm
and pause."[15]

Of *The Romance of a Plain Man,* Ellen Glasgow wrote, "All the
opening scenes on Church Hill are faithfully rendered," and she
lovingly recounts the details of the scenes and the names of the
people who lived there.[16] All the changing mores that many of the
Glasgow characters will regret are echoed in the changes that take
place in geographical Richmond. *Life and Gabriella* opens in an
old house on Leigh Street in what was termed the Court End in
earlier days, an area now almost totally razed by city planners.

[14](New York: Doubleday, Page, 1900), p. 366.

[15](Garden City, N.Y.: Doubleday, Doran, 1932), p. 5.

[16]*A Certain Measure,* p. 73.

When Gabriella returns from New York (c. 1912), her brother-in-law Charley, prefiguring Babbitt by at least ten years, boasts of the new Richmond rising from the ruins of the old. "We haven't left so much as an old brick lying around if we could help it. If you were to go back there to Hill Street [read *Leigh*], you'd scarcely know it for the hospitals and schools we've got there, and as for this part of the town—well, I reckon the apartment houses will fairly take your breath away. Apartment houses! Well, that's what I call progress—apartment houses and skyscrapers, and we've got them, too, down on Main Street."[17]

Charley drives up Franklin to show Gabriella the unnamed Monroe Terrace, Chesterfield, Gresham Court, the latter two still occupied by residents living in them when Charley drove past sixty years ago. He drives up Monument Avenue, "the handsomest boulevard south of Washington. It's all new, every brick of it." Gabriella misses the gardens, the shrubs, and flowers. She asks, "But where are the old people—the people I used to know?" Besides the apartment houses, Charley exults over the hospitals. He names the physicians; "they've all got their hospitals." The rootlessness of apartment living does not enter Ellen Glasgow's novels as a significant motif, but the loss of the individual in the collective environment is clearly implied. In later works, Monument was given the derogatory pseudonym of Granite Avenue. With its memorials to the heroes of the Confederacy, its mansions built by the nouveaux riches, and later its apartment houses, Monument obviously symbolized for Ellen Glasgow the vulgarization of the free spirit into the mass conformity of external show; it was a realtor's conception of the capital of the Confederacy, prefiguring the press-agent commercialism of latter-day chambers of commerce. As Ellen Glasgow moved away from naming specific places in her later works, she still saw her characters acting out their dramas in scenes explicit enough to be recognized by native Richmonders; the scenes evoked certain moods within the writer, and they served the psychological and philosophical ambience of her novels. If Richmond was primarily a social attitude for Cabell, it was, as she said of her Queenborough, "the distilled essence of all Virginia cities."

[17](Garden City, N.Y.: Doubleday, Page, 1916), p. 501.

In the last year of her life, Ellen Glasgow sent a New Year's greeting to a young soldier who had been raised on Third Street on Gamble's Hill. "As soon as I am well again, in April perhaps, I shall call my little white dog and set out for the terrace on Gamble's Hill. When you were a child, did you roll down those steep terraces? And do you remember, as I do, the gold of the buttercups?"[18] Ellen Glasgow died the following November in the big gray house which Richmond had swept past, leaving it a lonely relic among the antique shops. But the spirit of an older Richmond was still at work in the house; for three days after her death her sister Rebe and her brother-in-law Cabell Tutwiler closeted themselves in Ellen's study, destroying every last scrap of paper that would not redound to the glory of family and writer.

III

While Ellen Glasgow's social relationships in Richmond were not literary nor intellectual, they were in general pleasant enough. She could look on her fellow citizens with an amused, even affectionate, tolerance. James Branch Cabell, on the other hand, was early subjected to subtle social pressures that further inhibited an already intensely shy youth. His relationship with Richmond requires a more detailed recounting of family history. If the influence of Richmond on Cabell demands *biography,* let us recall that the word was chosen by Cabell to describe his major work.

Cabell's maternal great-grandfather, Mr. Thomas Branch of Petersburg, of obscure parentage and fired with Methodist zeal, flourished in unpropitious times and became the patriarch of a large and prosperous family. He moved to Richmond and established the Merchants' Bank; his sons and sons-in-law were the leading reestablishers of Richmond's economic life after the fall of the Confederacy. His oldest living son, James Read Branch, married into an old family, the Pattesons, but Cabell would write "that Grandmother did not ever weigh the fantastic notion of the Branches' being the social peers of the Pattesons." During the latter days of the war, Grandmother had brought her children to

[18]Cited with the kind permission of George V. Moncure.

live with her father, Dr. Patteson, in Richmond, as her husband
was serving in the Confederate army. Colonel Branch died in a
tragic accident soon after the war, but the dynamic Martha Louise
Patteson Branch saw that the children of this union married well.
The second daughter, born in Petersburg but raised in Richmond,
married Dr. Robert Gamble Cabell, Jr., on November 14, 1877.
Unlike the Branches, the Cabells were old family. Annie Branch,
protected from the poverty of Reconstruction by Branch money
and raised in the home of an adoring and aristocratic grandfather,
could never have suspected that she was socially vulnerable.

When Cabell returned to Richmond from William and Mary in
1898, he found an alteration in his parents' domestic relationship.
Dr. Cabell, with no word of explanation to his three teen-age sons,
and apparently little to his wife, had elected to move out. Whatever
the private disagreements between husband and wife may have
been, the personality of Cabell's mother must have had a bearing
on the separation. Anne Harris Branch, child of the "newly arrived"
Branches and "old family" Pattesons, had married at the age of
eighteen a man twelve years older than herself. Numerous reports
would have her beautiful and pleasure-loving. Her open nature
made her disregard the more rigid strictures of society. Presbyterian Calvinism was still a meaningful part of Richmond's social
fabric, but young Mrs. Cabell, freed from Branch Methodism by
Patteson Episcopalianism, would dare to smoke and drink cock-
tails before other ladies freely confessed to these pleasures. Unlike
her Patteson mother, Annie Cabell was not given to the pleasure
of reading; her pleasure was agreeable company. Cabell confessed
that he modeled the charming Meloir in *The High Place* on his
mother's personality. If "this bright light creature's very diverting
chat" does not savor of the intellect, the hero reasons, after all "he
had not married her in order to discuss philosophy." Among those
that Annie Cabell found agreeable company was her amusing,
man-about-town cousin, John Scott, only one year older than
herself. Mrs. Cabell either did not care what people thought of her
social attitudes or else was unaware of the censure her conduct
provoked in the upper levels of Richmond society. Judging from a
number of intangibles, and certainly in the eyes of her oldest son,
she may be credited with a large amount of innocence. Innocence
in a girl might be overlooked by an indulgent husband, but it

seemed out of place in a woman approaching forty, so that Robert G. Cabell, Jr., no prude but raised in the Presbyterian church, found his position as compromised husband, even if only in talk, intolerable.

The fifth child of the patriarch Thomas Branch of Petersburg was Sarah Frances Branch, and she married an Irishman, Frederic R. Scott. They were the parents of six sons and three daughters, and they too moved from Petersburg to Richmond. Their first child, John Walker Scott, was born January 19, 1858. He attended the University of Virginia and Harvard University. He traveled widely and he spent some years in Albemarle County as a gentleman farmer. In his forty-fourth year he began to give some thought to settling down to the practice of law. His younger brothers were already a part of that financial structure that Branch industry was rebuilding. His brother Frederic William Scott was a successful stockbroker and, with the death of their father, was looked upon as the head of the Scott family.

On Wednesday afternoon, November 13, 1901, John Scott went riding at the Deep Run Hunt Club. He dined with his family in their commodious mansion at 712 West Franklin Street, across from Monroe Park, later called on a young lady, and then proceeded to the Commonwealth Club at 401 West Franklin Street, some four short blocks from the Scott residence. He left the Commonwealth at 1:45 A.M. of the fourteenth, after ascertaining from a friend that he was in walking condition. He walked west on Franklin Street and passed the residence of his first cousin, Anne Branch Cabell, 511, where her widowed sister Elizabeth Branch Bowie lived on the third floor. It was the house that Dr. Cabell had quitted three years before, but young Mr. James Cabell was there, recently returned from employment in New York and now employed as a reporter for the Richmond *News*. Scott passed the iron gate of 515, the residence of Major E. T. D. Myers, on the corner of Belvidere and Franklin streets. There he met his death. An unknown assailant fractured his skull.[19]

For some ten days the four Richmond newspapers speculated on every aspect of the murder, in particular the motive. Revenge

[19] For a fuller account of this episode, see Edgar E. MacDonald, "Cabell's Richmond Trial," *Southern Literary Journal*, 3 (Fall 1970), 47-75.

soon emerged as the accepted theory, and in the rumors of arrest,
"a very important person," "a well-known citizen," or "a society
man" were widely referred to. In the minds of many Richmonders,
there were no doubts; the evidence pointed to the one man who
had the strongest motive: James Branch Cabell had murdered his
mother's lover. In less than two weeks after the murder, with
rumors and speculation at their height, all four newspapers lapsed
into total silence. People could air their opinions behind closed
doors, but the Scotts had effectively ended any public discussion
of the scandal. Cabell would later attempt to clear his name in the
court of public opinion, but he ran into the adamant opposition
of his cousin Fred Scott, who was determined to protect the Scott
family's reputation even at the expense of an innocent man. Cabell
never forgave his cousin.

Cabell's reaction to this period of stress in his life was in marked
contrast to his earlier trial in the court of public gossip in Williamsburg. His painful separation from Gabriella Brooke Moncure and
his intense unhappiness at the injustice of the homosexual rumors
at college left him without direction, with no vent for his feelings.
This time, however, the acceptance of three of his short stories by
Harper's, Smart Set, and *Argosy* in the same year as the murder,
1901, served to allay his sensibilities, and writing would prove the
needed outlet for his suppressed emotions.[20]

Just when Cabell learned of the role assigned him in this scandal
we cannot be sure until new evidence comes to light. Biographical
details seeded in his fiction make it appear that he was aware of his
being credited with murder before he learned of the slander against
his mother. Perhaps he thought at the time that proximity and the
old Williamsburg gossip would naturally accord him a role in
public speculation. His mother could observe with one of his characters in *The Cords of Vanity:* "People talk of course, but it is
only on the stage they ever drive you out into the snow-storm.
Besides, they don't talk to me." Cabell was absorbed in his writing
during this period, and Townsend in *Cords* most likely echoes
Cabell's attitude toward the gossip. "I did not greatly care what
Lichfield said one way or the other. I was too deeply engrossed;

---

[20]Cabell was always proud of the fact that when he submitted his first five short
stories to various magazines in 1901, three were immediately accepted.

first, in correcting the final proofs of *Afield,* my second book . . . ; secondly, in the remunerative and uninteresting task of writing for *Woman's Weekly* five 'wholesome love-stories with a dash of humor.' "[21]

The third son of Mr. Thomas Branch of Petersburg was John Patteson Branch. He married the daughter of a Methodist minister in Petersburg, and he remained a zealous Methodist. He established his family in Richmond in a large remodeled house at 1 West Franklin Street, and upon the death of Thomas Branch was looked on as the head of the family and its growing empire. The Branches and their in-laws were now among the "economic royalists" of Richmond, to use a term applied to them by one of their own.[22] They married well, but it was generally understood that the Branch contribution to marriage was money rather than family background. The separation of Robert Cabell, Jr., from Annie Branch and the sensational publicity surrounding the murder of John Scott had further impaired their social standing. The Cabell family had been handsomely memorialized in a monumental work that had appeared in 1895. A similar volume recording the virtues of the Branch forebears would do much to repair their social estate. And who could be more appropriate as its compiler than the scholarly victim of that society which was to be placated? Thus Mr. John P. Branch commissioned and financed the son of his maligned niece to produce *Branchiana.* Genealogical research was congenial work for James Branch Cabell, and he duly traced the ancestry of Thomas Branch back to its immigrant, Christopher Branch, who had arrived in Virginia commendably early, in 1619. As luck would have it, however, no one truly illustrious was to be found in the Branch line, and they fell into that middle category of respectable and pious good people, the counterpart of the "old citizens" in Richmond. Cabell's findings appeared in 1907, and the Compiler's Foreword to *Branchiana* is amusingly both an apology for the

[21]*The Cords of Vanity* (New York: Robert M. McBride, 1929), pp. 162-63.

[22]Walter Russell Bowie, *Sunrise in the South* (Richmond: William Byrd Press, 1942), pp. 126-27. Writing of Mary Branch Munford, his and Cabell's aunt, and her public-spirited husband, he observed, "Some of the other men in her family connection were persons of extraordinary driving force, which they used at times for community enterprises, but more often for their own social and business interests."

plainness of the Branch ancestry and a virtuous advertising of their marital fidelity. Implying that the noble connections of more illustrious families were frequently the result of extralegal bed-play, he added: "Shuffle over it as you may, the authentic forebearer of this family was merely an honest and God-fearing yeoman whose reputation is not attestedly enhanced by even the tiniest infraction of the Decalogue."[23] Cabell later had better luck when he went abroad for research in England, where he found an illustrious Branch ancestor, who was proudly offered to the local gods in 1911 as *Branch of Abingdon.*

The year 1907 recorded another stage of the events that kept alive the gossip surrounding Cabell's name. His mother determined upon a divorce, a step not lightly taken at that time. Dr. Cabell's desertion of his wife had undoubtedly played a large role in appearing to give verity to the slander of the John Scott case. Perhaps Anne Branch Cabell felt that a divorce could harm her name no further, that indeed a divorced woman stood better than one abandoned. There may also have been some thought that a divorce would cause embarrassment for Dr. Cabell, a husband who had treated her cruelly. The divorce was a simple matter of depositions recorded in a lawyer's office and presented to the chancery court.

At about the time his mother was granted a divorce, Cabell decided he would take his revenge on Richmond society by satirizing it in a "novel" that would expose its multiple hypocrisies. Its "hero," significantly named Townsend, would daringly be the philandering cad that gossip made of the reticent Cabell, and though called Lichfield, its setting would clearly be Richmond. *The Cords of Vanity* was begun early in 1907, and, following his usual penchant, Cabell reworked some of his short stories into the appearance of a very episodic novel. Thus the highly romantic stuff of magazine fiction is cemented together by a protagonist who is Cabell's age and who speaks in the first person. Much of the cement is thinly disguised autobiography. But Cabell's sentimentalism kept interfering with his irony. In the middle of the novel, he observed: "When I began to scribble these haphazard memories I had designed to be very droll concerning the provincialism of

---

[23](Richmond: Whittet & Shepperson, 1907), p. 9.

Lichfield; for, as every inhabitant of the place will tell you, it is 'quite hopelessly provincial,'—and this is odd, seeing that, as investigation will assure you, the city is exclusively inhabited by self-confessed cosmopolitans."[24] He went on to add that "comprehension [is] the grave of gusto," and confessed, indeed touchingly, "For the rest, Lichfield, and Fairhaven also, got at and into me when I was too young to defend myself. Therefore Lichfield and Fairhaven cannot ever, really, seem to me grotesque."[25]

Though exemplifying the cad, Townsend deplores the decline of romance and a race of heroic men (example: Col. James Read Branch, C.S.A.). Yellow journalism now records our vices; "in real life our peccadillos dwindle into dreary vistas of divorce cases and the police court." Townsend's uncle observes, "Blow, bugle, blow, and set the Wilde echoes flying!" And Cabell affects the style of that author. Undisguised biography comes to the surface:

Depend upon it, Lichfield knew a deal more concerning my escapades than I did. That I was "deplorably wild" was generally agreed, and a reasonable number of seductions and murders and sexual aberrations was, no doubt, accredited to me.

But I was a Townsend [Cabell], and Lichfield had been case-hardened to Townsendian vagaries since Colonial days; and, besides, I had written a book which had been talked about; and, as an afterthought, I was reputed not to be an absolute pauper, if only because my father had taken the precaution, customary with the Townsends, to marry a woman with enough money to gild the bonds of matrimony. For Lichfield, luckily, was not aware how near my pleasure-loving parents had come, between them, to spending the last cent of this once ample fortune.[26]

For Bulmer through the novel read Branch. Townsend's mother is clearly Cabell's mother as described on page 23, and her witticism "James and I just live downstairs in the two lower stories and ostracise the third floor" is given to Mrs. Townsend. The character of Stella Musgrave too appears modeled on a younger Annie Branch

[24]*The Cords of Vanity*, pp. 164-65.

[25]Ibid., p. 166.

[26]Ibid., pp. 161–62.

Cabell, and her description of her Methodist grandfather is patently a portrait of Thomas Branch of Petersburg. The psychoanalysts will note that Cabell kills off both Stella and Townsend's mother.

Cabell intended following *Cords* with a candid account of life in Richmond to have the punning title *Townsend of Lichfield,* but for his "comfort's sake" he gave up the idea. "I had looked forward to a liberal dealing with real persons—presented under such pseudonyms as would ward off libel suits, without ever becoming in the least impervious—and to some salutary loosing of long-pent-up malice."[27] He went on to observe that for Lichfield "immoral conduct did not exist until some open mention of it was printed in the local newspapers." Cabell never wrote his uninhibited exposure of Richmond society; however, its attitude of self-mockery, delight in subterfuge, rigid adherence to the outward proprieties despite the damning evidence would enter into every subsequent work from his pen. He would indulge in more thinly disguised biography in *The Rivet in Grandfather's Neck* and *Something about Eve.*

Another biographical detail is relevant here. While Cabell's literary efforts met with some modest success, he was far from being in a position to support himself from his earnings. When his brother married a wealthy heiress from North Carolina in 1911, Richmond gossip has Cabell remarking, "I suppose I too will have to marry money like my brother." When the essentially shy and reserved author met the well-to-do Mrs. Shepherd, mother of five children, at Rockbridge Alum Springs in 1912, he tells us it was not a matter of falling in love. It was a feeling of wholly dear contentment being near this older, maternal woman who appeared unaware and unconcerned with what Richmond people might think of her. Her light, engaging talk revealed no fear of censure. Her pleasure in meeting and being with people was totally unrelated to the restrictive dictates of Richmond's reigning social arbiters. Here was another defenseless Annie Branch. She really needed someone to protect her from her innocence, someone to prove she was "old family," in a book to be entitled *The Majors and Their Marriages.* Their first and only child would be named

---

[27]*Townsend of Lichfield* (New York: Robert M. McBride, 1930), p. 3. This title is given to the last volume of the Storisende Edition, a collection of miscellaneous material.

Ballard Hartwell, two of the happy genealogical discoveries in Priscilla Bradley Cabell's ancestry. Percie Cabell wore her newly brought-to-life honors with aplomb, and her preoccupation with the important things in life, such as good meals, a well-run house, and loving attention to one's family, was largely responsible for the healing of Cabell's neuroses concerning Richmond's social attitudes. With his acceptance as a respected householder, discretely amusing himself with gullible Yankee critics, he could in time write his Comedy of Redemption.

In *The Cords of Vanity* and *The Rivet in Grandfather's Neck,* however, Cabell set out to write the social comedies that Ellen Glasgow produced in her three best novels of Richmond life. But sentiment intruded on his irony. Allegory and Poictesme were later to give him a remove from his subject matter that would allow him to maintain his ironic pose. While Ellen Glasgow's tragic despair occasionally intruded on her irony, she could look on Richmond with amused detachment. Her neuroses lay elsewhere, with her father and her deafness, but Cabell could not write of Richmond objectively until after his major work was accomplished. In his cosmic comedies, Cabell appears to stand outside of time and place, but it would be difficult to find an American writer whose environment played a larger role in creating those stresses which result in literature.

IV

Whatever esteem Ellen Glasgow and James Branch Cabell won in American letters, their works were not widely read in Richmond. Numerous stories are told of the indifference of their friends to their writings. Richmonders loved to recount anecdotes about the families, foibles, and affairs of the two, but references to the novels brought shrugs. Hers were reputed to be high-minded and dull. "I hear they're depressing, and I certainly don't need that," would be a response accompanied with laughter. His were supposed to be risqué, but how could one tell, with all that make-believe? "I honestly can't make any sense out of it," would be admitted with engaging candor. But just as Henry James came to realize on his visit to Richmond that "the large, sad poorness was in itself a reference," perhaps we too should see in Richmond's "indifference" to Glasgow and Cabell as artists a deeper significance than the easy attribution of superficiality so frequently implied. The story-telling tradition throughout the South was primarily oral, allowing infinite variation, responding to the needs of varied auditors, coloring the basic myths of patriarch, quest, apotheosis. The tradition served in kitchen and parlor; it served as the pasturage of the lesser sentimentalists such as Page and Cooke as well as of the academically revered Warren and Faulkner. And despite their truly prestigious centenary celebrations, are Nebraskans devoted readers of Willa Cather?

The careers of Ellen Glasgow and James Branch Cabell reaffirm the observation that art is preeminently provincial, that it springs from a certain age and a certain locality. Richmond's class structure allowed Ellen Glasgow to write "English" novels, and when World War I accelerated the evolutionary into revolutionary changes, the results were her novels of manners, wherein her ironic gifts came to fruition. Cabell's pre–World War I work was flawed by its reflection of Richmond's ambivalent attitude toward itself, a mixture of public sentiment and private derision. World War I liberated Cabell, allowing him to be openly satirical in his philosophical comedies of disenchantment, and it provided a mundane society ready for sophisticated innuendo. The duality of Richmond's penchant for "Queen Anne façades and Mary Ann behinds" had become the national allegory of the American Dream versus the Gopher Prairie reality. As Cabell wrote Theodore Dreiser, "You and I regarded, as it were, the universe from very much the same point of view, and have been honored with, through many years, the same opponents."[28] Earlier, the temperamental disparity of Ellen Glasgow's parents had provided conflicting visions of life for a child who would dedicate her efforts to an attempt to bring them into a single focus, a "wholeness of perception." And young James Cabell had looked on in wonder at a society that could propound a comforting myth in public while admitting to a painful awareness of reality in private, a schizoid behavior that would obsess the young man, driving him to philosophical quests

[28]Margaret Freeman Cabell and Padraic Colum, eds., *Between Friends: Letters of James Branch Cabell and Others* (New York: Harcourt, Brace & World, 1962), p. 281.

for an ultimate unity. That which troubled them in youth they came to accept in age as the universal experience of the human heart. "When she was born," Ellen Glasgow asked herself late in life, "were ideas any more free in Oxford or Bloomsbury than in Richmond?"

If Richmond was a state of mind, a social attitude, a mythic symbol, it was also a geographical place, still recognizable despite the changes. One suspects that basically both writers felt comfortable there; they mocked it, they enjoyed its intimacy, they felt lonely there, it was home. After all, they were born there, but more significant, as far as Americans are concerned, is the fact they died there. Its literary flowers are few, but it's still a place with roots. And we still find talk about the people we grew up with vastly diverting.

Glasgow and the Southern Renaissance

Dorothy Scura

THIRTY of them attended that rather curious meeting in Charlottesville, Virginia, on October 23 and 24, 1931. They were all novelists, poets, literary critics, historians, playwrights, or biographers, and they all possessed various claims to the desgination "Southern." The author of *Sanctuary* was there, as were the authors of *Mrs. Wiggs of the Cabbage Patch, Jurgen, To Have and to Hold, Porgy,* and *Relativity: A Romance of Science.*[1] Some were at the threshold of a career, while others had their productive years behind them. Ellen Glasgow had proposed such a gathering, the University of Virginia had invited them as guests at its Southern Writers Conference, and they had accepted in what must have been a shared impulse to band together.

The official topic, which not many of them particularly liked, was "The Southern Author and His Public," and conversation ranged over this and other matters during three round table discussions and a number of social events. Because the conference stressed informality and because the discussions failed to probe deeply into any one subject, the event raised no waves in the literary world. As the evidence of the meeting suggests, it was primarily a pleasant Virginia house party to celebrate the birth of what we now accept as the Southern Literary Renaissance.

The manuscript of Ellen Glasgow's opening speech and James Southall Wilson's typed schedule of events remain the only two pieces of hard evidence from the conference. Other documents include Wilson's file of letters, newspaper accounts of the event, random references in personal letters of those who were present, and three magazine articles by authors who attended. The three articles—by Emily Clark, Josephine Pinckney, and Donald Davidson—cover the same ground, are fairly general and superficial, and

[1]William Faulkner, Alice Hegan Rice, James Branch Cabell, Mary Johnston, Du Bose Heyward, Archibald Henderson.

attempt no actual record of the two days. Du Bose Heyward's newspaper article is written in a similar vein.[2] A private letter by Sherwood Anderson, however, provides a franker account of the gathering and the participants.[3]

The schedule for the conference shows that activities were planned to keep the writers busy for both days at the university. The first session, at 11:00 A.M. on Friday, began with Glasgow's welcoming address and ended with an informal discussion by all the writers. Following a luncheon at Wilson's home (hosted by Wilson and Stringfellow Barr, editors of the *Virginia Quarterly Review*), there was a 3:00 P.M. auto trip to Castle Hill, the home of Amélie and Pierre Troubetzkoy. An informal dinner at the Farmington Country Club ended the day's schedule.

[2]All quotations in this paper from Glasgow's opening speech are from a rough manuscript of the talk now in the Ellen Glasgow Collection, University of Virginia Library.

Wilson's file on the conference, including the typed schedule of events, carbons of his correspondence with many authors, and the originals of the authors' responses, is in the James Southall Wilson Collection, University of Virginia Library. (In this file is a single letter to Wilson from Wolfe, which is a photocopy and not an original.) All quotations from letters in this paper which are not otherwise acknowledged are from this file.

For permission to quote from unpublished letters I am grateful to the following: Mrs. James Branch Cabell, Mrs. Donald Davidson, Mrs. John Gould Fletcher, Mrs. Archibald Henderson, Mr. Gerrard W. Glenn (for Isa Glenn), Mr. William Frederick (for H. L. Mencken), Mr. Allen Tate, Mr. Paul Gitlin (for Thomas Wolfe).

A copy of Du Bose Heyward's newspaper account of the meeting is in the Wilson Collection at the University of Virginia Library. The manuscript of the article is in the Heyward Collection at the South Carolina Historical Society, Charleston. Neither the newspaper account nor the manuscript reveals where the article was published. Richmond newspapers carried three stories about the meeting: "Noted Authors to be Guests of University," *Richmond Times-Dispatch,* Oct. 19, 1931; "Writers Gather at U. Va. Session," *Richmond News Leader,* Oct. 23, 1931; "Southern Authors Informally Swap Views at University," *Richmond Times-Dispatch,* Oct. 24, 1931.

The three magazine articles are: Emily Clark, "A Weekend at Mr. Jefferson's University," *New York Herald-Tribune Books,* Nov. 8, 1931, pp. 1-2; Josephine Pinckney, "Southern Writers Conference," *Saturday Review of Literature,* 8 (Nov. 7, 1931), 266; and Donald Davidson, "A Meeting of Southern Writers," *Bookman,* 74 (1932), 494-96. References to these articles will be cited by page number in the text.

[3]Anderson's letter was written on the day he left Charlottesville to Laura Lou Copenhaver, the mother of Eleanor Copenhaver, who would become his wife in 1933. The letter is published in Howard Mumford Jones, ed., *Letters of Sherwood Anderson* (Boston: Little, Brown, 1953), pp. 250-54. References to this published letter will be cited by page number in the text.

On Saturday an auto trip to Monticello was planned for 10:00 A.M., and a second round table discussion at Madison Hall was set for 12:00. At 2:00 P.M. Mr. and Mrs. Gerrard Glenn gave a luncheon for the group. (Glenn, the brother of Isa Glenn, the novelist, had successfully argued James Branch Cabell's *Jurgen* case in court in 1922.) The third round table discussion was planned for 3:00 P.M.; and the final event, a Colonnade Club tea, was held at the Club House on the West Lawn at 4:00 P.M. The well-designed conference was marked by informality, gracious hospitality, a series of elegant settings, and much opportunity for conversation and discussion.

If among Southern writers in 1931 there existed a personal feeling of excitement about the state of Southern letters—a feeling which Glasgow had recognized—there had also been public recognition of the renewal of Southern writing. Articles published by Herschel Brickell, Glasgow, and Howard Mumford Jones had documented some of the literary activity.

As early as 1927, Brickell had written in a *Bookman* article, "The Literary Awakening in the South," that "a casual glance at the recent literary output of the United States discloses immediately that H. L. Mencken's 'Sahara of the Bozart,' the South, has suddenly burst into colorful bloom." Brickell mentioned some sixty-nine writers—from Conrad Aiken to Stark Young—to support his contention that it seemed to him to be no "exaggeration to speak of a Renaissance of literature in the South."[4]

A year after Brickell's article appeared, Glasgow wrote in *Harper's Magazine* of "The Novel in the South."[5] First, she looked backward to assess the Uncle Remus stories and the work of Thomas Nelson Page, Charles Egbert Craddock, and James Lane Allen. Then, although she reserved her longest and most glowing tribute for her fellow townsman Cabell, she turned her gaze to the future and named "a little band of writers" who were "subjecting the raw material of life to the fearless scrutiny and the spacious treatment of art." Among those she cited were some who would attend the meeting in Charlottesville: Heyward, Green, Boyd,

[4]Herschel Brickell, "The Literary Awakening in the South," *Bookman*, 66 (1927), 138, 139.

[5]158 (Dec. 1928), 93-100.

Stallings, Glenn, and Clark. When she submitted the manuscript of the article to Cabell, he expressed his personal gratitude for her generous remarks about him, but he encouraged her to add more names to her initial list in order to make this "Southern renaissance" appear as extensive as possible.[6]

Near the close of the *Harper's* article, Glasgow named the ingredients necessary for great Southern novels: "And so it would seem that all qualities which will unite to make great Southern novels are the elemental properties which make great novels wherever they are written in any part of the world: power, passion, pity, ecstasy and anguish, hope and despair."[7] These words anticipate her opening address to her assembled colleagues in Charlottesville three years later.

Jones carried the Renaissance idea further in 1930 when he used as his title for a *Virginia Quarterly Review* article, "Is There a Southern Renaissance?"[8] He answered his question with a resounding yes, mentioned names already cited by Brickell or Glasgow, and concluded that "the South is the literary land of promise today." Thus by 1931 there must have been a general feeling among Southern authors that the rebirth of letters in their region was genuine, for it was a rebirth which they could easily observe and which had been documented in literary journals.

It was Glasgow, however, who originally gave voice to the idea of a Southern Writers Conference and pointed out to her friend Wilson that "it was unfortunate that Southern writers are too widely scattered even to meet each other."[9] That the idea for the meeting had been in her mind for some time cannot be doubted: for when Isa Glenn accepted Wilson's invitation to the conference, she wrote, "Miss Glasgow spoke to me of her intention of starting something of the sort, nearly two years ago: and I thought then, as I do now, that it's vitally necessary, if the South is to come in for what she deserves: for, as Ellen said then, we now have a larger

---

[6]Cabell wrote this in a letter to Glasgow dated September 17, 1928, now in the James Branch Cabell Collection, Clifton Waller Barrett Library, University of Virginia.

[7]P. 100.

[8]6 (1930), 184-97.

[9]Wilson, in a letter to Glasgow dated January 10, 1931, is quoting Glasgow.

number of first-rate authors in the South than has any other section of the country."

Nine months of diligent work by Wilson actually preceded the Charlottesville meeting, which seemed at the time to be so spontaneous and informal. On January 10, he had reminded Glasgow of her idea and suggested having a group of Southern writers come to the University of Virginia for "a day or two's pow-wow." Later in January, Du Bose Heyward of Charleston and Archibald Henderson of Chapel Hill met with Wilson in Charlottesville to talk about the project. Wilson assured Heyward and Henderson that the work would be done by Wilson himself and that the committee's functions would be advisory and honorary.

The first item of business at the initial meeting seems to have been to form a central committee of authors in whose names Wilson would issue invitations. From the beginning Glasgow was considered to be a member, and at the first meeting Heyward and Henderson insisted that James Branch Cabell be included. After much persuasion, Cabell reluctantly agreed if Stark Young, the novelist and drama editor of the *New Republic*, and Paul Green, the playwright, would be included to maintain a good balance.[10]

Willa Cather and John Crowe Ransom were invited to serve, but both refused. Ransom sent a telegram to Wilson explaining that he could not get away for the conference. Cather responded that any public use of her name might bring public intrusions and that she planned to spend time in California with her seriously ill mother. Thomas Wolfe was then asked to serve. Only thirty-one years old and "agonizing" over his second book, Wolfe wrote Wilson: "I want you to know that I am deeply sensible of the honor you have done me in placing me on a committee with such distinguished and talented people as you have: I know it is an honor I do not deserve." Thus the central committee was assembled: Glasgow, Cabell, Henderson, Heyward, Young, Green, and Wolfe.

Guests to be invited were then selected by the committee. Wilson submitted an inclusive list of authors to each committee member, who checked twenty to twenty-five names. Names not on the list could be added. Wilson then took the results of this poll and submitted a second list to committee members for them to

---

[10]Wilson quoted Cabell in a letter dated February 3, 1931, to Archibald Henderson.

check candidates. A final list was compiled by Wilson with names divided, according to the number of votes received, into a first and second list for invitations. As an author on the first list refused, one on the second list was invited.

If the mode of choosing the participants seems more like a method of selecting country club memberships than of evaluating serious writers, it is indicative of Wilson's delicacy in handling the personal side of the conference. His contacts with the committee were diplomatic and gentle, and his written invitations to the guests were masterpieces of tact: he offered accommodations at either the Monticello Hotel or the Farmington Country Club; he assured each guest of complete informality; and he provided protection so that each guest, if he chose, could avoid any scheduled event or outside invitation. The fact that so many writers came and had a good time shows the sympathetic understanding of Wilson and the University of Virginia faculty members who assisted him;[11] the fact that the meeting did not become a forum for penetrating discussion is probably also due to the atmosphere they created.

Many of those invited declined for various reasons. T. S. Stribling abruptly refused without explanation. Roark Bradford, and later Wolfe, begged off because of work. Bradford explained he would be busy at his typewriter on a plantation in northwest Louisiana in October. Irvin Cobb pleaded important other plans. Burton Rascoe, just out of the hospital, was not physically able to come, and Margaret Prescott Montague also refused for health reasons. Elizabeth Madox Roberts explained that she was in the midst of building a house and could not get away. In addition, Herbert Ravenal Sass, Lizette Woodworth Reese, and Stark Young sent regrets. Julia Peterkin had planned to attend but was prevented because her husband suffered an accident.

H. L. Mencken, who would have had the opportunity of seeing the Bozart in bloom, did not come either. Mencken had written Cabell in July: "Going to orgies at universities is very far out of my line, but I am already tempted." He said he would leave the

---

[11] Stringfellow Barr, as well as several other University of Virginia faculty members, aided Wilson during the conference by attending the scheduled events and by chauffeuring the authors and entertaining them.

decision to his wife, a former Goucher College teacher, "who is much less shy of the learned than I am."[12] Sara Haardt Mencken and her husband eventually claimed they could not come because of a prior engagement in New Orleans. Conrad Aiken also refused. He wrote from Rye, Sussex, that although the meeting would appeal to him in that he would be able to meet the authors of works that he found interesting, he also found the expenses of making a journey to Charlottesville prohibitive. In addition, he stated some objections to the conference: he deplored public dinners and speech-making; he distrusted the ultimate value of a scheduled conference; and he expressed contempt for the idea of sectionalizing the arts.

In contrast to the reservations Aiken had about the meeting, William Faulkner confessed no such serious concerns. Instead, the author of the just-published *Sanctuary* offered a fable to demonstrate both his acceptance and his apprehensions:

Thank you for your invitation. I would like very much to avail myself of it, what with your letter's pleasing assurance that loopholes will be supplied to them who have peculiarities about social gambits. You have seen a country wagon come into town, with a hound dog under the wagon. It stops on the square and the folks get out, but that hound never gets very far from that wagon. He might be cajoled or scared out for a short distance, but first thing you know he has scuttled back under the wagon; maybe he growls at you a little. Well that's me.[13]

And so they came to Charlottesville, these thirty southerners: William Faulkner from Mississippi and Alice Hegan Rice and Cale Young Rice from Kentucky. From South Carolina came Josephine Pinckney and Dorothy and Du Bose Heyward. From North Carolina came Archibald Henderson, Paul Green, James Boyd, Katherine Newlin Burt, and Struthers Burt. From Tennessee came Donald Davidson, Caroline Gordon, Allen Tate, and Mary and Stanton

[12]Mencken wrote this to Cabell in a letter dated July 24, 1931, which is now in the Cabell Collection, University of Virginia Library.

[13]Joseph Blotner, in *Faulkner: A Biography* (New York: Random House, 1974), pp. 705-16, tells of Faulkner's participation in this meeting. On p. 706 Blotner quotes from Faulkner's acceptance letter to Wilson. I did not see Blotner's account until after this paper was written.

Chapman. And from Virginia came Ellen Glasgow, James Branch Cabell, Mary Johnston, Sherwood Anderson, and Amélie Rives Troubetzkoy.[14]

A number of southerners who no longer lived in the South returned for the occasion: Emily Clark Balch of Richmond came from Philadelphia; Katharine Anthony of Arkansas, Helen Poteat Stallings (Mrs. Laurence Stallings) of North Carolina, Isa Glenn of Georgia, Herschel Brickell of Mississippi, and Irita Van Doren of Alabama—all came down from New York. U. B. Phillips, born in Georgia, and William E. Dodd, born in North Carolina, came respectively from Yale and the University of Chicago. John Peale Bishop, born in West Virginia, delayed his return to his home in Paris, France, in order to be present.

Although all those attending possessed some claim to being Southern, a few connections were rather tenuous. Sherwood Anderson, for example, was born in Camden, Ohio, and led a nomadic life before moving to Marion, Virginia, in 1925. During the meeting he declared that his best credential for being called Southern was that he had Italian blood. The novelist Struthers Burt was born in New York and divided his year with summers in Jackson Hole, Wyoming, and winters in Southern Pines, North Carolina. Stanton Chapman was a London native who had been naturalized in 1927. He was a Southerner by marriage, however, because Mary Chapman was a native of Tennessee. And the historical novelist James Boyd was born in Pennsylvania but had moved to North Carolina, the home of his ancestors, at the age of thirteen.

Many of those present at the 1931 meeting had contributed generously to the recent upsurge of literary activity in the South. Glasgow, for example, had published two of her comedies of manners (in 1926 and 1929) and was completing the third, *The Sheltered Life* (1932). The Storisende Edition of Cabell's work (1927–30), eighteen volumes of the Biography of Manuel, had been completed, plus two comic novels, *Something about Eve*

---

[14] Although she was included in the published account of those who attended, Princess Troubetzkoy did not attend the sessions; she did entertain the authors in her home. Davidson's published account mentions that Andrew Nelson Lytle, Lawrence Lee, and Agnes Rothery Pratt attended some of the sessions. Their names do not appear on Wilson's guest list.

(1927) and *The Way of Ecben* (1929), and a collection of essays on literary personalities, *Some of Us* (1930). Faulkner had published six novels; the three most recent were *The Sound and the Fury* (1929), *As I Lay Dying* (1930), and *Sanctuary* (1931). Although Anderson's only best-seller, *Dark Laughter*, had been published in 1925, between 1926 and 1931, when he was living in Virginia, he published four books: *Sherwood Anderson's Notebook* (1926), *Tar: A Midwestern Childhood* (1927), *Hello Towns!* (1929), and *Perhaps Women* (1931). For Paul Green, too, the late twenties had also been a time of great accomplishment. In 1927, for example, two of his plays opened in New York, *In Abraham's Bosom* and *The Field God;* the former won the Pulitzer Prize for that year. Also, his play *The House of Connelly* had just opened in New York. Davidson and Tate had both contributed to *I'll Take My Stand,* the Agrarian manifesto of 1930, and both had published volumes of poetry: Tate's *Mr. Pope and Other Poems* (1928) and *Three Poems* (1930), and Davidson's *The Tall Men* (1927). In addition, Tate had written biographies of Stonewall Jackson (1928) and Jefferson Davis (1929). Some other contributions of those present may not be so well remembered today, but a large number of writers at the gathering were actively publishing books in a variety of fields.

During the two days of the meeting two topics of discussion are mentioned in the printed accounts—book reviews and Southern stability. Rice, the Kentucky poet and dramatist, and Davidson, former editor of the Nashville *Tennessean* bookpage, lamented the lack of local criticism in the form of book reviews in Southern newspapers. Barr's explanation for this absence, which made the Southern writer dependent on the New York critics, was that southerners were not inclined to buy books (Clark, p. 2).

Green's laudatory words about technological progress seem to have provided the most tense moments of the meeting. During a discussion in which Bishop and Boyd praised the value of the fixity and stability of the Southern tradition, Green, "looking like a prophet out of the wilderness," in Clark's words, disclaimed these values and advocated the great benefits of the machine age. Green explained that Mr. Duke argued for the establishment of schools in his state so that people could become enlightened and thus make more money. And "through the worst intentions of the machine age," said Green, North Carolina was delivered "from slavery." Green termed the revolt against the machine age "nonsense" and announced that "any little runt who is driving a high-powered car at sixty miles an hour is going toward God." In response, Dodd assured those present that "the machine age was dead."[15] If Davidson or Tate responded to Green's shocking assertions, there is no record of what they said, although Davidson later wrote Wilson that at another time and place Green might have received more vocal response.

Anderson's letter to Mrs. Copenhaver provides a characteristic glimpse of Cabell at the conference. Anderson reported that Cabell had a "face like a baby's" and was "clever at retort, always with a streak of maliciousness" (p. 251). Cabell employed his mischievous spirit two years later in *Special Delivery* in what seems to be his version of the Charlottesville meeting:

Because of my own peccadillos in print I was privileged no great while ago to attend a gathering of some forty professional writers under frankly educational auspices. We responded, it may be, to our auspices. In any case, affairs had reached the stage called "an open discussion" of I never discovered just what, and the refrain of our morning-long liturgy stayed constant.

One after another these somewhat strange looking persons—for authorship, whatever it may do for the mind, does not beautify the body—arose and coughed. Thereafter each so deferentially cleared throat spoke with dauntless conviction of our duty,—of our multifold duties to the public, to art, to altruism, to posterity, to the American spirit (for it was generally agreed that our masterworks ought to be "autochthonous"), and I even heard two elderly persons of my own obsolete generation dwell upon our special duty toward that free-handed Deity who had blessed us with special talents. It all sounded most handsomely, and it made the business of writing any salable form of reading-matter seem a high-minded and painful pursuit wherein only seers and martyrs might hope to excel.

I listened, I admit, in extreme melancholy begotten by low envy of such elevated sentiments. My reflection was that for some reason or another such sentiments quite obviously caused their expounder's socks to wrinkle and to slide yet more downward, the

---

[15]Quotations in this paragraph are from Clark, p. 2, except for the last two quotations, which are from Davidson, p. 496.

higher that his moral fervor aspired. In the while that I wondered over this phenomenon the young woman who sat beside me remarked sotto voce, "But I write because I like to!"[16]

Anderson's own feelings about the discussion sessions were similar to Cabell's: "the meeting got bad—long, tiresome speeches from professors. Everyone began to think it was going to be like a dentists' convention" (p. 251).

The failure of the Charlottesville meeting to be as exciting and productive as one would wish may be due to the choice of the subject for consideration. John Gould Fletcher, for one, complained about the topic "The Southern Author and His Public" in his response to Wilson's invitation. Because he considered the theme too "academic" and not "deep enough," he suggested alternate subjects: "For instance, you might talk about the South and Industrialism, or the Proper Political course for the South to follow in order to control its own economy, or the question whether all present-day educational books used in the South are not tainted with the assumption which the present-world situation shows to be untenable, that an industrial and competitive system makes for progress." While Fletcher wanted the attention of those attending to be directed to large and publicly significant problems, Wolfe appealed to Wilson to direct the attention of the writers to themselves. He wrote Wilson that he was not interested in "literary chat," but in "the actual physical aspect" of the writer's work: "I do like to know how they work—how long they work at a time, how many hours a day, how much they can do in a day, how long it takes them to write their books."

The topic, however, remained as stated by the original committee, who probably felt it important because of the attention paid to it by Jones in his "Southern Renaissance" article the preceding year. Jones observed early in the article that although many Southern authors were writing books, their publishers found that readers in the Southern states did not buy books in important numbers and that the Southern writer was almost wholly dependent for recognition on such non-Southern literary journals as the *Saturday Review* and *Bookman*. Thus Jones's mention of the twin problems

[16](New York: Robert M. McBride, 1933), pp. 123–25.

of a meager reading public and of a shortage of influential organs
of review may have suggested the general topic for the Charlottesville meeting.

In her opening speech to the conference, Glasgow herself could
not come to terms with "The Southern Author and His Public."
The manuscript of her speech provides evidence of the difficulty
she faced. One marked-out but still legible paragraph reads:

By this time, you have observed, no doubt, that I have carefully
avoided the subject of our general discussion. Candidly, I have
little interest in publics. Like presidents, they fail to impress me
because I so seldom agree with them. Even when a public appears
in Roman dress on the stage, I immediately suspect that it is not
there for any good, but for purposes of assassination. So I find but
one approach to this topic, and that is with the question: How
much or how little should a writer participate, as we may say, in
his own public?

A second and third abortive attempt to discuss the problem are
also deleted.

As for the immediate topic for discussion, I hesitate, I must admit
to venture upon it, for it appears to me to be little more than a
thin crust—over what?

As for the immediate discussion, I admit shamelessly that I am
more interested in the Southern writer than I am in a public which
seems to me to be composed either of words or of a sanguine
illusion. What Southern writers may be, I am perfectly convinced
that there is no public.

Glasgow presided at the first event of the conference, and in a
humorous beginning to her opening address pointed out that she
spoke in Cabell's place.

When I was asked, as the only woman on this committee, to bid
you welcome to Virginia, I modestly replied that women come
before men only in shipwreck. But Mr. James Branch Cabell, who
imposes his duty upon me, is constrained to illustrate his theory
that after fifty the only thing worth doing is to decline to do anything. I, on the contrary, believe quite as firmly that the longer
one lives in this world of hazard and escapes disaster, the more
reckless one should become—at least in the matter of words.

She immediately observed "how elastic the term Southern writer may become when it is properly stretched" and noted that some of those present were not born in the South and some did not live in the South; but she quickly moved away from any parochial categorizing to call those present "not only Southern writers, but world writers." She explained that Southern writers were no longer expected to fall into "a kind of Swiss guard of defense," for not only was a defense of civilization "impertinent," but "the South needs defenders as little as it needs apologists."

She then moved to an examination of the problem of truth and distinguished between two kinds: the truth of life and the truth of art, which includes both history and fiction. Writers, she said, must learn to be tolerant of truths other than their own: "All we ask of any writer is that he shall be honest with himself, that he shall possess artistic integrity."

Then Miss Glasgow expressed her sympathy with "that outcast from the machine civilization—the well-bred person." After recounting her own early beginning in the 1890s as a "champion of the oppressed" and explaining that the protagonist of her first book was illegitimate and the son of a "poor white," she observed, "Always I was in the skin of the fox at every hunt and in the skin of the yellow dog under the wagon at every village fair." Then, however, since the situation had so reversed itself that it became fashionable and snobbish to be lowly, despised, and rejected, Miss Glasgow had switched her sympathies to embrace those persons whose breeding was evidenced by "simplicity and consideration for others."

Finally, she incorporated the conference topic into her speech by using it as a bridge to a new subject, the reasons for more compassion in contemporary German literature than in American literature. She asserted that she was actually more interested in American literature for what it does not say, than for what it does say:

If I might have chosen the topic for discussion, I should have avoided the Southern writer and his public, especially since that public is usually situated far away from the South, and have tried to discover why America which suffered so little from the world war in fact should have suffered more deeply in spirit than the devastated countries. It is historically and eternally true that only in material defeat is there spiritual victory.

Her praise of German literature was used to criticize the lack of compassion in American literature. She stated that "the only safe substitute for genius in American literature is brutality."

In her closing statement Glasgow identified herself as one who had never flinched before truth. Then she offered a peroration: "Only let us learn from Dostoyevsky that if nothing is more terrible than life, nothing is more pitiable. Love may go; sex may go . . . but as Russia knew yesterday and Germany has discovered today, pity survives. Otherwise, the machine age may as well destroy itself while it prepares the world for the insect."

It was a high-minded, serious address which appealed to the universal concerns of the writer. The timeless problems of truth and of compassion in literature took precedence over contemporary issues. The scheduled topic was almost completely ignored.

Glasgow's delivery of her speech must have been effective, for Davidson in his published account called the speech "brilliant and witty." And Tate wrote Young that "the more I think about grand Ellen Glasgow, the more I fall in love with her. None of her books is as grand as she is."[17] Anderson said of her: "Ellen Glasgow took charge. She is charming. She is quite old now, but had tremendous vitality . . . a kind of mental alertness, eagerness, and charm" (p. 250). Wilson told her she carried through the first day "triumphantly."

After the conference ended, there were, on the one hand, the inevitable disappointments in a meeting attended by such differing personalities, among whom there were such varying expectations. On the other hand, for those who came for a party and for satisfying the curiosity of meeting other writers, there seemed to be a consensus of pleasure. Clark—who had accepted the invitation with enthusiasm but whose main concern, as expressed in her letter to Wilson, was to be put up at the Farmington Country Club (of which she was a member) and to be given a room with a bath—made the meeting sound like a merry and charming house party.

---

[17]Young quotes Tate in a letter to Glasgow dated January 11, 1932. This letter is in the Glasgow Collection, University of Virginia Library.

In her *Saturday Review* account she wrote of "Morning at Monti-cello, among vistas so wide that thirty guests were easily lost among them; afternoon at Castle Hill, with Amélie and Pierre Troubetzkoy coming down the box driveway to meet the cars . . . sunset at the Colonnade Club with a black-trunked, gold-topped ash tree gleaming at the end of the colonnade; moonlight at the Farmington Club, the loveliest club in Virginia" (p. 2). Wilson preferred her sprightly account to the others and called it "the most interesting and delightful" of all.[18] Anderson's impression of the Farmington Country Club gathering was also a pleasant one: "After dinner at the club a big crowd gathered about Barr, Ellen Glasgow and myself. We got into an amusing wrangle over some abstract subject, more to hang conversation on than anything else. Presently all joined it. It was the first real thaw-out, fun, going it hot and heavy, good-natured raillery and good talk" (p. 252).

Heyward's newspaper account stated that the gathering had marked a cultural milestone in the South, and Boyd also com-mented on the social aspects of the meeting when he wrote Wilson congratulating him on the spontaneity and informality of an event that might have been characterized by neither of those qualities. Boyd surmised that the meeting was actually successful in not accomplishing anything definite.

Others, however, did not view the lack of definite accomplishment as quite the triumph Boyd did. Davidson and Tate, forged in the fire of a different kind of informal and stimulating meeting with the Nashville Fugitives, wrote Wilson letters which indicated their belief that the historical, elegant—perhaps soporific—Virginia set-ting may have impeded a real clash of ideas. Davidson mentioned in his published article that the meeting had "no name," "no program," and "no purpose" other than to bring writers together and see what would happen in the "pleasant and stately circum-stances of Mr. Jefferson's University" (p. 494). He pointed out that not much mention was made of regionalism, sectionalism, or any other "ism": "Most of the sleeping dogs that have now and then growled in Southern Councils dozed on unawakened" (p. 495).

[18]Wilson made this comment in a letter to Glasgow dated November 16, 1931, in which he congratulated her on her performance at the conference. He enclosed copies of the published accounts. The letter is in the Glasgow Collection, University of Virginia Library.

Nevertheless, Davidson called this first conference a "great success," and he wrote Wilson that he hoped to be invited to future ones. He admitted that it could not have gone off so well except under "Virginia auspices—certainly not for this first time, when nobody could tell how the wild men from the western wilderness would get along with the magician of Poictesme, or just what South Carolina (under literary circumstances) would say to North Carolina." He also carefully stated some serious considerations:

I am somewhat disturbed by the thought, however, that, at some other possible meeting-place, the swapping of ideas which was in the main so friendly and generous at Madison Hall, might easily turn into a fierce clashing of ideas. At one time during the past meeting, perhaps it was only the shade of Mr. Jefferson that prevented a schism. I could think of places where the remarks of Mr. Paul Green, for instance, might have been challenged more sharply than anybody felt like challenging them at our meeting. There's much to reflect on here. Perhaps the thought, if I dared to frame it, would be that it will take a prestige like old Virginia's to prevent internecine quarrels among Southern writers who have this or that idea of what is to be done about the South and its tradition. I am one of those who hope that Virginia's position, as of old, will favor Tradition, in a conservative and reconciling sense— for otherwise there is Mr. Paul Green, able, intense, ready to blow us all to bits.

Allen Tate, too, was not completely satisfied with the results of the meeting. Like Davidson, his pleasure had been somewhat tempered by thoughtfulness. He wrote Wilson, "Perhaps at later conferences we shall lose some of this amiability—an inevitable loss if we shall ever discuss the fundamental questions that confront Southerners today." Tate believed "that the leading question before Southern literature is the nature of its peculiar genius, and perhaps it will some time be appropriate for Southern writers, in the lack of political leadership, to point out certain features of the question that do not ordinarily pertain to the literary problem." Both Tate and Davidson, though they enjoyed the meeting and hoped it would become an annual affair, seemed disappointed at the lack of depth and seriousness in Charlottesville.

Pinckney described the gathering as being neither serious nor frivolous, but both. In searching for some meaning to the conference, she hypothesized a somewhat dubious value when she suggested that authors might not write such grim books if they got together, discussed their problems, and enjoyed themselves.

Anderson summed up the meeting quite simply: "There didn't seem to be any definite thing accomplished. There were a lot of talks I didn't hear. I think the Agrarians were the only ones trying to put over any definite program" (p. 253). It is possible that his stark analysis contained the most accurate evaluation.

Henderson, the University of North Carolina professor of mathematics and biographer of Shaw, criticized the results of the meeting with bluntness and candor. He wrote Wilson that the one purpose accomplished at the meeting, acquainting authors personally with each other, may have been good enough for this initial meeting, but that it was not "sufficient justification for the conference." His assessment proves that not everyone considered the topic for discussion unworthy and suggests that not everyone was dazzled by Ellen Glasgow's performance. Henderson thought the air of amiability and charm got in the way of something of value; he suggested that the meetings continue, but he insisted on a more serious approach:

The conference appears to have been almost wholly subjective: with few exceptions the expressed views were vague and inchoate, leading nowhere and never arriving. A conference of this sort is futile if it has not some large and significant objective, of a constructive sort. Next time, the fear which seemed to paralyze Heyward and others lest something be done, may have worn off.

All the conferences cannot be, as someone expressed it, "glorified house parties." And this first conference leaves all the major problems, and even the minor problems, both unattacked or even undiscussed. The blitheful, ostrich-like ignoring, by our handsomely dressed, prosperous authors, in their high-powered cars, of the existence of a reading public (without which they could not thus disport themselves or even exist) was the huge, ironic job of the conference. I am afraid this was a by-product of luxurious and vapid femininity.

Constructive ideas—not subjective vaporings—my dear Wilson—are what the poor South needs. A conference must go dead soon as it supply and nourish them not.

There were, perhaps, some small results from the Charlottesville meeting in 1931: Faulkner made his first acquaintance with the university he was to distinguish with his presence a quarter of a century later; Glasgow and Tate formed what would become a warm friendship; and Cabell transformed his experiences into an amusing essay in *Special Delivery* (1933). But as a forum for exchanging constructive ideas the conference seems to have been a failure, even though its success as a house party is well documented by the many enthusiastic letters written to Wilson after the event. And the general desire to continue the meetings was strong enough to support a second meeting in Charleston in 1932.

Thus the 1931 meeting was a recognition, as well as a celebration, of the development in Southern writing now known as the Southern Literary Renaissance. For this event Glasgow briefly asserted herself to play a leading role in Southern letters.[19] Age and illness would prevent her continuing in the part, for in 1933 she wrote Wilson from Baltimore, where she was undergoing medical treatment, to request that he arrange for her resignation from the committee, which was apparently still in existence at that time.[20] But even in her triumphant speech, which was so well received in Charlottesville, were the seeds of the literary conservatism that would have in any case precluded her continuing the role as a leader: her spirited defense of the well-bred and her equally spirited attack on what she termed "brutality" in modern letters.

Still, without meetings, the Renaissance continued to flower, and many of those present at the 1931 gathering made important contributions. Now, over four decades later, when the Southern Literary Renaissance is history, many of those thirty are all but forgotten; yet others—Faulkner, Tate, Anderson, Glasgow, Cabell, and Green, for example—have won a claim to a permanent place in literary history.

[19]Professor Frederick P. W. McDowell in *Ellen Glasgow and the Ironic Art of Fiction* (Madison: University of Wisconsin Press, 1963), p. 33, observes that Glasgow saw the beginnings of the Renaissance early and that with this Charlottesville meeting it seemed that she "might achieve substantial leadership in American letters."

[20]This letter, dated June 8, 1933, is in the Glasgow Collection, University of Virginia Library.

Postscript

At the meeting in Charleston on October 21 and 22, 1932, Du Bose
Heyward played Wilson's Charlottesville role and the committee
remained the same: Glasgow, Cabell, Henderson, Green, Young,
Wolfe, and Heyward. The typed schedule of events lists luncheons
at Fort Sumter and the Brewton Inn, dinner at the Charleston
Country Club, trips to Fort Sumter and to Magnolia and Middleton
Gardens. Two meetings were scheduled, one at the beginning on
Friday and one at the 3:00 P.M. closing on Saturday; no topic for
these meetings is noted.[21] Thus the very idea of the worthiness of
Southern authors convening annually may have finally floundered
on the shoals of a cocktail party given by the Junior League
Scribblers' Group in Charleston. Not a single member of the committee, with the exception of Heyward, attended the Charleston
meeting. Glasgow was ill and Cabell had a distaste for literary
gatherings that he had compromised for Charlottesville, but would
not for Charleston. Henderson's letter to Wilson after the Charlottesville meeting has been prophetic: lacking the substance of
constructive ideas, the conference died from lack of nourishment.

[21] For information about the Charleston meeting, I am indebted to Mrs. Granville T.
Prior of the South Carolina Historical Society, who provided me with copies of material
now in the Du Bose Heyward Collection.

The Novels

The Earliest Novels

Howard Mumford Jones

IN this, the centennial year of the birth of Ellen Glasgow, it seems appropriate to examine the birthpangs of her narrative art. I propose therefore to discuss her earlier novels, and if for a time my discussion shall seem severe, I beg you to hear me patiently and see where my argument comes out.

The novels of Ellen Glasgow fall into three unequal divisions. The first is made up of her two earliest books, *The Descendant* (1897) and *Phases of an Inferior Planet* (1898). These works have little to do with Virginia and are mainly set in New York City, a metropolis to which she returned in *The Wheel of Life* (1906). The second division begins in 1900 with *The Voice of the People* and extends to the publication of *Barren Ground* in 1925. Except for *The Wheel of Life* and for the last portion of *Life and Gabriella* (1916), a part of which is laid in New York City, the ten novels of this period are set in this commonwealth and reflect various stages in its history. The period also includes a book of short stories, mainly of the supernatural, *The Shadowy Third* (1923), which have some mild tenure of Virginian soil. The last period of her work runs from *Barren Ground* to the posthumously published fragment, *Beyond Defeat* (1966), and the five novels of this epoch include some of her very best: *The Romantic Comedians* (1926) and *They Stooped to Folly* (1929), comedies of manners in the sense of Meredith's comic spirit, humanely malign, volleying down his arrows of silvery laughter; *The Sheltered Life* (1932), one of her perfect books; and *Vein of Iron* (1935) and *In This Our Life* (1941), which have some of the stark quality of *Barren Ground*. But their iron, if I may make a wretched pun, is relieved by irony.

Whether Miss Glasgow independently decided that her life work was to write a fictional social history of Virginia or whether, as he claims, James Branch Cabell put the suggestion to her is less important than the fact that, like Balzac, looking back on part of her work and looking forward to what she wanted to do, she embraced the idea of a history of manners. As a consequence she has been judged by historians and critics in the light of this aim. I think the phrase is mildly misleading, for my reading of her work is that she really seeks to answer a question she phrased in a letter of 1935: "What is the motive that enables human beings to endure life on the earth?"[1] This question poses a moral and philosophical inquiry, not a social or a sociological one, but as the part of the earth she knew best happened to be Virginia, she rightly felt that an answer could be had in terms of the life she knew rather than in terms of the life she did not know—that is, if any answer could be found. The answer is, as I read her, spiritual fortitude.

If the historian or the critic takes the view that the novels of Virginia society are the enduring legacy of this writer to later times—and this view is justifiable—he will look upon a work like *The Descendant* with an indifferent or a hostile eye. What does *The Descendant*, what does *Phases of an Inferior Planet* contribute to the grand design? Apparently nothing; and this answer seems to be validated by Miss Glasgow's omission of both books from the two collected editions of her works. If Miss Glasgow made a fictional history of Virginia society her great artistic aim, these two books point in precisely the wrong direction, as does *The Wheel of Life,* which is also a novel of New York City. It is an amusing footnote to *The Wheel of Life* to know that Miss Glasgow conscientiously tramped the streets of that metropolis for days and days, searching for local color, but after she had published the novel and looked back on it, she confessed that in all its 474 pages there was but one sentence she could derive directly from this search for the local and the authentic.

The first two novels are the work of a literary apprentice, though an uncommonly gifted one. Compared with Hemingway's rather dreadful first book, *The Torrents of Spring,* or with F. Scott Fitzgerald's *This Side of Paradise,* they are relatively mature. Yet they suffer from a similar brashness, a desire to be at all costs, in our meaning of the term, sophisticated. I think there is more to them than is implied in this condemnation, but first let me see how

---

[1]Blair Rouse, ed., *The Letters of Ellen Glasgow* (New York: Harcourt, Brace, 1958), p. 193. See also p. 190.

severely they can be condemned. I shall dwell more upon *The Descendant* than upon *Phases of an Inferior Planet*.

The Descendant is the story of Michael Akershem, the bastard offspring of an unknown father and a Virginian mother who died in childbirth. His foster parents are unkind, as are the people in a village near which he lives, a town rather improbably called Plaguesville. Michael has brains, ambition, and sensitivity. Unable to stand the slings and arrows of life in the Virginia countryside, he runs away to New York. This takes up twenty-six pages. In New York he seeks work but finds none and almost starves. One day, fainting in a public square, he returns to consciousness to find his head pillowed in the lap of a kindly prostitute who gives him some money and disappears. When the money runs out, he is about to commit suicide. Unexpectedly, he lands a job on the editorial staff of *The Iconoclast,* a radical paper, the support of which comes largely from Driscoll, an older man who plays with radicalism but has a kind heart and some wealth. Akershem meets Rachel Gavin, also from Virginia, though nothing is made of the fact. She has gone to New York to paint, to live a Bohemian life, and to advocate the liberation of the female sex—she has, she says, a place in the most advanced flank of the New Woman's Crusade. Akershem and Rachel fall in love but do not marry. The liaison, however, destroys Rachel's capacity to paint. Since on philosophic grounds she will take no money from Akershem, she is supposed to earn her own keep and cannot. The cost of the little establishment leads Akershem to toy with the idea of a job on a more moderate journal. Tension between Akershem and his mistress increases, among other reasons because Akershem has been drawn to Anna Allard, a better-balanced young woman than is Rachel and a girl who retains her status in New York society. Michael now offers to marry Rachel, but she refuses him, closes her studio, and flees the country. To help him get out *The Iconoclast* Michael had taken on a wild-eyed anarchist named Kyle, who now reproaches Akershem for softening his radical views; and in a sudden office quarrel Michael shoots and kills Kyle. Driscoll, who has hitherto viewed the whole situation with genial cynicism, though he is ill, does what he can to have Akershem's sentence for manslaughter reduced from ten to eight years. Released from jail and having contracted tuberculosis in prison, Akershem is recognized on the street by

Rachel, now an established artist recently returned from Europe. She still loves him. She takes him to her apartment and tries to nurse him back to health, but he dies in her arms.

An essential weakness of *The Descendant* is evident in the concluding paragraphs:

Then in a moment it was over, and he lay looking up at her, his face carved in the marble whiteness of pain, his brilliant eyes un-clouded. There was a harder battle to fight before the end would find him.

In his face the old fearless spirit which could be quenched but by dust shone brightly.

"Give me half a chance," he said, "and I will be even with the world at last."

But upon his lips was set the blood-red seal of fate.[2]

This is bad prose. Except in fiction dying men do not utter such perfectly modulated defiances as: "Give me half a chance, and I will be even with the world at last." Other phrases are just as brassy: "carved in the marble whiteness of pain," "the old fearless spirit which could be quenched but by dust," "the blood-red seal of fate." This style is no better than that in *St. Elmo;* and it is a tribute to Miss Glasgow's genius that she advanced from this staccato brassiness to the exquisite modulations of General Arch-bald's soliloquy in *The Sheltered Life.*

The central difficulty in *The Descendant* is that the management of the story and of the leading characters comes out of other books, not out of life observed and transmuted by the imagination. Miss Glasgow tells us in a notable passage in *A Certain Measure* that she had a sudden vision of the child Michael Akershem sitting in the dust by a Virginia road, the image with which the novel begins. I have no doubt that she did. What did she do with the image? The image of a miserable little boy, a bastard ill treated by adults and quite solitary in his sorrow, is also out of *Oliver Twist,* the harsh stepmother and the henpecked stepfather derive from *Great Expectations,* and there is nothing specifically Virginian about the little boy or the dusty road. He could have been sitting by a dusty road in Wisconsin or California, and he and his wicked stepmother and his stealthy escape to a passing circus with the aid

[2](New York: Harper & Bros., 1897), p. 276.

of a benevolent but sheepish adult—these, like his social ostracism, would have been just as valid. The starving and talented genius lost in the big city but rescued by a kindly prostitute with a heart of gold who puts money in his hand and disappears—the young man and the prostitute are anticipated by Victor Hugo and George Gissing and various other sentimental or "realistic" nineteenth-century worthies. When Akershem is on the verge of suicide and is rescued at the last minute by a benevolent bystander, one's mind goes back to Jean Valjean and the episode of the bishop's candle-sticks in Hugo's *Les Misérables.* Female virtue in Bohemia is the theme of du Maurier's *Trilby,* the conversation piece of all New York in the late nineties. The lover torn between a conventional woman and an emotionally undisciplined one you will find in Hardy's *Jude the Obscure;* and the death by tuberculosis of a suffering lover you weep over as the curtain goes down on the last act of either *La Traviata* or *La Bohème:* all Miss Glasgow has done is to reverse the role of the sexes. In this connection it is significant that Mariana, the heroine of *Phases of an Inferior Planet,* is an aspiring opera singer, and that the first encounter between her and Algarcife, the male lead, too closely parallels the first act of Puccini's sentimental masterpiece. Substitute a wilting geranium for Mimi's candle in *La Bohème* and the trick is done. In that novel, by the by, Algarcife and Mariana live in a New York boardinghouse with which Miss Glasgow had had some experience, but that did not prevent the boardinghouse from being translated into an Americanized version of the *pension Vauquer* in Balzac's *Le Père Goriot.* The witticisms of Algarcife's fellow boarders may be better than, but are suggested by, the labored wordplay of Goriot's companions in that famous story. Melodrama depends upon the exaggeration of situations and characters to secure a cheap and easy and immediate emotional effect.

At first glance the style in the two books seems to be no more than a vehicle for what is false, theatrical, and facile. The author writes, too much of the time, at the top of her voice. Here, for example, in *The Descendant,* is a situation that illustrates both the striving for a false emotionalism and the style through which the emotionalism is supposed to affect the reader. When she falls in love, Rachel Gavin has, too conveniently for theatrical symbolism, been at work on a picture of the Magdalen, that standard nineteenth-century epitome of the fallen woman. Suddenly, having become Akershem's mistress, she cannot paint. One then reads this direful prose: "She shivered and shrank back; she looked upon her unfinished picture—the great Magdalen; she stretched out her hands with a bewildered, appealing gesture. 'O God, anything but that—anything but that. O my God! O my God!'" This is opera, not reality. But worse is to come: "She threw herself upon her knees beside it, her bowed head [and this is incredible] resting against the outlined hem of the painted woman's garment [painted woman!]. . . . She had reared the temple of her aspirations upon her own heart, and she saw it shiver and crumble to its foundations, a dart hurled by her own faithless hand." A little later: "It was as if a devil and an angel warred within her, one chaining her to the flesh and to earth, the other drawing her upward to the heaven of the mind." A wandering critic now strolls in, inspects the picture, and tells Rachel her heart is not in her work. This infuriates her, and there follows an episode as theatrical as anything in Alexandre Dumas. Startled at the word *heart,* she springs up and paints furiously without pause for six mortal hours. In this frenzy she finishes the Magdalen, which is instantly transformed into a masterpiece. The canvas, we read, has been changed into something "strong and bold in its unrestrained drawing of pose, the repentant droop of the head, the passion and misery and sin." This is not all. The colors seem to "take fire and glow with a living flame."[3] To parallel this magic transformation one has to go back to Oscar Wilde's *The Picture of Dorian Gray* of 1891, which in the nineties it was daring to read.

In the nineties, it is true, advanced thinkers found little difficulty in reconciling the flippant epigrams of Wilde with the pessimism of Schopenhauer or in fusing the gloom of Ibsen with the optimism of Herbert Spencer, who, though he called God the Unknowable, nevertheless argued that the cosmos, if you would but let its operations go forward without interference, would by and large improve the human condition. The paradox of Ibsen is that almost all individuals fail, but mankind pushes on to a mysterious third empire, an empire in which the spirit of man shall at length reenter its heritage, as we learn from the conclusion of Ibsen's vast his-

---

[3]See ibid., pp. 115–17, for the whole episode.

torical drama, *Emperor and Galilean.* The paradox of Wilde is that
although in the view of the art-for-art's-sake school, life is futile,
art is immortal, unchangeable, perfectible. In a queer way Wilde
tried to draw together the world of epigram and the world of
progress, this in a small book, *The Soul of Man under Socialism,*
published two years before Miss Glasgow's *The Descendant.*

I have said nothing about the plot of *Phases of an Inferior
Planet,* which turns upon the conflict of individual demands of
science—in this instance, evolutionary science—and the demands
of art, in this case, musical art. The heroine, Mariana, is an opera
singer with more ambition than voice; the hero, Anthony Algarcife,
who seems to feel that with the most primitive laboratory facilities
he can correct his masters about the theory of acquired characteristics, is a "radical." They marry. A child is born and dies. Mariana
leaves the boardinghouse to try her luck in Europe; Anthony, on
the verge of suicide, is somewhat improbably persuaded to become
an Episcopal clergyman preaching fervent sermons which he secret-
ly contradicts in magazine articles he writes as an anonymous
biologist. This time the woman dies in the arms of the man, and
Algarcife, again about to kill himself, is suddenly called upon to
mediate a strike in a mill. The plot is no great advance over that of
The Descendant, and the style, as I have hinted, is peppered with
brittle epigrams. Thus in recording the conversation of the boarders
in the lodging house where Mariana and Algarcife live, Miss Glasgow sets off these verbal firecrackers in the space of two pages:

. . . as a method of self-destruction, there is none more efficacious
than an exclusive diet of . . . potatoes. Allow me to pass them.

Food may be important but important things should not always
be talked of.

Do you know, sometimes I wonder if social intercourse will not
finally be reduced to a number of persons assembling to sit in
silent meditation upon the subjects which are not spoken of.

We are a nation of prudes, and there is no vice that rots a
people to the core so rapidly as the vice of prudery.

I hold that indecency can only exist where beauty is wanting.
All beauty is moral.

Our one consolation is the knowledge that if we could possibly
have been uglier we should have been so created.

Personalities in conversation should be avoided as sedulously as onions in soup. They are stimulating but vulgar.[4]

However amusing any one of these sententiae may be, they are taken from the conversation of five of the characters, who all talk alike. I find it difficult to believe that boarders in a rooming house, even in New York's Bohemia, thus perpetually scintillated.

So far I have argued in the character of a prosecuting attorney. What now can be said for the defense? I think a great deal.

In the first place the writing and publishing of *The Descendant* are events almost as incredible as the transformation in six hours of Rachel Gavin's portrait of the Magdalen. At the age of twenty-two an unknown Southern belle, lonely, self-educated, rebelling against her family and the social tradition that confined her intellectual energy, often ill, conscious of growing deafness, suffering from the death of her mother, a loss that exposed her to the sternness of her father, abetted almost in secret by a sister, having twice destroyed the manuscript of a novel and completing one on a third try, ignorant of the world of publishing, of literary agents, of book contracts, of royalties, through a series of happy accidents gets her manuscript accepted by that prestigious American firm, the house of Harper. The publishers make no special effort to push her book, which they publish anonymously. An enchanting minor mystery then develops—who is the author? Perhaps Harold Frederic, whose *The Damnation of Theron Ware* (1896) had fluttered many dovecotes?

Before publication, in March 1897, *Publishers Weekly* says the book is "the story of a hero at odds with society who allies himself with the forces that make for anarchy and who openly defies law and order; a book said to be thought-compelling." "Forces that make for anarchy."[5] Readers shudder. Only three years earlier Coxey's army of the unemployed had marched on Washington; only last year William McKinley had been elected president because William Jennings Bryan, who thundered that you should not

---

[4]*Phases of an Inferior Planet* (New York: Harper & Bros., 1898). These sentences will be found sprinkled over pp. 11–13.

[5]*Publishers Weekly*, Mar. 13, 1897, p. 481.

crucify mankind on a cross of gold, was a revolutionary and an anarchist; only this year had the depression of 1893, after forty-eight months, begun to expire.

In 1897 the Century Club of New York announced that its library would henceforth be closed to the New York *World* and the New York *Journal,* apparently for their radical views, and in Boston the Public Library refused general access to certain works by French and German socialists. In April 1897, Anthony Comstock, the roundsman of the Lord, seized the entire edition of a translation of Maupassant, an author, said Miss Glasgow later, who taught her the art of fiction. The book was *Mme. Tellier's Girls.* In the summer Comstock caused the arrest of George H. Richmond, a New York bookseller, for vending Gabriele D'Annunzio's *Triumph of Death,* described in the warrant as an immoral, lascivious, and improper work. The American Bible Society, however, congratulated the Russian Bible Society in September for its success in circulating the Bible in the empire of all the Russias, and in July a sanitary Bible for the use of courtrooms had been invented. It was proposed to erect a monument in Edinburgh to the author of *Treasure Island,* an official life of Lord Tennyson was announced, and Lippincott said they were about to publish in a single volume "The Beauties of Marie Corelli," whose novel *The Sorrows of Satan* had had an enormous readership in 1895. In December the first edition of *Who's Who in America,* then called *Who's Who the Country Through,* appeared.

The name of the author of *The Descendant* was made public on June 12, 1897, by the publishers, who said that except for the last few chapters, the book was written before the author was twenty-two. The statement naturally increased interest. Not surprisingly, therefore, *The Descendant,* according to William W. Kelly's bibliography of Ellen Glasgow, went through three printings in 1897, a fourth in 1900, and a fifth in 1905. In consequence of this success Miss Glasgow had no difficulty in placing *Phases of an Inferior Planet* with Harper's, who insured simultaneous publication in London through the firm of William Heinemann. Both editions went through two printings, and might have received more, but the firm of Harper and Brothers was thrown into bankruptcy in December, 1898. One could read, however, in *Publishers Weekly* for May 27, 1898, that Miss Glasgow is a Southern girl, whose knowledge of the seamy side of life is as marvellous as that of [Beatrice Harraden, who wrote *Ships That Pass in the Night*]. Miss Glasgow's reputation was made but a short time ago with "The Descendant." Her recent novel is called "Phases of an Inferior Planet," a fourth- or fifth-rate Bohemia in New York City being the "inferior planet." Poor authors, struggling artists, impecunious journalists, and starving scientists are the characters. An intense love story told with painful truthfulness has its rise and fall in this environment.

The notice goes on to compare the new novel with *The Open Question,* a much discussed book by C. E. Raimond (Elizabeth Robbins), another problem novel on the dangers of marriage between close relations. It is clear that both of Miss Glasgow's books received respectful attention in their time.

In its last issue for January, 1898, *Publishers Weekly,* as was its custom, reviewed the publishing year for 1897. It found *The Descendant* worth notice, even among the more than 1,000 titles in fiction, American and foreign, the year had seen printed. *The Descendant,* it said, is the work of a young Southern girl, Miss Glasgow, and, in spite of some shortcomings, the book is "an exceptionally strong and promising novel. It is a study of heredity and socialism, often painfully disagreeable and showing lack of experience, but remarkable in its power of holding the attention, and in the daring unconventionality it betrays."[6]

Literary historians, forgetting that fiction is a commerical product that has to compete on the marketplace for its existence, stress only its competitiveness on the intellectual and artistic planes. *The Descendant* had to sell in competition with Sienkiewicz's immortal *Quo Vadis?*, Ralph Waldo Trine's gassy *In Tune with the Infinite,* James Lane Allen's *The Choir Invisible,* Hall Caine's *The Christian*, Richard Harding Davis's *Soldiers of Fortune*, Rev. Mr. Sheldon's *In His Steps*, one of the best sellers of all time, and Kipling's *Captains Courageous. The Little Colonel* by Annie Fellows Johnston had appeared two years earlier; *The Wonderful Wizard of Oz* was to follow it in three years. These were the popular successes. As for intellectual eminence, 1897 was the first appearance of Josiah Royce's *The Concept of God,* John Fiske's

---

[6]See, inter alia, the advertisements of Harper and Brothers in *Publishers Weekly,* and items in various notes and comments for Aug. 13, Oct. 1, 1898, and Jan. 28, 1899.

Old Virginia and Her Neighbors, William James's *The Will to Believe*, Bishop Spalding's *Thoughts and Theories of Life and Education*, Conrad's *The Nigger of the Narcissus*, Bernard Shaw's *Candida*, and a novel by Henry James. Looking back on 1897 from the vantage point of January 29, 1898, *Publishers Weekly* took a somewhat reserved view of Henry. It said: "Few books are more talked about than Henry James's 'What Masie Knew,' presenting repulsive aspects of the divorce question; Mr. James also wrote 'The Spoils of Poynton.'"[7]

Now, *The Descendant* is not necessarliy a masterpiece because in the year of its publication it competes on the market with the poems of Thomas Bailey Aldrich or gets more space in a review of the publishing year than did a novel by Henry James. But its history reveals two things: first, that though readers recognized defects in the book, they did not write it off as merely bungled work; and second, that it took its place in a new literature advancing the American capacity to think in terms of evolution, heredity, the relativity of morals, and social conventions. Has it, with its sequel, other merit?

The answer is that it has. The links between these early books and Miss Glasgow's maturer work are threefold: style, technique, and theme.

I have said the style in both books is artificial and metallic. It is a style that virtually compels the author to look at her characters from the outside. She does not in these books enter anybody's consciousness as she enters that of Judge Honeywell in *The Romantic Comedians*. The prose is angular and geometrical. But it also has weight and precision, it wastes no words, and it defines the visible world. If the balance of phrases in the epigrams is mechanical, this was fine practice work for the witty comparisons in the maturer novels. Here, for example, is a sentence from *Life and Gabriella:* "Her pretty vacant face with its faded bloom resembled a pastel portrait in which the artist had forgotten to paint an expression."[8] The comparison has wit, but note how unobtrusively "face" is balanced against "portrait" in this sentence and "faded bloom" offsets "forgotten to paint." For a fuller dis-

[7] *Publishers Weekly,* Jan. 29, 1898, pp. 218-19.

[8] *Life and Gabriella* (Garden City, N.Y.: Doubleday, Page, 1916), p. 5.

cussion of style in Miss Glasgow one turns to Monique Parent's monograph on her published in 1960. Here I merely emphasize that the specificity of language in the early books is an admirable vehicle for a writer to whom the visible world exists. She gives us not the gray, undifferentiated universe of Henry James, but a world of shapes, colors, and things.

She solves technical problems in *The Descendant* and in *Phases* that she is to solve more subtly in later work. One is the treatment of time, always a central element in her fiction. A characteristic novel tends to develop an initial situation richly, the development including veins of reminiscence that explain how the situation came about—an obvious parallel is almost any Ibsen play—and the initial situation develops its own climax. Then there is a time-gap, sometimes bridged by somebody's memory in the latter part of the novel. Toward the end of a book all the elements of the story, time past, present, and, by anticipation, time to come cumulate in a denouement. Such is the general structure of *The Sheltered Life.* But this pattern of development is also evident in *The Descendant* and *Phases,* although in *The Descendant* the first principal episode, the growth of love between Akershem and Rachel, is preceded by the prologue of Michael's boyhood and his arrival in New York.

A second important element is the use of a chorus that comments on the action, sees it at a distance, and anchors the story in specific time and place. The chorus, as in Greek tragedy, is only half aware of issues. Miss Glasgow, I think, took this device from George Eliot and Thomas Hardy, each of whom employs peasants, villagers, farmers, and the like smaller folk for the purpose. The slaves in *The Battle-Ground* and the villagers and farmers in *The Miller of Old Church* are examples of this technique, but Algarcife's fellow lodgers in *Phases of an Inferior Planet* show us an early use of this device.

One striking technical change is, however, evident. In *The Craft of Fiction* by Percy Lubbock, a book Miss Glasgow read with care, that critic distinguishes between the novel as scene and the novel as panorama. The first is put together like scenes and acts in a play; the second is a continuum of narrative. Thus Wilkie Collins's *The Moonstone* is composed of separate dramatic units like building blocks, whereas Henry James's *The Spoils of Poynton* flows like a river. In her first two novels Miss Glasgow inclines to the scenic novel; in her later ones she tends to the panoramic. The weakness of the first method is that the story may proceed by jerks where the latter method permits the novelist to fuse into a single line of narrative an exploration of the consciousness of a character, a sense of growing tension, and the lapse of time. Perhaps theme is more important than technique or style.

All accounts agree upon the enormous amount of reading the young girl from Virginia did in philosophy, political science, the theory of evolution, and the like topics. The accumulated weight of nineteenth-century intellectualism poured upon the novelist and as a consequence her first two books are overintellectualized, which accounts for what I have referred to as a certain metallic quality in their style. But this very fact enables us to trace to its fictional beginnings some of the major concerns of the future artist as she gradually shaped her personal view of the world. Like others in her generation, she was troubled by determinism, or the theory that all we are and do is fixed by causes beyond our control, of which heredity and social environment are most important. Blood, race, family, social custom—these are the stuff out of which she builds her manifold interpretations of life in Virginia. In a naive way heredity and environment "explain" the leading characters in her first two books—the bastardy of Akershem, Rachel's determined effort to escape a social pattern she was born to, Algarcife's temperament, and Mariana's French inheritance. Each couple is unable to conquer the environment in which we find them.

But Miss Glasgow is also a product of a tradition, a tradition that puts special emphasis upon individual freedom no less than upon the contradictory theory of Calvinism, which holds that man has no freedom of the will. In her later books she pictures rebels and victims. The latter succumb, dwindling as some of them do into the genteel old maids and futile bachelors of her Virginia novels; the former, though they may be defeated by inheritance and circumstance, win an inner victory, a clarity of vision, a maturity of values, as do Christopher Blake in *The Deliverance,* Millie Burden in *They Stooped to Folly* and Asa Timberlake of *In This Our Life.* Hints of this inner victory appear in the first two novels, however weakly. Algarcife is saved from suicide by a demand that he go forth and mediate between strikers and their employees;

Rachel returns from Europe a maturer and compassionate woman to comfort the broken Akershem; and, I suppose, in a naive sort of way, when Mariana comes back to New York reconciled to the fact that her physical endowment will forever prevent her from being a great operatic star, this, rather than her social success, is the point of her return in spirit to Algarcife.

Commentators on Miss Glasgow have spoken again and again of her dislike of evasive idealism, the source in her mind of all the genteel hypocrisies she delighted to condemn. She condemns it in these two books. Rachel escapes from Virginian gentility but she does not escape evasion, for she assumes that to secure a fuller life, the experience of love, and status in the world of art, all she has to do is to be "free," not realizing that freedom carries with it human responsibility. Hypocrisy and evasion also condition the attitudes and the conduct of Mariana and Algarcife in *Phases of an Inferior Planet;* only with great pain does Algarcife learn that human beings are not mere biological productions, and not even simple minds to be hoodwinked by sermons that are for him mere rhetorical exercises. His upside-down evasive idealism is finally forced to face reality when he is called out to settle a strike.

Like all major novelists Miss Glasgow comes at last to intelligent compassion as the key to life and art. Compassion, however, is a hard mistress, for the reason that it can easily slide into contempt on the one hand and into a maudlin pity on the other. Compassion is not self-evident in her first two books, which, I fear, take refuge in contempt and in sentimentality more often than they express compassion. Yet the compassion is there, now disguised as melodrama, as in the scene of Rachel leaning against the portrait of the Madonna, and now as snobbery, as Miss Glasgow writes down what, from her superior point of view, are the little falsities of conversation among her characters. But genuine compassion exists. An example is a brief episode in *The Descendant,* where Akershem, who has impulsively rescued a newsboy from a cable car and broken his leg in his recklessness, is visited by Driscoll. One reads:

And yet, John Driscoll, looking down upon him, started and fell back, wonder-stricken by the evanescent light upon his face. All the good deeds he might have done, all the pure thoughts he might have thought, seemed to circle in a humanized radiance about his head. A fleeting look, and yet John Driscoll felt a sudden chill of regret, for that one moment had shown him the man, not as he was, but as he might have been had not the corroding grasp of shame fastened upon his soul—had the sins of the fathers passed in honor on the head of the child.[9]

This is not good writing, but the essential note is there, the note of wisdom. Miss Glasgow's view came to be that of Meredith, from whom she took the title of one of her better novels:

> In this our life
> No villain need be. Passion spins the plot—
> We are betrayed by what is false within.

Or, in her own terms,

in looking back through a long vista, I can see that what I have called the method of constant renewal may be reduced to three ruling principles. Obedience to . . . self-imposed discipline has enabled me to write novels for nearly forty years, and yet to feel that the substance from which I draw material and energy is as fresh today as it was in my first youthful failure. As time moves on, I still see life in beginnings, moods in conflict, and change as the only permanent law. But the value of these qualities . . . has been mellowed by long saturation with experience—by that essence of reality which one distils from life only after it has been lived.[10]

Saturate *The Descendant* and *Phases of an Inferior Planet* with experience, and the resulting essence of reality will be called *Barren Ground, The Sheltered Life, They Stooped to Folly,* or *In This Our Life.*

[9] *The Descendant,* pp. 67–68.

[10] Glasgow, *A Certain Measure: An Interpretation of Prose Fiction* (New York: Harcourt, Brace, 1943), pp. 208–9.

The Prewar Novels

Frederick P. W. McDowell

WHILE the judgment may continue to stand that Ellen Glasgow's best novels were published from 1925 to 1932 and include *Barren Ground, The Romantic Comedians, They Stooped to Folly,* and *The Sheltered Life,* still some of her fiction before World War I has undeniable strength, considerable aesthetic merit, compelling social and psychological insight, interesting characters, and substantial vigor. Her novels beginning with *Barren Ground* represent her in her maturity and reveal austere control of her art. Yet with acceptance by readers and critics, climaxing a long struggle for serious recognition, went a certain hardening and rigidity, in evidence at least in her last two books, present at times even in her best late work, and disturbing in her monolithic pronouncements upon the state of Southern letters during the 1930s, in which she condemned some of the very tendencies, themes, and attitudes that she had done so much to domesticate into Southern fiction. *Virginia* (1913) is the best of these early novels and can stand comparison with the best of her later works. And at least two other novels from this period merit extensive analysis. *The Deliverance* (1904) and *The Miller of Old Church* (1911).

The novels which I do not have the time to discuss are less important in an absolute sense than the three that I shall treat. Yet the other four novels from these years which found a place in the Virginia Edition of 1938 have their merits. In *The Voice of the People* (1900) the minor characters such as Marthy Buff, Judge Bassett, Miss Chris, and Mrs. Dudley Webb reveal the born chronicler of manners, social usages, and powerful if inert traditions; and her presentation of social change, with the eclipse of the Virginia aristocracy by the rebellious proletariat and lower middle class, is interesting as it indicates an acceptance with her mind of its inevitability and a reluctance with her emotions to accept its full implications. As for *The Battle-Ground* (1902) such precisely rendered feminine types as Miss Lydia and Mrs. Lightfoot, the haunting death of Virginia Ambler in war-torn Richmond, and the utter waste involved in Dan Mountjoy's defeat give it some distinction despite its overromanticized depiction of antebellum life in Virginia. *The Romance of a Plain Man* (1909) is concerned with the rise of a Southern tycoon, but the term *romance* suggests what is indeed the case, that the book lacks the ruthless realism which characterizes Dreiser's portrait of Frank Cowperwood in *The Financier.* Moreover, Ben Starr's sexual tensions, which result from his defensiveness toward the aristocracy into which he marries, are all too weak in Miss Glasgow's realization of them. But again the re-creation of aristocratic manners and the challenges posed to them by the emerging middle class is discerning—Miss Mitty Bland's ambition to think just like her ancestors did and General Bolingbroke's horror that any woman of his acquaintance should know enough about sex to condemn a candidate for governor because of his profligacy ("What's the world coming to, I ask, when a maiden lady isn't ashamed to know that a man leads an impure life?"). In *Life and Gabriella* (1916) Miss Glasgow was less concerned with the outcast and the alienated individual (like Oliver Treadwell in *Virginia*) or with the victim of conventions in a changing age (like Virginia Pendleton in *Virginia*) than she was with the psychology of the individual who rises above the claims of a static culture. She is less persuasive, however, in presenting the forceful, commanding, and gallant woman in Gabriella Carr than she is in portraying the victims of outworn mores. Gabriella is the least attractive heroine in Miss Glasgow's fiction, a first version of the Dorinda Oakley in *Barren Ground,* who is also finally more admirable than appealing. Yet Dorinda is enough of the outcast and is so thoroughly assimilated to the broomsedge fields that her assumptions of superiority are much less obtrusive. Nevertheless, in *Life and Gabriella* Miss Glasgow again excels, at least in the opening chapters, when she dramatizes Southern manners and the absurd excesses which result from Mrs. Carr's inability to face—other than hysterically—the consequences of the disagreeable, in this case the infidelity of her other daughter's husband. Accomplished and interesting as these other books often are, *The Deliverance, The Miller of Old Church,* and *Virginia* are more consistent aesthetic successes. If these three books lack the full artistic and philosophical maturity revealed in her later comedies of manners, they exemplify a greater impatience

with constricting traditions, a more forthright rebelliousness, a
greater independence of temper, a more confident authority, and
a freer mind. Though she is not in these books as finished an artist
as she will later become, she is, there is reason to think, a more
attractive one.

Unfortunately, *The Deliverance, The Miller of Old Church,* and
Virginia must now be relegated to the category of "lost literature,"
books that still have something important to say but have dropped
out of the literary consciousness at large and are virtually impossible to procure. Only four of Miss Glasgow's novels have survived
on publishers' lists, the excellent but not always typical *Barren
Ground,* and these peripheral works, *Vein of Iron, In This Our
Life,* and *The Voice of the People.* If one regrets that these earlier
novels are not available, he must also deplore the fact that her later
comedies of manners are out of print. I would be happy if my
critique may suggest again the excellence of at least a half dozen
of Miss Glasgow's books and encourage publishers to take them up.
At a time when women and literature and women in literature
have become engrossing enquiries in higher education, it is distress-
ing that key works on these subjects such as *The Miller of Old
Church, Virginia, The Romantic Comedians, They Stooped to
Folly,* and *The Sheltered Life* are not at hand for study and for
classroom use.

The Deliverance centers upon the psychic conflicts of Christopher
Blake, who as a child during the Civil War and the Reconstruction
has been brought up by his fanatical sister, Cynthia, in resentment
of his family's fallen fortunes. As a study of the modulations
through which perverted passion can take a man, the book is
masterly. And it achieves its authority from the way in which
Christopher's resentment and passion are regional and racial emotions as well as an individual's. The festering sense of material and
cultural loss engendered by defeat in war and the humiliation
experienced during the Reconstruction have their embodiment in
Christopher Blake, the deposed and deprived descendant of the
Virginia aristocracy, who is unable, perhaps justifiably, to accept
with resignation his altered status. He and his family work to keep
his blind mother ignorant of the evil days upon which their house
has come. Since she is blind, she does not know that she is living
in the former overseer's house rather than at Blake Hall; she does

not know that her once affluent children are now reduced to poverty and that the family has lost political power and social prestige. She does not even know that the South has been defeated in the Civil War. Just as the South in the later nineteenth century tended to live only in the past and to evade the realities of military and economic eclipse, so Mrs. Blake lives in the past and worships the the traditions which she accepts as binding, though privately she regards some of the more romantic of them with an almost brutal cynicism. Though she thus sees them for what they are, she would, under no circumstances, disown them.

But Christopher is not without his sensitivity, his largeness of nature, and his intelligence. These qualities ultimately deflect him in his single-minded pursuit of revenge. Or, more properly, they impress upon him the heinous quality of his schemes once he is about to realize them. Too late, he sees that his design, now that it has been elaborated, cannot be prevented from its completion. He has had the diabolical inspiration to corrupt Will, the impressionable grandson of his adversary, Bill Fletcher, who had stolen Blake Hall and plantation in the confusion prevailing during Reconstruction. Will Fletcher, weak rather than vicious, is ruined when Christopher deliberately sets about making him a drunkard and an idler and encourages him to defy his grandfather so that the rupture between them will be hastened.

Christopher evades for long the truth which his conscience tries to force upon him, that in seducing Will he has manipulated another human being, using him for his personal ends as his ancestors had used their Negro slaves. It is, in another form, the crime of Thomas Sutpen in *Absalom, Absalom!*, who rejects the purely human claims which others make on him in the pursuit of an abstractly conceived ambition. Only through the agency of his love for Maria Fletcher does Christopher finally realize that his crime against a human being is worse than Fletcher's theft of the Blake lands.

In Christopher Blake Miss Glasgow has managed to incorporate a capaciousness and an elemental quality deriving from his contact with the soil and the grievances of his region. His vindictiveness is more than personal in its origins, and his rapport with nature has the effect of sometimes endowing his passion with a positive sanction, to the point even of persuading the critical observer Guy

Carraway (or the reader) of its legitimacy. If his final scheme is reprehensible and small-minded, Christopher himself is not. Therein lies his tragedy and perhaps the tragedy of the postwar South, which tended to brood over its afflictions rather than act positively to lessen their effect. Christopher's accord with nature and his willingness to sacrifice himself for his family give a largeness to his being, a largeness that is reminiscent of the figures in Greek tragedy. In that he gives up his best years and his best energies for his family, he is their ritual sacrifice; in that he deliberately cultivates the demonic in pursuit of his revenge, his family and, symbolically, his region are the sacrifices. Like the protagonist in a Greek tragedy, Christopher comes to an ultimate agonizing recognition of the flaw in his nature. If his resentment against Bill Fletcher as the opportunist who has battened on the misfortunes of others is justified, it is also destructive in its psychic damage to Christopher. Like Hamlet he is too sensitive, ultimately, for the vindictive role that convention, circumstances, and his own vehement nature have forced upon him; and he comes to see that "he had sold his birthright for a requital which had sickened him even in the moment of fulfilment."[1] When he falls in love with Maria Fletcher, he feels as much resentment as exaltation, a resentment caused by a reluctant recognition that love for Maria will compel him to forgo the passion that for so long has sustained his spiritual life.

The waste of Christopher's powers is implicit in his realization that he has striven to preserve an ethos that has not been worth his heroic efforts or the sacrifice of his entire life to it. More quickly than Cynthia, he rebels against aristocratic pride and exclusiveness, the ideas of caste and class, though he appreciates her own self-effacement and stoic renunciations. Once he begins to feel love for Maria Fletcher he can no longer agree with Cynthia that the intelligent yeoman Jim Weatherby is unworthy of Lila Blake, their sister, simply because he is a plebian. Ultimately, as one aspect of his "deliverance," Christopher sees that his ancestors, though they possessed charisma, command, and courage, were also effete, hedonistic, even trivial in their outlook and values. When at

---

[1]*The Deliverance* (New York: Doubleday, Page, 1904), p. 427. Subsequent references to this book will be by page number within the text.

the end he decides to take the blame for Will's murder of his grandfather, he looks up during this moment of crisis at the portrait of
a formerly revered ancestor who had once said, "I may not sit with
the saints, but I shall stand among the gentlemen," and mutters to
himself, "Precious old ass!" Thus is Christopher delivered from the
tyranny of past traditions upon him and from the moral coarseness
and apathy which have been in part his heritage. Graciousness,
poise, generosity, and physical courage are positive attitudes that
he has also inherited, but their influence does not countermand
that of Blake decadence upon him until it is almost too late.

Christopher realizes at last the lengths to which the evasive
idealism of his ancestors would take him if he were to align himself
with it forever. As a symbol of these values and of the backward-
looking South after the Civil War there is the blind but redoubtable
Mrs. Blake. For the most part she convinces as a symbol because
she is so perfectly envisioned as a person, largely as a result of her
brilliant, witty, and cynical conversation and the values which she
expresses through its means. In her vocal expression of tradition
and social values, she becomes, as it were, the living voice of her
region. Like the South of which she is emblematic, she extols
romance, fine manners, and time-tested social institutions such as
marriage and the Episcopal Church. Perhaps like the South, she
recognizes the falsity inherent in most of what she extols, but the
appearance, in her view, is often more important than the reality.
Or to be more exact, the appearance must be revered, though one
also has the obligation of recognizing the appearance as an appearance (at least the worldly wise will see such hypocrisy for what it
is, even while they condone it).

It is as a spokeswoman for these contradictions in the chivalrous
South that Mrs. Blake is so remarkable a portrait. She puts first
what she considers to be first, though under the eye of eternity
she must know that it cannot be first. In this view gentility is
superior as a value to a sincere morality or a deeply felt religion,
if there has to be a choice between them, as she implies in this
observation: "Remember to be a gentleman, and you will find that
that embraces all morality and a good deal of religion" (p. 479).
She is a romantic by disposition in extolling love, but a cynic to
the degree that she acknowledges the limitations of romantic feeling as a viable basis for social stability. Love is not so important as

marriage, which in its turn is to be regarded as a faintly punitive rather than an exalted experience:

"My child, there was never a book yet that held a sensible view of love, and I hope you will pay no attention to what they say. As for waiting until you can't live without a man before you marry him—tut-tut! the only necessary question is to ascertain if you can possibly live with him. There is a great deal of sentiment talked in life, my dear, and very little lived—and my experience of the world has shown me that one man is likely to make quite as good a husband as another—provided he remains a gentleman and you don't expect him to become a saint" (p. 398).

Even if the individual knows that love will fade, he is still expected to do his part to preserve the social fabric. A man, above all, has no right to be an individual to the extent of pleasing himself by not marrying:

"For a man to go twenty-six years without falling in love means that he's either a saint or an imbecile, my dear; and for my part, I declare I don't know which character sits worse upon a gentleman" (p. 104).

"I'm sure Providence expects every man to do his duty, and to remain unmarried seems like putting one's personal inclination before the intentions of the Creator" (p. 161).

Above all, the woman must not put her personal inclinations above what society expects from her:

"I married for love, as you certainly know . . . but the marriage happened to be also entirely suitable, and I hope that I should never have been guilty of anything so indelicate as to fall in love with a gentleman who wasn't a desirable match" (p. 198).

More is expected of the woman than of the man. If the man is discreetly profligate, he may well acquire an added glamor, but the Southern woman, like Caesar's wife, must be above suspicion: "Oh, the family was all right, my dear. I never heard a breath against the women" (p. 270).

One other focus in the novel is provided by the Calvinist local storekeeper, Susan Spade. In her exaggeratedly grim and earnest view of retribution, she reflects without knowing it the fatality which will overtake Christopher. That aspect of Calvinism which holds that as a man sows so shall he reap is exemplified in Christopher's fate. But she is also a humorous character largely because she cannot see the absurdity of a religion whose adherents, without imagination, judge only by the letter of dogma. She also embodies the same evasive idealism as Mrs. Blake but reflects, in addition, an asceticism quite foreign to her upper-class counterpart. As a kind of one-woman rustic chorus and as the voice of nemesis, she reflects upon Maria Fletcher's misfortunes in a vindictive, self-gratulatory way which she does not see as being at all self-righteous:

"She ain't bewitched me, an' what's mo', she's had too many misfortunes come to her to make me believe she ain't done somethin' to deserve 'em. Thar's mighty few folks gets worse than they deserve in this world, an' when you see a whole flock of troubles settle on a person's head you may rest right sartain thar's a long score of misbehaviours up agin 'em. Yes ma'am; when I hear of a big misfortune happenin' to anybody that I know, the first question that pops into my head is: "I wonder if they've broke the sixth this time or jest the common seventh?" The best rule to follow, accordin' to my way of thinkin', is to make up yo' mind right firm that no matter what evil falls upon a person it ain't nearly so bad as the good Lord ought to have made it."

"That's a real pious way of lookin' at things, I reckon," sighed Eliza [Field] deferentially . . ." but we ain't all such good churchgoers as you, the mo's the piety."

"Oh, I'm moral, an' make no secret of it," replied Mrs. Spade. "It's writ plain all over me, an' it has been ever sence the day that I was born. 'That's as moral lookin' a baby as ever I saw,' was what Doctor Pierson said to ma when I wan't mo'n two hours old. It was so then, an' it's been so ever sence. 'Virtue may not take the place of beaux' my po' ma used to say, 'but it will ease her along mighty well without 'em'—" (p. 368).

The Deliverance has some flaws, notably the way in which love is supposed to regenerate Christopher Blake. In this aspect of the denouement too much is asserted without being conclusively dramatized. Christopher's conversion is too complete and finally too easy, lacking the authority exerted, for example, by Raskolnikov's regeneration in *Crime and Punishment*. Maria Fletcher is too confident a spiritual agent, too assured that her own suffering has given her an ultimate degree of wisdom. She is also too passive and abnegating before Christopher. The suspicion obtrudes that he may be raising her to a more exalted social station as well as undergoing a spiritual renovation. The conversion is too enclosed, too little related to the milieu of which both are parts. J. R. Raper has succinctly expressed this kind of reservation: "For all its criticism of evasive idealism, *The Deliverance* seems, in light of the true psychological problem of the modern South, to be a call for the reconciliation of all southern whites under the banner of a modified aristocratic ideal with the black man playing the familiar role of excluded scapegoat."[2] But Raper also says that we should be grateful that Ellen Glasgow had gotten as far as she had in 1904 in the repudiation of lifeless conventions.

All reservations aside, *The Deliverance* is distinguished for its evocation in the Virginia tobacco fields of unspoiled nature, for its analysis of the lives of men and women close to the elements, for its psychological acuity, for its depicting of characters who are alive at the same time that they are social symbols, and for the creation of an imaginative universe in which Miss Glasgow has convincingly embedded some of the mythic aspects of a Southern civilization immediately anterior to her own time.

The Miller of Old Church is remarkable for its unity of tone, its consistency of texture, and its admixture of objectivity and sympathy revealed in the novelist's point of view toward her people, their milieu, and their problems. The conspectus of the novel is broad, encompassing with authoritative grasp the social classes to be found in turn-of-the-century Southside Virginia and their interactions with each other. It is a novel with social transition as its subject, in which talented representatives from the poor white class are emerging from their former obscurity to wrest political power from a declining aristocracy. Behind the shifting social scene, as if perhaps to emphasize its ultimate unimportance, lies an unspoiled landscape, with all its beauty and suggestion of primitive power. In no other of her novels is the beauty of the countryside quite so integral a component. As in Hardy's books the sympathetic characters are alien to its influence. Without seeming at all

[2]J. R. Raper, *Without Shelter: The Early Career of Ellen Glasgow* (Baton Rouge: Louisiana State University Press, 1971), p. 198.

derivative, *The Miller of Old Church* is the most Hardy-like of Ellen Glasgow's novels. The Darwinian view projected of nature and of life in society, the stress upon the baleful coincidence (Molly Merryweather arrives just in time not to prevent Abel Revercomb's disastrous marriage to Judy Hatch), the chorus of rustic peasants, and the presence of an overarching landscape are some aspects of this novel which may have derived from the books of her much admired Hardy.

This is Miss Glasgow's one novel in which the lower-class hero is fully convincing. More fire went into Miss Glasgow's envisioning of Abel Revercomb, the miller, than into the more tentatively conceived Nicholas Burr of *The Voice of the People* or Ben Starr of *The Romance of a Plain Man.* She feels more unalloyed sympathy with Abel's aspirations, possibly because the aristocrats are more desiccated and contemptible in Miss Glasgow's view of them than they are in *The Voice of the People,* for example. More erotic feeling also went into his characterization than Miss Glasgow was usually capable of. Abel is an enterprising man of Populist leanings, a self-developed man of credible intellectual pretentions and political ambitions, a man toward whom his creator does not condescend. In love he suffers from a tendency to idealize—at least from a wish to make Molly Merryweather more consistent and more ardent than she is by nature. But for the most part he sees things as they are, in contrast to the evasive aristocrats who ought to be the community leaders but who have renounced their responsibilities. There is the same conflict in the lovers between the man's compulsion to possess the beloved absolutely and the woman's resistance to such domination, a subject which D. H. Lawrence was soon to exploit in his fiction.

The course of true love is anything but smooth. In her heroine Molly, as in another of the women in the novel, Blossom Revercomb, Miss Glasgow consummately realized one feminine type, more frequent in rural nineteenth-century Anglo-Saxony than in modern urban culture, the woman whose ardor is in conflict with a chastity deriving from a hereditary Puritan temperament and a sexually repressive culture. Molly's conflicts with the miller are as much conflicts between both sides of her divided self as they are between the ardent man and the hesitant woman. If anything, this same conflict is more intense as it determines the affair between the protorake Jonathan Gay and the warm but chaste Blossom, who will not submit to him without marriage. Symbolically, at about the halfway point in the novel, Molly must choose between coming into her aristocratic heritage or marrying the miller. At the end Abel insists that she give herself to him completely, something which she had not been able to do earlier. Her father, the elder Jonathan Gay, had stipulated in his will that she would lose her inheritance if she married without the consent of the Gays. Molly's confusion is at least explicable as she tries to adjust these contrary absolute claims being thrust upon her. Her true inheritance stems from her mother; and to the peasant strain and the integrity which it represents she is ultimately loyal in her willing, if still hesitant, submission to the miller at the novel's end.

Miss Glasgow presented rural types persuasively and sympathetically in this novel. Reuben Merryweather, a man of sensibility and intelligence but of limited education and personal force, suffered most from the unfair caste system prevalent before the war, the limitations of which the miller has been able to surmount. Reuben is convincing as a rural saint, probably because he figures only incidentally in the action. His death at seventy on a fine spring afternoon following his conversation with the ninety-year-old, eternally vital Adam Doolittle is invested with a pathos that escapes sentimentality. Reuben is only one of the people who have had to suffer from the tyranny of the false saint, the aristocratic Mrs. Gay, who is so pure that nothing disagreeable can ever be mentioned in her presence. His granddaughter remains illegitimate because her father, the elder Jonathan Gay, could not marry Janet Merryweather, the woman he had compromised: the whole affair would have been too much for Jonathan's sister-in-law, the delicate Mrs. Gay, with her reputed weakened heart, even to acknowledge. Janet, the rustic woman whose disappointments drove her to insanity and death, is the communal sacrifice to the obstructive purity and reticence of the inflexibly innocent Mrs. Gay.

The other Revercomb men do not possess the miller's intelligence and enterprise. His brother Abner, the father of Blossom, is morbidly introverted, while Archie, the younger brother, is the drifter and shiftless pleasure-seeker. Sarah Revercomb, the mother of these men, is one of Miss Glasgow's finest creations. She is the self-assured Calvinist whom other people regard as monolithic because she never admits a mistake or a weakness. Her sympathies are limited in the ordinary concerns of life because to express them would be an unwarranted self-indulgence. Her religious fundamentalism is so intense and so incongruous as to be a source of humor for the detached reader while it is a source of distress to those who must in the novel come to terms with it.

It is in the presentation of the rural populace in *The Miller of Old Church* that Miss Glasgow reaches one peak of her artistry. Nowhere else are the rustics so engaging, nowhere else is the humor that they or their remarks inspire so genuine, and nowhere else are they so organic to the meaning of the novel. They provide local color and do much more. They are humorous in two ways: they are capable of seeing things as they really are, without the veneer of polite manners and in their incongruous aspects; and their simplistic comments on morality, the relationships between the sexes, and general ideas are in themselves comic. In the early pages Solomon Hatch descants at length on the connection between a reluctance to undergo immersion and the tendency to succumb to immorality, and so underlines the tendency of the populace to regard religion, morality, and ideas in the most literal light. But if the rustic is in his philosophy of life too single-minded, Jonathan Gay illustrates the lack of seriousness, characteristic of the Cavalier temper, which results in disaster for him. If old Adam Doolittle is a realist and a pessimist when he philosophizes on the Darwinian aspects of nature, he generally eschews the unpleasant because, for a ninety-year-old man, life is too short for one to be preoccupied with the disturbing. He prefers, therefore, not to think of the possibility that the elder Gay may have been murdered in revenge by Abner Revercomb:

"I'm too old at my time of life to take up with any opinion that ain't pleasant to think on, an', when all's said an' done, pure murder ain't a peaceable, comfortable kind of thing to believe in when thar's only one Justice of the Peace an' he bed-ridden since Christmas. When you ax me to pin my faith on any p'int, be it for this world or the next, my first question consarnin' it is whether that particular p'int happens to be pleasant. 'Tis that little small argyment of mine that has confounded Mr. Mullen more than once, when he meets me on equal ground outside the pulpit. 'Mebbe 'tis an' mebbe 'tisn't,' as I remarked sociably to him about the matter of eternal damnation, 'but you can't deny, can you, suh, bein' outside the pulpit an' bound to speak the truth like the rest of us, that you sleep a long sight easier in yo' bed when you say to yo' self that mebbe 'tisn't?'" [3]

In this view of things he reflects, in its most reductive form, the evasive idealism of the aristocrats such as Mrs. Gay and Jonathan Gay. At the corn-shucking the peasants comment on Molly Merryweather and her illegitimacy with the same lack of sympathy for the woman involved in sexual irregularity as their counterparts in the aristocracy might reveal. So Solomon Hatch expresses himself, to be echoed in his opinion by the others present:

"Why, to see the way she trails her skirts, you'd think she was the real child of her father. Ah, it's a sad pass for things to come to, an' the beginnin' of the end of public morality, when a gal that's born of a mischance can come to act as if a man was responsible for her. It ain't nothin' mo' nor less than flyin' in the face of the law, which reads different, an' if it keeps up, the women folks will be settin' up the same rights as men to all the instincts of nature" (p. 298).

This passage manifests the same rationale as that behind Mrs. Gay's rigorous application of the double standard of sexual morality, a standard which forbade her, for example, to extend sympathy to Janet Merryweather.

Miss Glasgow reveals the aristocracy in this novel as played out. It is undoubtedly her purpose to show it at its nadir of strength and influence, and she makes her point. But the novel might have possessed additional intonations and complications if there had been a vocal aristocrat who exemplifies some of the positive qualities which Miss Glasgow usually ascribed to this class even in its decline. There is no Tucker Corbin or General Archbald to exert the force of civilized values; the role of the mystical-materialist saint in this novel is assumed by Reuben Merryweather, from the lower class. Molly Merryweather at her strongest and most gracious may connote the reinvigoration of the aristocratic stock with an infusion of the Merryweather blood from below; but she ultimately

---

[3] *The Miller of Old Church* (Garden City, N.Y.: Doubleday, Page, 1911), p. 8. Subsequent references to this book will be by page number within the text.

chooses the miller from her mother's class, as we have seen, rather than the Gays from her father's.

The effete aspect of the aristocracy is associated in *The Miller of Old Church* with the destructive dominance of feminine influence and its concomitant evasive idealism. Three major figures, all triumphs of characterization, reveal the debilitating influence of an idealized conception of woman: Mrs. Gay, Jonathan Gay, and Kesiah Blount. Foremost is Mrs. Gay herself, whose pernicious power stifles the lives of others. She "had surrendered all rights in order to grasp more effectively at all privileges" (p. 72); the chief of these privileges is the exercise of power over others, which she enjoys though she or no one else will admit that this is the fact. She is a mythical figure in that she represents the heightened femininity which a male-oriented society reveres. But she is also conscious of her mythical role: she only regrets that there are no Byrons, de Mussets, or other exalted sinners for her to uplift and regenerate in her unromantic era. She also uses the values of sanctified custom for her own ends and is destructive, insidiously so, because no one can ever be honest in her presence. She is either the ultimate or the proximate cause of the elder and younger Jonathan Gays' deaths, of Janet Merryweather's madness and early death, and of Blossom Revercomb's bereavement. In this novel Miss Glasgow thus demonstrated the link between the Victorian idealizing of woman and moral decadence. Because a "pure" woman could not in all conscience face the unpleasant, she encouraged the easy rather than the upright moral course. It is easier in the present to avoid the unsettling fact, though one may compound its later adverse effects by so doing. It is because Jonathan Gay had been taught to consider his mother's sensitivity rather than a respect for the truth that he dies tragically.

Miss Glasgow's analysis of the Cavalier mentality in Jonathan Gay is discerning. Jonathan is not so much evil and criminal in tendency as indecisive and apathetic, a drifter rather than a wrongdoer, a man who recognizes what he ought to do but settles for what is easiest to do, a man whose easy fatalism courts disaster. Christopher Blake's restlessness of temperament is accentuated in him. Mrs. Gay's example only encourages his specious rationalizations and his self-deceptions. His death is a high price for him to pay in order to preserve his mother's peace of mind. Just as much as Janet Merryweather, Jonathan Gay is the tribal scapegoat offered up to his goddess mother, a sacrifice that is tacitly rather than ever explicitly acknowledged. It is most ironical, too, that Jonathan is murdered when, at Molly's bidding, he goes to make amends to Blossom. Mrs. Gay had also concurred with those who united to ruin the life of Kesiah Blount, her sister, a woman who finds revolt impossible because she is plain. She had had artistic talent but her family were adamant in their disapproval of her going to Bohemian Paris to study: "It was out of the question that a Virginia lady should go off by herself and paint perfectly nude people in a foreign city" (p. 75).

The Reverend Orlando Mullen is only one of the people who regard Mrs. Gay as a saint, a paragon among women. Mr. Mullen is entirely conventional in his point of view as befits one who reveals "less the ambition to excel than the moral inability to be peculiar." Nowhere is he more approving of convention than when he preaches his sermon on woman. The sequence in which he extols in church the submissive and clinging woman is one of the most amusing in the novel. He voices ideas that are really absurd, though he and his audience are incapable of so judging them. In his sermon he thus reveals the same unconscious, society-wide hypocrisy as do the Gays and the rustics when he describes with enthusiasm the constricted sphere of activity open to a virtuous woman. Part of Miss Glasgow's summary of this sermon demands quotation:

Woman . . . was created to look after the ways of her household in order that man might go out into the world and make a career. No womanly woman cared to make a career. What the womanly woman desired was to remain an Incentive, an Ideal, an Inspiration. If the womanly woman possessed a talent, she did not use it—for this would unsex her—she sacrificed it in herself in order that she might return it to the race through her sons. Self-sacrifice—to use a worn metaphor—self-sacrifice was the breath of the nostrils of the womanly woman. It was for her power of self-sacrifice that men loved her and made an Ideal of her. Whatever else woman gave up, she must always retain her power of self-sacrifice if she expected the heart of her husband to rejoice in her. The home was founded on sacrifice, and woman was the pillar and the ornament of the home. There was her sphere, her purpose, her mission. All things outside of that sphere belonged to man, except the privilege of ministering to the sick and the afflicted in other households (p. 130).

The unconscious duplicity behind all this rhetoric was to present a constricted existence as a glorious one.

The excellence of *The Miller of Old Church* becomes firmer the more it is subjected to careful scrutiny. It is one of the most compendious of Miss Glasgow's books; its scope is broad, and the modes of experience which it encompasses, from the tragic to the comic, make it distinctive. It also reveals an effortless quality, as if it were a spontaneous ebullition from Miss Glasgow's full knowledge of the society of which she wrote. The book is impressive in its truth to life and in its truth to the requirements of art.

An even more commanding distillation from Miss Glasgow's total immersion in her culture and region is to be found in *Virginia,* one of the masterpieces of early twentieth-century fiction. There is no doubt of Miss Glasgow's command of her subject, and this command is evinced through her consistent ironic vision. The irony holds her people at a distance and allows her to see them objectively, to comment, as the omniscient narrator, upon the scene which she has set in front of her. An intensity accompanies this irony, and sometimes breaks its mold to become compassion, particularly in the later portions of the book, though compassion even here will revert to the more detached ironic perspective.

Actually, this diversity of modes characterizes the whole novel. In Book One, "The Dream," there is such alternation of modes of a different sort. Subjective sympathy—or compassion—is scarcely present except as the irony modulates on occasion to mellowness. In this section the contrast is, rather, between the ironic social commentary and the lush, romanticized descriptions of dawning love and sexual attraction. The assimilation of the love affair between Virginia and Oliver to the verdant Southern spring at once intensifies the idealism of the participants and their ardor. Miss Glasgow conveys how erotic Virginia and Oliver really are and, at the same time, how unconscious they are of this eroticism or how they explain it away, regarding their emotion as transcendent spiritual feeling, the calling of soul to soul, and so on. Although Miss Glasgow outdid contemporary romancers in these sequences, they ultimately serve an ironic purpose when, far along in the novel, the reader reverts to these earlier scenes and contrasts the bleak aspect of Virginia's later years with the emotional fullness of her courtship.

The irony is mostly verbal in the first part of the novel, though there is also much irony in situation established by the time the novel ends. Miss Glasgow's ironic vision is expressed through statements which eventuate in a balanced critical appraisal of the scene before her. In her diction she often reinforces her saturnine perspective by an aphoristic, epigrammatic, concentrated style. The irony not only implicitly criticizes the society, or the person, or the belief being described, but is delayed in its full effects and thereby permeates and pervades the whole novel. Miss Glasgow achieved perfection for this kind of utterance in *The Romantic Comedians* and *They Stooped to Folly,* though in some ways she reveals a more robust sensibility in *Virginia.*

The opening chapters evoke with fullness of control an entire society, the Virginia of the middle eighties, as they range from the industrial enterprises of Cyrus Treadwell to the educational efforts of Miss Priscilla Batte of the Dinwiddie Academy for Young Ladies, from the saintly Pendletons to the trapped Negress Mandy, from the ancestrally subservient Mrs. Peachey to the rebellious writer Oliver Treadwell, from the cowed and repressed wife in Belinda Treadwell to the capacious and capable "new woman" in her daughter Susan.

In the paragraphs which sum up Miss Priscilla Batte, Miss Glasgow manifests her mastery of the distanced commentary. She is thoroughly alive as narrator to the incongruities in Miss Batte's situation, wherein intellectual incompetence is the measure of success as a teacher, and to the subtle hypocrisies in a society which supports the academy. Both teacher and society opt for the static present moment and ignore (and wish to bury) all challenges to spiritual tranquillity. It is a culture which, above everything, judges by surfaces and external characteristics and in which the need to think independently would be the last indignity:

With the majority of maiden ladies left destitute in Dinwiddie after the war, she had turned naturally to teaching as the only nice and respectable occupation which required neither preparation of mind nor considerable outlay of money. . . . Just as the town had battled for a principle without understanding it, so she was capable of dying for an idea, but not of conceiving one. She had suffered everything from the war except the necessity of thinking independently about it, and, though in later years memory had become so sacred to her that she rarely indulged in it, she still clung passionately to the habits of her ancestors under the impression that she was clinging to their ideals.[4]

The fact that Oliver Treadwell is a writer and an intellectual disturbs this supposed servant of the intellect, lest his influence undermine the attitudes with which she has indoctrinated Virginia Pendleton. Miss Batte fears especially that he may wish to write poetry instead of Confederate history from the Southern point of view: "I've always heard that poetry was the ruination of Poe," she laments. When Virginia before marriage champions Oliver as an original thinker, Miss Priscilla is dismayed. A woman's mind in her view and Dinwiddie's (and even Oliver's) is to be trained in acquiescence, not in aggressiveness or originality:

Her [Virginia's] education was founded upon the simple theory that the less a girl knew about life, the better prepared she would be to contend with it. Knowledge of any sort (except the rudiments of reading and writing, the geography of countries she would never visit, and the dates of battles in ancient history) was kept from her as rigorously as if it contained the germs of a contagious disease. . . . [For Miss Batte] a natural curiosity about the universe is the beginning of infidelity. The chief object of her [Virginia's] upbringing, which differed in no essential particular from that of every other well-born and well-bred Southern woman of her day, was to paralyze her reasoning faculties so completely that all danger of mental "unsettling" or even movement was eliminated from her future. To solidify the forces of mind into the inherited mould of fixed beliefs was, in the opinion of the age, to achieve the definite end of all education. When the child ceased to wonder before the veil of appearances, the battle of orthodoxy with speculation was over, and Miss Priscilla felt that she could rest on her victory (pp. 17–18).

Part of the irony of all this is the elevation of spiritual tyranny to the status of cosmic beatitude.

[4]*Virginia* (New York: Charles Scribner's Sons, 1938), Virginia Edition, pp. 9–10. Subsequent references to this book will be by page number within the text. The unrevised text of 1913 (Garden City, N.Y.: Doubleday, Page) is more commonly available in libraries than the limited Virginia Edition or the Old Dominion Edition of 1929 (Garden City, N.Y.: Doubleday, Doran), also a revised text; but since I quote extensively from *Virginia,* I decided to use the latest revised text. The Virginia Edition text is considerably, though not in many instances substantively, revised. The fact that the best texts are not widely available poses a problem for Glasgow scholars.

The evasive idealism of the Southern gentry and middle class comes in for similar satiric scrutiny. The Reverend and Mrs. Pendleton, Mrs. Peachey, and Miss Batte are its chief exemplars, though even worldly men like Oliver Treadwell, Cyrus Treadwell, and John Henry Pendleton are not free of the taint, particularly as they think of woman. In describing the Pendletons Miss Glasgow managed to convey the essence of the mid-Victorian point of view in America, which reached its apogee in the South: antebellum culture gave the South a more clearly defined standard for its continued evasiveness in the present, since nothing in the present could compare with what had once been in a glorious past. The South in *Virginia* merely presents in a more accentuated and appealing form the distaste inspired by unpleasant realities of any sort, a distaste which characterized the nineteenth-century way of life in all Anglo-Saxon civilizations.

It is in this way that *Virginia* attains its universal significance. It is impossible, finally, to discuss it in terms only of Dinwiddie, the state of Virginia, or the South itself. One is finally drawn to use such terms as *genteel American* or *Victorian* in fixing the social and intellectual dimensions of the novel. The term *Victorian* enlarges its perspective to make it a critique in part of Anglo-Saxon civilization as a whole. Though the novel so consummately reflects its own age and time in its own region, it transcends its period because it is finally concerned with the universal human failing of self-deception, the universal human recoil from the unpleasant, the universal tendency to prefer a palatable untruth to the harrowing facts. These aspects of human psychology and behavior, though universal, reached their culmination in the middle of the nineteenth century. In their primness, provinciality, and complacency the Pendletons, of course, are typical representatives of these characteristics:

He [Gabriel Pendleton] had never in his life seen things as they are because he had seen them always by the white flame of a soul on fire with righteousness. To reach his mind, impressions of persons or objects had first to pass through a refining atmosphere in which all baser substances were destroyed, and no fact had ever penetrated this medium except in the flattering disguise of a sentiment. Having married at twenty an idealist only less ignorant of the world than himself, he had immediately devoted his gifts to embellishing the actuality. Both cherished the conviction that to acknowledge an evil is in a manner to countenance its existence, and both clung fervently to the belief that a pretty sham has a more intimate relation to morality than has an ugly truth. Yet, so unaware were they of weaving this elaborate tissue of illusion over the world they inhabited, that they called the mental process by which they distorted reality, "taking a true view of life." To "take a true view" was to believe what was pleasant against what was painful in spite of evidence: to grant honesty to all men (with the possible exception of the Yankee army and a few local scalawags known as Readjusters); to deny virtue to no woman, not even to the New England Abolitionist; to regard the period before the war in Virginia as attained perfection, and the present as falling short of that perfection only inasmuch as it had occurred since the surrender.

As life in a small place, among a simple and guileless class of gentlefolk, all passionately cherishing the same opinions, had never shaken these illusions, it was but natural that they should have done their best to hand them down as sacred heirlooms to their only child. Even Gabriel's four years of hard, fighting and scant rations were enkindled by so much of the disinterested idealism which had sent his State into the Confederacy, that he had emerged from them with an impoverished body, but an enriched spirit. Combined with his inherent inability to face the facts of life, there was an almost super-human capacity for cheerful recovery from the shocks of adversity. Since he had married by accident the one woman who was made for him, he had managed to preserve untarnished his innocent assumption that marriages are arranged in Heaven; for the domestic infelicities of many of his parishioners were powerless to affect a belief that was founded upon a solitary personal experience. Unhappy marriages, like all other misfortunes of society, he was inclined to regard, as entirely modern and owing mainly to the decay of antebellum institutions. "I don't remember that I ever heard of a discontented servant or an unhappy marriage in my boyhood," he would say when he was forced against his will to consider either of these disturbing problems. Not progress, but a return to the "Ideals of our ancestors," was his sole hope for the future; and in Virginia's childhood she had grown to regard this phrase as second only to that other familiar invocation: "If it be the will of God" (pp. 27–29).

Evasive idealism is evinced in the Pendleton distrust of the aesthetic as representing the reprehensibly pleasurable or the immoral. The Pendletons, including Oliver's wife, Virginia, recoil from the kind of realism which he wishes his plays to exemplify. The Pendletons prefer the time-tried and the reassuring to the innovative and the truthful. Virginia as a girl had been allowed to read only those books that edify, according to the narrowest possible prescription:

That any book which told, however mildly, the truth about life should have entered her daughter's bedroom would have seemed little short of profanation to both the rector and Mrs. Pendleton. The sacred shelves of that bookcase . . . had never suffered the contaminating presence of realism. The solitary purpose of art, in Mrs. Pendleton's eyes, was to be "sweet," and she scrupulously judged all literature by its success or failure in this particular quality. It seemed to her as wholesome to feed her daughter's growing fancy on an imaginary line of pious heroes, as it appeared to her moral to screen her from all suspicion of the existence of immorality. She did not honestly believe that any living man resembled the "Heir of Redclyffe," any more than she believed that the path of self-sacrifice leads inevitably to happiness; but there was no doubt in her mind that she advanced the cause of righteousness when she taught these sanctified fallacies to Virginia (p. 41).

Gabriel, in his turn, has never been able to surmount a suspicion that his son-in-law's literary endeavors are not quite wholesome. By the very confidence he has in his fixed opinions, he has the power to irritate profoundly the aspiring artist, when, in Oliver's early days of literary success, the rector declares that he has no objection to plays provided that they are elevating:

"By the way, I haven't spoken of your literary work," the rector remarked, with the manner of a man who is saying something very agreeable. "I have never been to the theatre, but I understand that it is losing a great deal of its ill odour. I always remember when anything is said about the stage that, after all, Shakespeare was an actor. We may be old-fashioned in Dinwiddie," he pursued in the complacent tone in which the admission of this failing is invariably made, "but I don't think we can have any objection to sweet, clean plays, anyway, with an elevating moral tone to them. They are not worse, anyway, than novels" (p. 190).

Virginia Pendleton represents, for better or for worse, "the feminine ideal of the ages." She represents it in its purest, least self-conscious form—not in any calculating sense, as Mrs. Gay does. She is Oliver's ideal at first, by virtue of the racial ethos which he has assimilated. Only when he develops beyond Dinwiddie's provinciality does he find Virginia's passivity, gentleness, self-sacrifice, fine breeding, and unselfishness inadequate. If women in the Victorian South (and in the Victorian age in England and America) were trained to efface themselves before their husbands, brothers, sons, and fathers, it is no wonder that the men in this novel unite in "a belief in the supplementary being of woman." If woman is to find fulfillment in marriage, she should not, like the otherwise conformist Virginia Pendleton, think with active ardor about her lover; rather, she should remain passive in the hope that he will notice her, and she should remain ladylike rather than passionate in demeanor. If Virginia goes beyond convention to think of her lover as a person to whom she responds emotionally, she stops short of thinking about her greatest fulfillment in marriage, the presence of a child. To think specifically of the process involved in begetting one is for the gentlewoman a sign of the greatest indecorum, not to say of coarseness of nature:

And with a reticence peculiar to her type, she never once permitted her mind to stray to her crowning beatitude—the hope of a child; for, with that sacred inconsistency possible only to fixed beliefs, though motherhood was supposed to comprise every desire, adventure, and activity in the life of woman, it was considered indelicate for her to dwell upon the thought of it until the condition had become too obvious for refinement to deny (p. 157).

After Virginia's marriage the course of true love eventually does not run smooth; or perhaps it runs too smooth for too long a time for Oliver's love for his wife to last. The novel proceeds, structurally and ideologically, by a rise and decline pattern, the decline in Virginia's personal fortunes being marked by a process of erosion. The high point in Virginia's life is the night when she succumbs to Oliver's kisses in the rectory garden, and she and Oliver become affianced lovers. The first book builds to this climax in Virginia's life; the last two books, roughly two-thirds of the novel, chronicle the attenuation of her once firm personal, social, and spiritual situation.

In her development of the relationship between Virginia and Oliver, Miss Glasgow demonstrates that both are responsible and not responsible for its decay. At first, Virginia and Oliver are helpless before their passion; likewise, they seem to be helpless to keep it fresh and unspoiled after marriage. Virginia sacrifices her beauty for her family's well-being; she has also been taught to regard the sensual as degrading. The physical aspect of love is only temporary, she thinks, its chief purpose being to lead her mate ever closer to the beauties of the spirit. Though she is an excellent wife in the caretaking sense, like many other married women of the time, she has no proficiency as a mistress. Virginia either mortifies that side of her nature or regards it as an inconvenience. She has been taught, however, to be as she is; the men of the age encouraged her, since they often found sensual satisfactions outside marriage. Rather ironically, she thinks that Oliver lacks that side to his nature since his ardor has decreased as far as she is concerned. The irony in her reflections about her husband's continent nature resides in the fact that he has by then taken his leading lady, Margaret Oldcastle, as his mistress. Virginia's emotions are intense but her interests are narrow. As Miss Glasgow says, Virginia is matchless as a wife but as a mental companion she scarcely exists. It is a measure of Miss Glasgow's art that she continually enlists our sympathy for Virginia and our interest in her fate, despite the fact that, as Louis Auchincloss points out,[5] she bores everyone in the novel. She has archetypal dimensions in a racial sense as embodying an evocative if artificial ideal that her contemporaries appreciate more in the abstract than in the concrete; but it is such dimensions that preserve our involvement with her and her fate.

To her that hath shall be given; to her that hath not shall be taken away even that which she hath. This paraphrased text succinctly describes Virginia Treadwell's situation as the years take their toll from her while Oliver flourishes as a result of his new affluence and Virginia's former efforts in his behalf. The pathos emanating from the situation of a good woman whose generosity and unselfishness and courage are heroic being deprived of the love that she needs to sustain her becomes intense; and as Virginia's spiritual deprivations increase, the power of the book grows. Virginia ought to have lived in a static rather than a dynamic time, or married someone less exposed than Oliver to the forces of change. She is powerless to deal with change because she cannot admit to it, nor does she have the intellectual force to handle the strange and the unexpected. Moreover, she has been taught to avoid intro-

[5]Louis Auchincloss, *Ellen Glasgow* (Minneapolis: University of Minnesota Press, 1964), p. 22.

spection as morbidity, and so can only imperfectly analyze her situation when it grows too adverse to be ignored. And yet her behavior is also self-willed. She comes to realize that her unselfishness has really been selfishness in another guise. But only intermittently can she acknowledge such unsettling truths. Characteristically, she lives for the intensity and harmony of the moment rather than for a harmonious existence in the future which by some miraculous means will, in any case, repeat the auspicious present. Virginia's virtues thus often prevent her from seeing her situation as it is. She is also the victim of the very processes of life and change themselves, and it is in this aspect that she achieves her universal significance. Ritualistically she offers herself to the Cosmic Powers in return for the life of her sick son. The sacrifice is accepted, Harry recovers from the dreaded diphtheria, and Virginia's loveliness and sexual vitalism pass away forever. *Sic transit gloria mundi*—a glory never to be retrieved for her.

The stature of *Virginia* results from the way in which the universal and the particular, the transcendent and the contingent, are interlocked. Virginia's tragedy is not just her own but that of the Victorian woman's lack of insight, awareness, and flexibility. It is every individual's appointed fate, also, that youth and vitality wane, but that vitality outlasts the fresh beauty of youth. It is not that Virginia's spirit has dimmed; it is that her body no longer inspires the passion that it once did, and that with sexual love gone, there is nothing for her to put in its place that will enable her to interest others. She is thus the social as well as the racial and cosmic victim. Her fate is the more pitiable because she has not discarded her high standards and noble intentions: they are merely irrelevant in a different age.

Virginia is impressive also by the breadth of its canvas as by the intensity of the personal conflicts in it. The Treadwells extend the novel beyond the drama of the personal. All of them except Belinda are concerned with activities that transcend in part the provincial. Cyrus Treadwell is an entirely believable tycoon and domestic tyrant in this age of transition during which "the ashes of a vanquished idealism" were to yield to "the spirit of commercial materialism." Seen from the outside, he has all the intransigent reality that is lacking in Ben Starr in *The Romance of a Plain Man*. The mean-souled materialist is a partly real and a partly mythic

figure. Cyrus achieves both dimensions in the novel, as the fore-
runner of Jason Compson and the Snopes tribe in Faulkner's world
or as an analogue to the Mangan of Shaw's *Heartbreak House.*
Basically, he is not one of the sons of light. The New South,
moreover, is present as an actuality in this novel, wherein the life
of Dinwiddie is fostered, and also strangled, by the dominating
Treadwell tobacco factory and the encircling railroads controlled
by Cyrus. His daughter Susan represents the new kind of woman
who would come to the fore in the twentieth century, one who
breaks constructively from the paralyzing traditions that benumb
Virginia Treadwell. Susan is a woman who learns to command
circumstance rather than bow to it. Through Cyrus the problem
of race is vividly dramatized in his miscegenation with Mandy, the
Treadwell laundress. He refuses to recognize the child he has
fathered or to help him when his life is in danger, simply because
it is easier to sin than to acknowledge the sin. Mandy is seen
sympathetically as the trapped animal that does not understand
its sufferings rather than as the alluring, sensual mistress of the
white man. Through Oliver, Miss Glasgow confronted the older
culture, represented in Virginia and her parents, in Miss Batte and
Mrs. Peachey, with the enterprising spirit of modernity. He is
flexible and adaptable, but lacks central stamina and some dimension of the integrity that would ensure an authentic as opposed
to a popular reputation.

One of the most incisive aspects of *Virginia* is Miss Glasgow's
presentation of the gap between the generations, a gap as profound
as that which develops between Virginia and Oliver. Though their
children share the emancipated attitudes of Oliver, they are more
at home with Virginia. But they would agree with him that Virginia is too old-fashioned quite to exist in their newer world. Lucy
with her amorous boldness and Jennie with her impatience with
the evasive idealism of the Pendletons and her concern at any cost
with the truth are, in actuality, Virginia's antitypes. Miss Glasgow
presents the misunderstandings between mother and daughters
with tolerance, a sympathy for both sides in the conflict, and a
humorous sensitivity to the incongruities involved in the staid
Virginia's attempts to penetrate issues that elude her understanding.

Although she was to write more tightly ordered novels, Miss
Glasgow never achieved quite the same authority as social historian

and vigorous critic of men, women, and manners as she did in *Virginia*. The focus in her later novels was narrower. *Virginia,* published when Miss Glasgow was forty, may well represent the last expression in her novels of an unalloyed youthful confidence. If the novel may sometimes seem brash in its coruscating irony, it is never superficial. Miss Glasgow ranges over an entire civilization with authenticity, possibly because it was just far enough behind her for her to see it with both detachment and affection.

Virginia is not so heady a book as *They Stooped to Folly,* nor is Virginia Pendleton quite so legendary as Eva Birdsong in *The Sheltered Life. The Sheltered Life* reveals a deeper compassion since Eva is a more appealing victim than Virginia. She is also a more evocative symbol of the arrested traditions of the Old South. *The Sheltered Life* earns its position as Miss Glasgow's best novel because the social realities presented in it lend themselves more convincingly to the mythical and archetypal dimensions of Southern culture. George Birdsong lacks Oliver's seriousness but is not so repellent as Oliver turns out to be; and Eva Birdsong has intelligence and genuine accomplishments as a musician, a whole worldly side which Virginia lacks. Eva also has the awareness to appraise her situation, even if she cannot admit to others her husband's infidelities and must support the same cross of ladylike behavior that Virginia must. But there is aesthetic loss in the later book as well as aesthetic gain. The vigor and asperity of Miss Glasgow's ironic vision in *Virginia* give it a strength which the later elegiac novel does not always attain. In any case, the two books represent the twin summits of Miss Glasgow's achievement in the two phases of her career.

The Comedies of Manners

C. Hugh Holman

IN Ellen Glasgow was the rebellious yoking of two incompatible traditions and attitudes toward life. "I had the misfortune . . . to inherit a long conflict of types," she said in 1943, "for my father was a descendant of Scottish Calvinists and my mother a perfect flower of the Tidewater, in Virginia. Her ancestors had been broad Church of England and later agnostics. This conflict began in my soul as far back as I can remember."[1] She spent her youth and young womanhood in open, angry, and often anguished rebellion against the dark Calvinism of her father's grim Presbyterian world and, it seems from her revealing, fascinating, romantic—and perhaps somewhat romanticized—autobiography, *The Woman Within,* identified herself almost pathologically with her mother and her mother's Tidewater world and her mother's wrongs.

Between 1897 and 1922 she wrote thirteen novels in which she pursued the ideals of realism and instructed the world in what she was learning from Darwin, Henry George, Schopenhauer, Nietzsche, and the Fabian socialists, among whom she counted herself. Up to the age of forty-nine, her life, aside from this realm of thought and creativity, had been one of ill health, growing deafness, suffering, bereavement, anger, unhappy love affairs, humiliation, and despair—or at least, looking back upon it, she saw it so. But after 1922, after she was reconciled to the end of her engagement to Henry Anderson, she found herself in what she later called "one of those blessed pauses that fall between the 'dark wood' of the soul and the light on the horizon."[2] In that "blessed pause" she did almost all her best work, and she was certainly correct when she said, "Between fifty and sixty I lived

---

[1] Blair Rouse, ed., *The Letters of Ellen Glasgow* (New York: Harcourt, Brace, 1958), p. 329. Hereinafter cited as *Letters.*

[2] *Letters,* p. 341.

perhaps my fullest and richest years."[3] During those years she produced *Barren Ground* and the three Queenborough novels, *The Romantic Comedians, They Stooped to Folly,* and *The Sheltered Life.* She explained this success to J. Donald Adams, saying: "So long as I was held fast in the toils of life, suffering within my own ego, it was impossible to project my whole self into my novels"— by which, I submit, she really meant "keep my whole self in large part out of my novels."[4]

She declared late in life that she ended her history of manners in Virginia with *Life and Gabriella*—conveniently forgetting those two failures, *The Builders* and *One Man in His Time.* With *Barren Ground,* she said, "I broke away from social history."[5] *Barren Ground* was also the book in which she rediscovered and understood at least the secular implications of her father's dark Calvinism, seeing behind its theological symbols a pragmatic truth about life, the grim philosophy of fortitude, which despite her angry and tearful rejection she could finally no more escape than could Thomas Carlyle or Nathaniel Hawthorne or Herman Melville.

Into the story of Dorinda Oakley she could pour herself— perhaps with too few restraints. "If falling in love could be bliss, I discovered presently," she wrote in *The Woman Within,* "that falling out of love could be blissful tranquillity."[6] She heaped upon Dorinda her suffering, her bitterness, her sense, as James Branch Cabell put it, of "the outrageous unfairness of heaven's traffic with Ellen Glasgow,"[7] and then she gave Dorinda the victory. At the end of the novel she wrote: "The storm and the hag-ridden dreams of the night were over, and the land which she had forgotten was waiting to take her back to its heart. Endurance. Fortitude. The spirit of the land was flowing into her, and her own spirit, strengthened and refreshed, was flowing out again toward life. . . . This was what remained to her after the years had taken

[3]Ellen Glasgow, *The Woman Within* (New York: Harcourt, Brace, 1954), p. 273. Hereinafter cited as *Woman Within.*

[4]*Letters,* p. 121.

[5]*Letters,* p. 339.

[6]*Woman Within,* p. 244.

[7]*As I Remember It* (New York: McBride, 1955), p. 233.

their bloom. She would find happiness again. Not the happiness for which she had once longed, but the serenity of mind which is above the conflict of frustrated desires."[8] If this is overwriting, it is—like much of her overwriting—the result not of overexpressing or sentimentalizing Dorinda but of speaking too plainly and strongly for herself.

Barren Ground was a critical success, and in the serene mood which followed it—"I wrote *Barren Ground*," she said, "and immediately I knew I had found myself"[9]—she was ready to do her best work. "I always wanted to put my best into my books—to make them compensate, in a way for . . . the long tragedy of my life," she wrote Stark Young. "The only thing I have saved out of the wreck is the gift of work."[10] The gift of work was enough. Out of "the tranquil immunity of a mind that had finished with love"[11] and had come to honor the tragic virtue of fortitude, she was to fashion the Queenborough novels before the pendulum of the conflict continued its swing and the dark vein of iron took total command.

Always she had borne—silently and in the novelist's way—a didactic burden. Her novels had been instructive exempla through which she had taught her place and region the error of their ways or had explored and assuaged the ache of her own disasters. Now in the serene and tranquil autumn of her life, she seems almost instinctively to have discovered a release from this didactic burden, and in that release to have found in the comedy of manners a form in which she could utilize her skill, her wit, her concern with style, her deep-rooted insider's knowledge of Virginia aristocracy, and her slowly developed novelistic skill to their best advantage. The force in the life-long conflict between her father, who "was of Valley stock and Scottish in every nerve and sinew,"[12] as she said, and her Tidewater mother had seemingly reached an equilibrium in this calm time between her fifty-second and her sixtieth years.

---

[8]*Barren Ground* (Garden City, N.Y.: Doubleday, Page, 1925), p. 509.

[9]*Woman Within,* p. 243.

[10]*Letters,* p. 112.

[11]*The Romantic Comedians* (Garden City, N.Y.: Doubleday, Page, 1926), p. 305. Hereinafter cited as *Comedians.*

[12]*Woman Within,* p. 299.

The equilibrium, of course, was temporary, for the harsh world of her father was to grow in strength and find its expression in her celebration of endurance in *Vein of Iron,* which she defined admiringly in 1935 as the "Scottish strain of fortitude that has come down from the earliest pioneers in the Valley," [13] and finally in the gathering darkness of *In This Our Life.*

In 1926, weary from the three-year struggle with *Barren Ground,* Miss Glasgow felt, she says, "the comic spirit . . . struggle against the bars of its cage. . . . It was thirsting, as I was, for laughter; but it craved delicate laughter with ironic echoes." [14] In this mood, she embarked on *The Romantic Comedians* (1926), wrote it quickly, and then followed it with *They Stooped to Folly* (1929), and completed what she recognized as a trilogy with *The Sheltered Life* (1932). Over the three novels hovers the comic spirit, and a conscious delight. "The last thing I wished to do," she said, "was to transfix the wings of my comic spirit. . . . For I had come at last to perceive, after my long apprenticeship to veracity, that the truth of art and the truth of life are two different truths." [15] The completed trilogy she called "The Tragicomedy of Manners" and said, "These [novels] depict the place and tragicomedy of the individual in an established society. They illustrate the struggle of personality against tradition and the social background." [16]

The comedy of manners was ideally suited to her purposes, her mood, and her art. It is a form that asks that its characters be placed in a sharply definable social situation, usually one that is elegant and sophisticated, and that the manners, beliefs, and conventions of that society be the forces that motivate the action. Its style is witty; its thrust satiric. It usually places in its fable an emphasis on the "love game" and centers on at least one pair of somewhat immoral lovers. The comedy of manners on the stage and in the novel also demands a highly developed craftsmanship and a delight taken by author and audience alike in finished artistry, in conscious and successful artifice. That definition describes

[13] *Letters,* p. 191.

[14] *A Certain Measure* (New York: Harcourt, Brace, 1943), p. 214. Hereinafter cited as *Measure.*

[15] *Measure,* pp. 212–13.

[16] *Letters,* p. 206.

the individual novels in the Queenborough trilogy and the trilogy
as a whole, although there is a steady deepening of the seriousness
and broadening of the scope of the books as the trilogy progresses.
The Romantic Comedians is almost pure comedy. If there is, as
she said, "tragedy in the theme," it is also "tragedy running on
light feet."[17] In *They Stooped to Folly* the cast is larger, and the
action, which is also compressed into a year, is given historical
perspective, however lightly, by allowing us to see three "fallen"
woman living according to the social codes of three historical
periods. Thus the past, which is only a faint reference point in
The Romantic Comedians, assumes a depth and takes on a tinkling
resonance in *They Stooped to Folly.* This deepening seriousness
continues to grow in *The Sheltered Life,* where the action covers
more than eight years but reaches backward in time to set Queenborough and its aristocrats against a pattern of Southern history
extending back before the Civil War. The seriousness of the issues
at stake has also intensified. The unhappiness of December un-
wisely wedded to May, which had all the lightness of Restoration
comedy in *The Romantic Comedians,* has deepened into issues
that now literally are matters of life and death. Yet, as I shall try
to show, all three novels are truly comedies; none is fundamentally
tragic, and over them all echoes the "silvery laughter" of Meredith's
comic spirit.

To appreciate fully both Miss Glasgow's accomplishment and
the comic implications of the Queenborough novels, it is necessary
to look at her role as narrator. For, however much the three novels
vary, Ellen Glasgow remains remarkably consistent as their teller.
Everywhere she is present; although she has learned most of the
lessons of point of view and author-effacement which the realists
taught—particularly those lessons taught Henry James, for whom
she actually had only a qualified liking—she has suited them to her
own purposes.

Louis D. Rubin once observed: "It is a good rule of thumb for
the Glasgow novels that whenever the author begins identifying a
character's plight with her own, begins projecting her personal
wishes and needs into the supposedly fictional situation, then to

---

[17]*Measure,* p. 223.

that extent both the character and the novel are weakened."[18] Looking at it from a different direction, Louis Auchincloss said, "She was unable sufficiently to pull the tapestry of fiction over her personal grievances and approbations. The latter are always peeping out at the oddest times and in the oddest places."[19] These observations are generally true of the early novels, and they are particularly true of *Barren Ground.* Always in the fourteen novels before *The Romantic Comedians,* Miss Glasgow had personal and emotional involvements with one or more of her characters, who spoke as her surrogates and through whom she achieved vicarious solutions to the tormenting problems to which she was victim in life. In these novels, from time to vexing time, the thin but essential line between the author's actuality and the fictional world she created was crossed, as it was to be in the novels of Thomas Wolfe. In a discussion of the implied author in which he cites *Barren Ground* as an illustration of "authorial intrusion," Louis Rubin reminds us that "it is not the narrative's fidelity to truth as such that the reader of a novel must be made to accept, but rather the story-teller's fidelity to the story."[20]

Ellen Glasgow's great accomplishment in the Queenborough novels is that her stance as implied author is always outside the action of the stories she tells, although she tells them with an insider's sure, somewhat affectionate, but by no means gentle satiric knowledge. Yet, somewhat like the puppet master role that Thackeray assumes toward audience and actors in *Vanity Fair,* her attitude is clear, her presence is authoritatively felt, and her persistent irony is a function of style and of her defining for us, without crossing the line between the fact of personal experience and the fiction of imagination, a reality against which the appearances of the novels are to be seen. It should come as a surprise to no one who has studied the Queenborough novels that she considered *Tom Jones* the "best of all English and American novels."[21]

[18]*No Place on Earth* (Austin: University of Texas Press, 1959), p. 14.

[19]*Ellen Glasgow* (Minneapolis: University of Minnesota Press, 1964), p. 42.

[20]*The Teller in the Tale* (Seattle: University of Washington Press, 1967), pp. 13–14.

[21]*Letters,* p. 108.

In the Queenborough novels, Ellen Glasgow was given the grace to view her characters with the disinterestedness of a creator rather than to suffer with them as surrogates of her anguished self. And this quality allowed her to use her intimate knowledge of an ordered and mannered society without self-service, to re-create her world like a true Maker, and in its gravest moments to flood it with the silvery laughter of Meredithian comedy. Even in the darkening close of *The Sheltered Life,* the author seems to stand without, above, removed, like dead Troilus in Chaucer's *Troilus and Criseyde,* in "the hollowness of the eighth sphere," who

> . . . down from that high station . . . began
> To look upon this little spot of earth
> Enfolded by the sea, with full contempt
> For this unhappy world . . . and at the last
> He looked down on the place where he was slain,
> And laughed within himself at all the woe
> Of those who wept and sorrowed for his death,
> Condemning all our work that so pursues
> Blind lusts that cannot last.[22]

Ellen Glasgow, in her role as narrator or implied author, maintains a figurative distance quite as great as Troilus's literal one.

Out of this distance and her skill and style emerges a very self-conscious yet effective artifice, so that the Queenborough novels are consciously *written* novels, and a part of their success rests upon our delight—a delight common to most high comedy— in the artificer joyfully at work at her hard-earned, highly wrought craft. (And, in an aside to the current biographers who are appalled at the way she ordered and designed her life and her career, one might add that it is possible to see that ordering too as a triumph of the artificer over reluctant materials, of the will over fate.)

We can sum up the Queenborough novels as the comedy of the missed delight, the hunger for the unknown timeless instant of joy, the sorrow of the aged for the passing of what Chaucer called "The blinde lust, the which that may not laste." Martin Seymour-Smith, in a gross oversimplification, says of Ellen Glasgow that she had

---

[22]*Troilus and Criseyde,* book V, stanzas 260, 261, as modernized by Theodore Morrison in *The Portable Chaucer* (New York: Viking Press, 1949), pp. 577–78.

"the limiting view that consists of specifically sexual disappointment followed by stoical acceptance."[23] Certainly in novels before *The Romantic Comedians* we see that pattern appearing regularly, and it continues in the Queenborough novels. And in them, too, although they are novels of age rather than youth, the missed delight is directly linked with sex; hence the passage of time is portentous, and time is the great enemy for the characters. Of old General Archbald, meditating on his past life and the married Englishwoman he had loved and lost half a century before, she said: "Like other men all over the world, he had sacrificed to gods as fragile as the bloom of light on the tulip tree. And what was time itself but the bloom, the sheath enfolding experience? Within time, and within time alone, there was life—the gleam, the quiver, the heart-beat, the immeasurable joy and anguish of being."[24]

Actually most of the major characters in the Queenborough novels fall into one of two groups: the old who remember, long, regret, and are sad; and the young who declare their right to their own lives and will almost certainly lose it. To see such persons in such potentially tragic situations as figures in a comedy requires, as Troilus had had, a vantage point in space or philosophy from which they are viewed. For Ellen Glasgow that vantage point was essentially her father's dark faith, a view of civilization, and a sense of the triviality of hedonism. I think there is no need to argue that Ellen Glasgow is speaking her own view in *The Romantic Comedians* when she refers to Mrs. Upchurch's "conventional mind [which] preferred to hold a world war, rather than original sin, responsible for Annabel's misguided behaviour."[25] She seemed to be applauding when General Archbald, in *The Sheltered Life,* declared that "Mankind was still calling human nature a system and trying vainly to put something in its place."[26] It is the author who, in *The Romantic Comedians,* concludes that "a symbol [Duty] . . .

[23]*Funk & Wagnalls Guide to Modern World Literature* (New York: Funk & Wagnalls, 1973), p. 50.

[24]*The Sheltered Life* (New York: Doubleday, Doran, 1932), p. 148. Hereinafter cited as *Sheltered.*

[25]*Comedians,* p. 285.

[26]*Sheltered,* p. 145.

is better than an abyss to fall back upon."[27] And when the young
fling themselves eagerly upon the sword of the First World War,
General Archbald concludes with a wryness that is certainly Miss
Glasgow's that "what the world needed . . . was the lost emblem
of evil."[28] When in *A Certain Measure,* she refers to Queenborough
as "a shallow and aimless society of happiness-hunters, who lived
in a perpetual flight from reality, and grasped at any effort-saving
illusion of passion or pleasure,"[29] it is the portion of her self in-
cubated in Scotland, nurtured in the Valley of Virginia, and trained
by her Presbyterian father that is speaking.

The view she expressed of civilization is one that puts its
pretenses to serious test. General Archbald, whom she declared in
the preface to be "a lover of wisdom, a humane and civilized
soul,"[30] supposed that "the wonder in every age was not that
most men were savage, but that a few men were civilized."[31] And
he later qualified even this limited optimism saying, "a Red Indian
lurks in every man we call civilized."[32] Curle Littlepage, in *They
Stooped to Folly,* was, Miss Glasgow said, a man who "may make
the world a desert and call it progress."[33] And his father, Virginius
Littlepage, brooded over the modern world in these terms:
"Modern life especially appeared without dignity and even without direction, an endless speeding to nowhere."[34] She characterizes
civilization as immature: "In America," she said, "the cult of the
immature had prevailed over the order of merit,"[35] and she condemned what she called "the worship of adolescents and other
myths of primitive culture."[36]

When she moved from this larger frame of beliefs to the small,
dry, and dying aristocratic world of Queenborough, the dislike of
its values became intense. Of Queenborough she said, "I felt that
I required the distilled essence of all Virginia cities rather than the
speaking likeness of one"[37]; yet declaring her freedom from the

---

[27]*Comedians,* p. 300.   [28]*Sheltered,* p. 373.   [29]*Measure,* p. 203.

[30]*Measure,* p. 203.   [31]*Sheltered,* p. 147.   [32]*Sheltered,* p. 252.

[33]*They Stooped to Folly* (Garden City, N.Y.: Doubleday, Doran, 1929), p. 256.
Hereinafter cited as *They Stooped.*

[34]*They Stooped,* p. 336.   [35]*Sheltered,* p. 260.   [36]*Sheltered,* p. 306.

[37]*Measure,* pp. 211-12.

bondage of literal fact, she said that "I have not failed . . . to make two trees grow in my Queenborough where only one was planted before me in Richmond,"[38] so Richmond was clearly and recognizably in her mind. (It is tempting to play with the name Queenborough: the queen is certainly Elizabeth the Virgin Queen, and so Queenborough is Virginia City, which is Richmond. But Queenborough is very close in sound to Queensberry, and the marquis of Queensberry's rules are very precise regulations strictly governing a conflict, a boxing match; hence the name suggests very formal and stylized rules of conduct.) This Queenborough is committed to "evasive idealism that had become a second nature . . . to the whole community"[39]; it existed in "an epoch when faith and facts did not cultivate an acquaintance."[40] Like Mrs. Upchurch in *The Romantic Comedians,* Queenborough "was natural only when it was artificial."[41] It tried to create a "sheltered life," a "smiling region of phantasy"; its smile was often like that animated grimace of Eva Birdsong's, which finally settled into a rictus. Like Judge Honeywell and "like most lawyers and all vestrymen, [it] was able to believe automatically a number of things that [it] knew were not true."[42] It existed as an interlocking protectorate of families which might disapprove, as General Archbald knew, but would rally around a member through clan loyalty: "All the old families that were not rotten within would close round him [if he supported his granddaughter's marriage to a plain man]," he said, "just as they would close round him if he had forged a cheque or murdered his uncle"[43]; as, indeed, they had rallied round the Goddards, who "had united in the heroic pretense that plain murder was pure accident. By force of superior importance, they had ignored facts, defended family honour, shielded a murderer for the sake of saving a name, turned public execration into sympathy, and politely but firmly looked the law out of countenance."[44] The special gift of Queenborough society was its "capacity to believe anything or nothing,"[45] to "subordinate happiness, even love to pride,"[46] to make the highest art of conversation and

---

[38]*Measure,* p. 213.   [39]*Comedians,* p. 199.   [40]*Comedians,* p. 251.

[41]*Comedians,* p. 190.   [42]*Comedians,* pp. 250-51.   [43]*Sheltered,* pp. 102-3.

[44]*Sheltered,* p. 174.   [45]*Sheltered,* p. 24.   [46]*Sheltered,* p. 245.

appearance. Ellen Glasgow says: "Even in Queenborough, where until recent years, conversation had been the favourite and almost the only art patronized by the best circles, wealthy citizens were beginning to realize that, if books look well in a library, pictures lend even more emphatically the right note in decoration to the walls of a drawing room."[47] Using this view of the world and this attitude toward a decaying Virginia aristocracy, Ellen Glasgow in the Queenborough novels made a cool, detached presentation of the world she knew best, loved sincerely, and had an amused and tolerant contempt for.

Fundamental to her artistry was the choice of her narrative point of view. In all three novels she elected the same basic approach, and it is one that is markedly Jamesian in concept. She elected to report, essentially through the witty and epigrammic voice of the implied author, that aspect of the consciousness of major characters which is capable of being verbalized directly. Each of the novels begins with a long and unbroken presentation of such a center of consciousness. The first ten chapters of *The Romantic Comedians,* 124 of a total of 346 pages, is a report of the thoughts and feelings of Judge Gamaliel Honeywell; but those thoughts, although presented directly, have passed through the alembic of Ellen Glasgow's skillful and sometimes scornful reporting. In a typical remark, that "he had been happy with Cordelia, as a man may be happy in a marriage with any agreeable woman when he stops thinking about it,"[48] we hear a direct witty interpretation by the implied author. It is difficult for a remembering reader ever to overcome the effect of such reporting as this statement: "It is astonishing, he reflected, with the slow but honourable processes of the judicial mind, what Spring can do to one even at sixty-five—even at a young sixty-five, he hastened to remind himself."[49] This distance and this tone well established, Miss Glasgow then begins in the eleventh chapter to shift the point of view to the consciousness of other characters, Annabel, Mrs. Upchurch, and Amanda, and it shifts often, frequently for ironic effect.

In *They Stooped to Folly,* the first part, 138 of 351 pages, is centered with equal force and much the same effect in the con-

---

[47]*They Stooped,* pp. 28–29.   [48]*Comedians,* p. 13.   [49]*Comedians,* pp. 1–2.

sciousness of Virginius Littlepage. The second part, 143 pages, is predominantly, although not exclusively, in the consciousness of his wife, Victoria, but the consciousnesses of other characters also are entered from time to time. The third part, 104 pages, moves freely among the consciousnesses of several characters, quite clearly for ironic contrast. In the concluding chapter of the first part, for example, we are told of Virginius's "sense of universal futility" that "joy he had never known in its fulness. He had had his years or his seasons, but never his moments."[50] Were it not for Ellen Glasgow's style and the dry wit of her reporting, the sympathy that we naturally feel for Littlepage might almost have moved to the sentimental, if not the maudlin. But should style have surrendered temporarily to sentiment, it could not long remain in that position. Fifteen pages later we are in the consciousness of his wife, sorrowing in the memory that Virginius had been Virginius rather than "the young Lochinvar of her mind" and that "she had missed some finer essence of living, some purer distillation of joy."[51] If—as I doubt—Ellen Glasgow is saying, "Oh, the pity of it all!" she is saying it not in tears but in laughter. This principle of ironic juxtaposition—one of her basic comic devices—is well illustrated by two sections late in the novel. In one, at the end of chapter 7, Louisa Goddard reflects on the changes which she considers improvements: "Nothing was worth all the deceit, all the anguish, all the futile hope and ineffectual endeavor, all the pretense and parade, all the artificial glamour and empty posturing of the great Victorian tradition."[52] On the following three pages, Virginius is sorrowful over these changes, over the loss of "the true feminine character which had never flowered more perfectly than in the sheltered garden of the Southern tradition."[53] The posture the implied author is asking the reader to assume is not with either Virginius or Louisa but above them and superior in knowledge and insight to either.

In her preface to *The Sheltered Life,* it seems to me that she writes in 1938 from the deepening despair of her later years about a comedy of manners which she considered one of her two best books (the other was *Barren Ground*),[54] placing an emphasis on

---

[50]*They Stooped,* pp. 134–35. [51]*They Stooped,* p. 151. [52]*They Stooped,* p. 331.
[53]*They Stooped,* p. 333. [54]*Letters,* p. 342.

its "tragic" qualities at the expense of its comedy, and leading to a series of later critical distortions. If the book is not comedy, as I think it is, then the alternative is not tragedy—the people lack stature and the action significance—but pathos and sentimentality. In the preface she describes the form of the book as a function of point of view: "In *The Sheltered Life,* where I knew intuitively that the angle of vision must create the form, I employed two points of view alone. . . . Age and youth look on the same scene, the same persons, the same events. . . . Between these conflicting points of view the story flows on, as a stream flows in a narrow valley. Nothing happens that is not seen, on one side, through the steady gaze of the old man, seeing life as it is, and, on the other side, by the troubled eyes of the young girl, seeing life as she would wish it to be." [55] The first of the three parts, "The Age of Make-Believe," 125 of 395 pages, is told through the consciousness of Jenny Blair Archbald, aged nine going on ten. The second part, "The Deep Past," only 40 pages, is General Archbald's recollection of the past—a section of which Miss Glasgow said in 1944, " 'The Deep Past' contains the writing I should wish to be remembered by in the future," [56] a judgment in which most of her critics join her. The long, 225-page third part, "The Illusion," alternates between Jenny and the general. Certainly parts 2 and 3 succeed as well as anything Ellen Glasgow ever wrote. The weakness in the book—and I consider it the least totally successful of the Queenborough novels—is a function of two things. General Archbald is intended to be the protagonist, not merely because Miss Glasgow so asserted to Allen Tate the year of its publication but also because that is the common structure of the Queenborough novels, as we shall see a little later. But beginning with 125 pages located in Jenny Blair's consciousness violates the structural pattern Ellen Glasgow had established for the Queenborough novels and has led many critics to see her as the protagonist. Furthermore, setting the story in motion when Jenny Blair is only nine placed a heavy burden on Miss Glasgow's ironic style, with the result that in this section almost alone among the Queenborough novels, the distance of author from character and action is uncertain. Furthermore, Jenny at nine is incapable of some of the thoughts that she is

[55] *Measure,* pp. 200-201.   [56] *Letters,* p. 354.

assigned. May I cite one example: "What was it about Mrs. Peyton, Jenny Blair asked herself, gazing at the ashen hair and the long, thin face, with its pale skin the texture of a withered rose, that made her remember a Confederate flag in the rain? She wasn't, of course, in the very least like a Confederate flag. No lady could be. Yet Jenny Blair never looked at her that she didn't think of a flag going by in the rain to the inspiring music of bands."[57] Now this figure is a most effective one, suggesting gallantry and defeat, brave display and heartrending, futile courage. It is, however, Ellen Glasgow and not Jenny Blair who is thinking it. It is one thing for the implied author to couch a character's consciousness in the author's ironic language; it is quite a different thing to give the character thoughts and insights clearly beyond her years. This is the old problem that Ellen Glasgow had had in earlier novels and notably in *Barren Ground*. Its effect here is to give the hard selfishness of Jenny Blair—whose true role is much like that of Annabel in *The Romantic Comedians* and Milly Burden in *They Stooped to Folly*—an authorial sanction that is not intended. The novel never completely recovers from the skewing of attitude that occurs in part 1. And the weakness is a function of an uncertain distance between author and subject. For a short time—enough to cast doubts but not completely to destroy illusion—Troilus descends from the eighth sphere, Ellen the Maker finds some middle ground between Olympus and earth, and the silvery laughter is muted but by no means stilled.

In fiction as consciously and meticulously constructed as the Queenborough novels, meaning is a product of structure. And the structure of each of these three novels, like the use of the Olympian implied author and of shifting centers of consciousness in them, is remarkably similar. They might be grouped as a trilogy under the common title *April in Queenborough,* for their time-settings are April, and, indeed, in them,

> April is the cruellest month, breeding
> Lilacs out of the dead land, mixing
> Memory and desire, stirring
> Dull roots with spring rain.[58]

[57]*Sheltered*, pp. 107-8.

[58]T. S. Eliot, *The Waste Land*, ll. 1-4, published by Harcourt Brace Jovanovich, Inc.

The reference to T. S. Eliot is not accidental; those lines define in miniature the central fable of the Queenborough novels, and Miss Glasgow's emphasis on April cannot be accidental. Robert Holland examined Ellen Glasgow's work as pictures of a wasteland and Virginius Littlepage as a character much like Eliot's Prufrock.[59] And it should be remembered that she was enthusiastic about that most Eliot-like of Southern poems, Allen Tate's "Ode to the Confederate Dead," which she called "a great poem, because it strips away not only appearances but experience itself, and bares some dark and nameless quality of being."[60]

Each novel has the same basic plot situation. In Queenborough, a society of now empty and sterile forms, people in late middle or old age who have surrendered themselves to these forms try vainly to rebel and to achieve a previously unexperienced happiness through sexual love before it is too late. The young whom they love rebel against them, Queenborough, and their now outmoded set of values without even trying. In *The Romantic Comedians,* Judge Gamaliel Honeywell, who in his youth had been in love with Amanda Lightfoot but had married Cordelia, whom he did not love, now made a widower by Cordelia's death, marries the young Annabel Upchurch in a search for lost youth; she does not love him and finally leaves him. In *They Stooped to Folly,* a successful middle-aged lawyer, Virginius Littlepage, has had a successful but dull and nonecstatic marriage to Victoria, and now dreams of an affair with Mrs. Dalrymple, of somewhat sullied reputation and generous curves, but finally lacks the courage to realize it. His sister Agatha, a ruined woman of the Victorian era, still stays upstairs in disgrace. His secretary, Milly Burden, has had a child out of wedlock by Martin Welding, whom his daughter Mary Victoria has married but who leaves her. Remorseless Milly is seeking her own life. In *The Sheltered Life,* young Jenny Blair Archbald falls in love with middle-aged George Birdsong, the philandering husband of her friend, the famous beauty Eva Birdsong. Her grandfather, General David Archbald, an eighty-three-year-old lawyer who married because he had accidentally but innocently compromised a woman he did not love, and who had lost the one

---

[59]"Miss Glasgow's Prufrock," *American Quarterly* 9 (1957): 435–40.

[60]*Letters,* p. 229.

woman he had loved because she was already married, is the contrasting center of consciousness to Jenny Blair. Eva Birdsong, ill, sees Jenny and George in an embrace and kills him.

The protagonist of each book is an elderly or aging man. Each, like General Archbald, "had longed to seek and find his one brief hour of delight."[61] Each, like Judge Honeywell, felt "that he had missed the secret of life . . . that he had lost beyond recovery something indescribably fresh and satisfying."[62] These men remind us of Lambert Strether of James's *The Ambassadors,* but they experience Strether's awakening to their unlived lives much later than James's protagonist does. They are now at or close to old age, and they have sacrificed youth, middle age, dreams, imagination, and vital instincts to "the moral earnestness of tradition."[63] It was true of them, as Ellen Glasgow wrote of Asa Timberlake in *In This Our Life:* "For the sake of a past tradition he had spent nearly thirty years doing things he hated and not doing things he liked; and at the end of that long self-discipline, when he was too old to begin over again, he had seen his code of conduct flatten out and shrivel up as utterly as a balloon that is pricked."[64] Each in his own way shared Judge Honeywell's "natural aptitude for evading unpleasant truths."[65] Each, like Virginius Littlepage, had a "hidden flaw in his nature which made it harder for him to commit a pleasure than to perform a duty, which made him hesitate and fail in the hour of adventure."[66] Jenny Blair reports accurately of General Archbald: "Mamma told me he was so queer when he was young that everybody was surprised when he made a good living. I asked him about that and he laughed and said that he made a good living by putting an end to himself."[67] It is easy enough to see in these protagonists aspects of Ellen Glasgow's life and attitudes about which she could on occasion be almost lugubriously self-pitying. But here they are used, not as personal experience but as transmuted material for fiction, not as a basis for tragedy or self-pity but for genial comedy.

Each of the novels also has a collection of women who are embodiments of the tradition of Queenborough, often in its most

[61]*Sheltered,* p. 32.   [62]*Comedians,* p. 180.   [63]*Sheltered,* pp. 32–33.

[64]Quoted by Louis Auchincloss, *Ellen Glasgow,* p. 36.

[65]*Comedians,* p. 13.   [66]*Sheltered,* p. 19.   [67]*Sheltered,* p. 283.

admirable form. The wives Cordelia Honeywell, Victoria Littlepage, and Erminia Archbald are capable, practical, intelligent, and devoted women; and each contributes enormously to her husband's success and ease of living, if not happiness. Only Victoria Littlepage is alive during the forward action of one of the books, and she is one of the triumphs of *They Stooped to Folly*. There is a comic poignancy to her being shown to have the same regrets and unfulfilled dreams of ecstacy as Virginius has. In each there is an embodiment of tradition in the form of a lost romance: Amanda Lightfoot, who remains faithful to Judge Honeywell; Mrs. Dalrymple, who beckons to Mr. Littlepage's dreams of joy; Louisa Goddard, who has loved him silently all these years; Eva Birdsong, the model of beauty, sacrifice, and fidelity to George and to General Archbald; and the Englishwoman whom Archbald briefly and passionately loved in his youth. There are other middle-aged widows who represent the society and dominate the men of their world: Mrs. Upchurch, the cheerful pragmatist; Mrs. Burden, committed to the lower-middle-class prejudices; Mrs. Archbald, the General's efficient daughter-in-law. There are also women in each novel whose lives were sacrificed to the tradition: Amanda Lightfoot, Agatha Littlepage, and Etta Archbald. This society of Queenborough is a thoroughly feminine world, dominated by wives, aunts, mothers, and daughters. It is they who have shaped for each of the protagonists a world such as that of General Archbald, of whom Ellen Glasgow says: "He had had a fair life. Nothing that he wanted, but everything that was good for him."[68] But good though the life they make for the protagonist is, Ellen Glasgow is not gentle with them. Mrs. Archbald she accuses of "persevering hypocrisy . . . the triumph of self-discipline"[69] and says, "Even her realm of phantasy was a small, enclosed province, peopled by skeletons of tradition and governed by a wooden theology."[70] Toward Eva Birdsong, considered by some critics, for reasons I fail to see, an admirable person, she is particularly and devastatingly severe: "She had never drawn a natural breath since she was married,"[71] and Miss Glasgow tells us that she doesn't work in the garden, doesn't love flowers, prefers hothouse

[68]*Sheltered,* p. 163.   [69]*Sheltered,* p. 243.   [70]*Sheltered,* p. 98.
[71]*Sheltered,* p. 207.

plants, and never wanted a child. She is as sterile, lifeless, and artificial as the dazzling smile which she can turn on as though by a switch. Only toward Victoria is Ellen Glasgow kindly.

Of crucial importance in each of the Queenborough novels is a young girl who is modern, headstrong, hedonistic, and selfish, and around whom the action of the novel revolves. These young girls are startlingly alike in character and attitude. Jenny Blair Archbald speaks for them all when she declares, "All I want to do is to live my own life."[72] Millie Burden gives the wish an Emersonian twist when she says, "I shouldn't consent to take my experience from you second hand."[73] Ellen Glasgow says, "The actual boundary between youth and age is the moment when one realizes that one cannot change life."[74] These modern young ladies are far from that line.

It seems plain to me that these novels are intimately related and mutually complementary ironic portraits of the same hedonistic society, judged against the serious, even grim, standards of Ellen Glasgow's later years. That they are comedies, albeit quiet ones, is a result of attitude, tone, and style. The implied author of the Queenborough novels gained for Ellen Glasgow a fortunate freedom for wit and epigram. She has often been criticized for a tendency of her style to intrude on her narratives, but the Maker and Voice of Queenborough has a defined position from which she can exercise her gift for wit and epigram freely. In 1928, writing of *The Romantic Comedians,* and while *They Stooped to Folly* was in press and *The Sheltered Life* was getting under way, she said: "The style of writing was what I gave most thought to from the first page to the last."[75] The Queenborough novels are loaded with epigrams, such as "Necessity is the reluctant mother of endurance."[76] "Edmonia had been born with the courage of her appetites."[77] "Mrs. Upchurch . . . had a small mind but knew it thoroughly."[78] "Her ideas were so correct that it was sometimes difficult for her to make conversation."[79] "The worst of all possible worlds would be one invented by good women."[80] "The

---

[72]*Sheltered,* p. 180.   [73]*They Stooped,* p. 41.   [74]*Comedians,* p. 317.

[75]*Letters,* p. 90.   [76]*Comedians,* p. 197.   [77]*Comedians,* p. 16.

[78]*Comedians,* p. 20.   [79]*Comedians,* p. 57.   [80]*Comedians,* p. 78.

virtue of perfect behavior lies, not in its rightness, but in its impenetrability."[81] "That prevalent class which our rude ancestors dismissed as scatterbrains, but which superior persons today cherish as intelligentsia."[82] "The Judge was tolerant of any views that were not brought into vocal conflict with his own."[83] "A mind so sprightly that it was not troubled by convictions."[84] "The long Victorian age . . . when womanhood was exalted from a biological fact into a miraculous power."[85] Mr. Littlepage's father "had found it less embarrassing to commit adultery than to pronounce the word in the presence of a lady."[86] "It really takes two to make an influence."[87] "Poor Aunt Agatha had fallen like a perfect lady."[88] Mr. Littlepage was reconciled to a war "that diverted Mary Victoria's mission from the Congo, where faces were incurably black, to the Balkan kingdoms, where, he charitably assumed, they were merely sallow."[89] "Judge Honeywell, whose faith, however flexible, was triumphant over logic (who could recite the Apostle's Creed so long as he was not required to practice the Sermon on The Mount, and could countenance Evolution until it threatened the image of its Maker)."[90] "Though a trifle heavy in figure, she [Isabella] was nimble in mind and vivacious in conversation, a little too wide for the sheath skirt which was just going out, and not quite broad enough for the modern ideas which were just coming in."[91] As every reader of Ellen Glasgow knows, such a group of epigrams could easily be tripled or quadrupled from any single one of the Queenborough novels. The voice here is plainly that of Ellen the Maker, indirectly telling us what opinions we should have about her characters and their world and actions. In one sense the pleasure that we take in these comedies of manners is a direct result of our participation with her in her delight at the happy exercise of her urbane craft. What finally lingers longest in our minds after we read the Queenborough novels is this invisible and omnipresent Maker—sophisticated, detached, amused, gently satiric—fashioning the world she knows best into a comic object.

[81] *Comedians*, p. 149.   [82] *Comedians*, p. 166.   [83] *Comedians*, p. 221.

[84] *Comedians*, p. 121.   [85] *They Stooped*, p. 13.   [86] *They Stooped*, p. 30.

[87] *They Stooped*, p. 81.   [88] *They Stooped*, p. 85.   [89] *They Stooped*, p. 12.

[90] *Comedians*, p. 218.   [91] *Sheltered*, p. 225.

The line between comedy and tragedy is definite but paradoxically indefinable. It helps, perhaps, to say, as Walter Kerr does, that tragedy is the record of man's struggle to realize his ultimate capabilities, the reflection of his nobility of spirit and the magnitude of his possible action, and that comedy is the record of his limitations, the restraints of the frail flesh, the blind lusts of the mighty. It is in her record of such limitations that the people of Queenborough—good and wise, like General Archbald; weak and foolish, like Virginius Littlepage; trapped and frantic, like Eva Birdsong; or self-serving and adolescent, like Jenny Blair—live. And it is in the definition of such limitations imposed by society and human weakness upon the self that Ellen Glasgow is most truly a writer of comedy.

In his tone poem *Ein Heldenleben,* Richard Strauss dramatizes the life of his hero from the early days of arrogant defiance, through the hard struggle for recognition, to the great battles for victory, to the calm triumph of success, and, finally, to a period of quiet peace. In the section preceding the final one—the period of late middle-age, of success—Strauss uses recapitulations of his own great tone poems to suggest the garnering of the victor's laurels. It seems to me that Ellen Glasgow's career follows a quite similar structure. In her early career she defied the household gods of her Virginia aristocracy; in her middle years she struggled through to personal and artistic success against great handicaps and harsh events; in the sixth decade of her life, having won a victory at a high cost, she moved into a serene and tranquil time when she could look at her subject, her life, and herself with a hard-won detachment and allow the comic spirit to dictate to her both a mood and a mode for ordering and recapitulating her life. It is to this period and this mood that the Queenborough novels belong, and as the clear expression of the triumph of spirit over flesh, of will over fate, of detachment over despair, and as the embodiment of a personality and a style in works of high craftsmanship, they have seldom been surpassed in the American novel of manners.

It seems to me that *The Romantic Comedians* is, as she herself immodestly asserted, unsurpassed as an American comedy of manners. It is almost without flaw—the only serious one that I can find being her failure to play out the scene in which the judge learns of

Annabel's leaving him. *They Stooped to Folly* has a broader theme than *The Romantic Comedians* and is almost as perfect in execution, although it is less compact and its characters are less intimately related to a single action. *The Sheltered Life* has a theme that is deeper and a meaning that covers more of the territory of historical and moral record, but it is flawed by the weakness of the point of view at the beginning and by a tendency from time to time for Miss Glasgow to lose some of the essential detachment that never wavers in the first two of the books. But taken all in all, the Queenborough novels form a triptych of Virginia aristocratic life and manners that treats them with knowing affection and yet submits them to the gently corrosive irony of a great comic wit. They succeed admirably in that difficult and rare genre, the American comedy of manners.

The Ideas

Ellen Glasgow's Civilized Men

Blair Rouse

WHAT is a civilized person? Who is civilized? What is a civilization? The dictionaries do not provide much help in understanding these widely used, more often misused, words. I shall not impose the ineptness of a host of lexicographers. A few will suffice. The *American College Dictionary* informs us that *civilization* is "1. An advanced state of human society, in which a high level of art, science, religion and government have been reached. 2. Those people or nations that have reached such a state. The type of culture, society, etc. of a specific group. 4. Act or process of civilizing." This dictionary also tells us that *civilized* means "1. Having an advanced culture, society, etc. 2. Polite; well-bred; refined. 3. Of or pertaining to civilized people."[1] *Webster's New World Dictionary of the American Language* says that *civilization* is "1. The process of civilizing or becoming civilized. 2. The condition of being civilized, social organization of a high order, marked by advances in arts, sciences, etc. 3. The total culture of a people, nation, period, etc. . . . 4. The peoples and countries considered to have reached a high stage of social and cultural development." And this volume further informs us that *civilized* means "1. Advanced in social organization and the arts and sciences. 2. Of people or countries thus advanced. 3. Cultured and courteous; refined."[2] *The American Heritage Dictionary of the English Language* says that *civilization* is "1. A condition of human society marked by an advanced stage of development in the arts and sciences and by corresponding social, political, and cultural complexity. 2. Those nations or people regarded as having arrived at this stage. 3. The type of culture and society developed by a particular group, nation, or region, or by any of these in some particular epoch.

[1](New York: Random House, 1958).

[2](Cleveland and New York: World, 1962).

4. The act or process of civilizing or of reaching a civilized state."
And this aid to learning defines *civilized* as: "1. Having a highly
developed society and culture. 2. Of, pertaining to, or characteristic of a people or nation so developed. 3. Polite or cultured;
urbane; refined."[3]

Enough of this! It may be that dictionaries can be useful only
to those who already know the answers. Certainly the information
offered in these three reasonably representative abridged dictionaries provides glorious examples of question-begging in almost
every other word. "Advanced"? Advanced from what to what?
A "high level"? A high level as measured against what base? Any
"total culture" is a civilization? "Countries and people considered
to have reached a high stage of social and cultural development"?
Considered by whom? Judged so by what criteria? And to be civilized is to be "polite" or "well-bred" or "refined" or "cultured"
or "courteous" or "urbane"? Surely these alleged synonyms are
thin, superficial, and beg many questions. What seems especially
noticeable—and discouraging—in these lexicographical struggles is
that *civilization* and *civilized* appear to be labels for largely material attainments of groups of human beings or the outward
modes of action of such groups. A case might be made that some
of these definitions suggest the possibility that these words denote
more than materialistic achievements and surface appearances.
Nevertheless, the questions as to what civilization is and what it
means to be civilized are begged, not answered.

Moreover, scholars who have written of civilization and, by
implication, of civilized men, may treat these words in as cavalier
a manner as the makers of dictionaries. Ellsworth Huntington
wrote *Mainsprings of Civilization,* a book in which he devoted
many pages to showing how heredity, geography, and climate
shape culture and history. But I find in his book no definition of
civilization or *civilized.* He apparently assumed that any fool
would know what these familiar words mean and, of course, that
the fool's meanings would correspond with his own notions. An
interesting assumption.

Lord Clark, in his book *Civilisation,* is rather discouraging.
"What is civilisation?" he asks on page 1. He replies, "I don't know.

[3](Boston: Houghton Mifflin, 1969).

I can't define it in abstract terms yet. But I think I can recognize it when I see it; and I am looking at it now." (He was standing on the Pont des Arts in Paris.) On page 14 he ventures the possibility that civilization involves "a sense of permanence." And on page 17 he comes a bit closer to defining *civilized* when he says, "Civilized man . . . must feel that he belongs somewhere in space and time; that he consciously looks forward and looks back."[4] Now this may suggest that such individuals have some sort of sense of history or historic consciousness—but, in their own peculiar ways, so did the Australian aborigines before contact with Europeans very largely destroyed their culture.

Occasionally Ellen Glasgow used *civilized* and *civilization* with the imprecise denotations already examined. More often, however, she reserved the word *civilized* as a citation of merit for a small number of her characters, all men. And from time to time, in letters and essays, she showed that, for her, one who should be called civilized must possess attributes found with decreasing frequency in a world, or at least the world of Western culture, which one might very doubtfully think of as civilized and, hence, a civilization.

Certainly Ellen Glasgow did not measure civilization by material achievements. So-called technological progress could not provide measurements for civilization. Nor did outward appearances of politeness, courtesy, refinement, urbanity, and other surface ornaments of the supposedly well bred gentleman necessarily guarantee that he was a civilized man. (Ellen Glasgow was only too aware of well-bred mobs that had participated in lynchings.)

To be civilized demanded, for Ellen Glasgow, a condition of the inner man: a complex of spirit, of morality, of character which might be revealed in outward appearances and more certainly in conduct, but which appearances alone could not certify. Manners are indeed one evidence of the civilized man, but only if his manners are the outward evidence of an inner existence.

It has been observed that many of Ellen Glasgow's women appear stronger in relation to most of the males in her novels. In other words, Miss Glasgow has been thought of as a novelist who portrayed weak or victimized or, occasionally, evil men but admi-

[4]Kenneth Clark, *Civilization* (New York: Harper & Row, 1970).

rable and often very strong women. One who has read the novels thoughtfully will, of course, recognize this oversimplification. True, she was harsh in her portrayal of many of her men, often showing them as weak, foolish, ludicrous, or villainous. But though she created a number of admirably strong women, such as Dorinda Oakley in *Barren Ground,* she also created a number of women who were victims in various ways, targets of her irony and even of her malice and scorn, as well as some women meant to be seen as less than admirable pillars of strength and virtue. At least one—Angelica in *The Builders*—is evil personified. She is psychopathic, perhaps, but nevertheless evil in what she does and in her effects on others.

At this point it may be well for me to defend myself against possible accusations of male chauvinism. Miss Glasgow created the male characters whom she considered civilized, not I. She specifically named several of these portrayals of men as her characterizations of civilized persons. And Miss Glasgow, not I, refrained, at least as I observe her portrayals and statements, from naming any civilized women. Does this mean that she thought that women were not or could not be civilized—in her understanding of the word? Perhaps so. However, I doubt that this is necessarily the truth of the matter. The answer to the problem may lie simply in the fact that the women she chose to portray did not fit the category or possess the attributes of her *civilized person.* It may be interesting to speculate later concerning some of Ellen Glasgow's more admirable women and to try to determine why she did not name them among her civilized persons.

Although she did not eliminate factors of culture from her concept—arts, sciences, and government evidently have their importance—Ellen Glasgow found social, moral, and spiritual values far more imperative if one should deserve the accolade of *civilized.* Her civilized men possessed these inner controls of their actions in relation to others and in relation to themselves.

The men whom Miss Glasgow considered civilized are Tucker Corbin in *The Deliverance* (1904), Marmaduke Littlepage in *They Stooped to Folly* (1929), General David Archbald in *The Sheltered Life* (1932), and John Fincastle in *Vein of Iron* (1935). I believe that Asa Timberlake of *In This Our Life* (1941) also belongs to this select group. Possibly Judge Bassett in *The Voice of the*

People (1900) might be seen as one of the civilized had Miss Glasgow's delineation of him been more completely developed. She did not name Virginia Pendleton's father, the rector, in *Virginia* (1913), among her civilized men, nor am I able to include him as an addition according to my own judgment. He was a most admirable man, a fearlessly heroic soul. But he was imprisoned in the intellectual and emotional fog of "evasive idealism." He and his wife and, indeed, most of his class, as portrayed in *Virginia,* believed sincerely in what they thought of as taking a "True View" of life—which actually meant closing their minds and hearts to things unpleasant and even to outrageous evils so that, in the name of high ideals, they evaded the presence of evil and refused to acknowledge its existence.

Let us look at the men of the Commonwealth of Virginia whom Ellen Glasgow did find civilized.

Tucker Corbin is one of the Blake household, who, with the Fletchers, occupy the central interest of *The Deliverance,* published by Miss Glasgow in 1904. In a novel replete with the depiction of hatred, intellectual as well as physical blindness, and misconceived heroism, Tucker stands forth as one who has known suffering, disappointment, and defeat but has never surrendered to hatred or despair. The unhappy Blake home is the overseer's cottage in which the aristocratic Blakes were forced to live after being dispossessed of "Blake Hall" by their one-time overseer Fletcher. In this place Tucker Corbin is the one individual who is not tormented by hatred of Fletcher, as is young Christopher Blake, or blinded to truth, as is the physically blind Mrs. Blake, who is deluded by her family so that she believes the Confederacy has been victorious and that she is still living in "Blake Hall."

Some of Ellen Glasgow's more rewarding characters are persons, usually men, who have been harshly wounded physically or psychically. In an otherwise bitter novel of 1878, Tucker Corbin, the maimed Civil War veteran of *The Deliverance,* breathes kindness, good sense, and an awareness of beauty. He has suffered cruel injury, yet he has learned how to live a fruitful life. He is endowed with riches of spirit which permit him to overcome his disabilities and to find a deep happiness in the small details of his daily life. More than an aristocrat by birth and class, he is an aristocrat of the mind and soul. His afflictions have strengthened rather than embittered him. Yet he is neither sentimental nor blind to suffering. He is no Pollyanna any more than he is a victim of self-pity. Tucker Corbin is, indeed, a truly civilized man.[5]

Certainly Ellen Glasgow believed that he was civilized, for in *A Certain Measure* she wrote:

Tucker was a civilized soul in a world which, by and large, is not, and may not ever become, civilized. His true companions in my books are General Archbald in *The Sheltered Life* and John Fincastle in *Vein of Iron*. This rare pattern of mankind has always attracted me as a novelist. I like to imagine how the world would appear if human beings were really civilized, not by machinery alone, but through that nobler organ which has been called, *the heart in the intellect* (italics added).[6]

In this phrase, "the heart in the intellect," Ellen Glasgow gave the key to her conception of what it could mean to be civilized: there must be the heart, signifying the inner spirit, soul, feeling, emotion; but there must also be the controlling force of intellect, of the mind functioning with tempering wisdom. Part of a conversation between Tucker and his embittered niece, Cynthia Blake, suggests the quality of this man, the first of Miss Glasgow's civilized men:

"I didn't notice things much myself when I was young. The only sights that seemed to count, somehow, were those I saw inside my head, and if you'll believe me, I used to be moody and out of sorts half the time, just like Christopher. Times have changed now, you'll say, and it's true. Why, I've got nothing to do these days but to take a look at things, and I tell you I see a lot now where all was a blank before. You just glance over that old field and tell me what you find."

Cynthia followed the sweep of his left arm. "There's first the road, and then a piece of fallow land that ought to be ploughed," she said.

"Bless my soul, is that all you see? Why, there is every shade of green on earth in that old field, and almost every one of blue, except azure, which you'll find up in the sky. That little bit of cloud, no bigger than my hand, is shaped exactly like an eagle's

[5]In this essay, I draw on pertinent material in my *Ellen Glasgow* (New York: Twayne Publishers, 1962).

[6](New York: Harcourt, Brace, 1943), pp. 38-39.

wing. I've watched it for an hour, and I never saw one like it. As for that old pine on top the little knoll, if you look at it long enough you'll see that it's a great big green cross raised against the sky."

"So it is," said Cynthia, in surprise; "so it is."

"Then to come nearer, look at that spray of turtlehead growing by that gray stone—the shadow it throws is as fine as thread lace, and it waves in the breeze just like a flower."

"Oh, it is beautiful, and I never should have seen it."

"And best of all," resumed Tucker, as if avoiding an interruption, "is that I've watched a nestful of young wrens take flight from under the eaves. There's not a play of Shakespeare's greater than that, I tell you."

"And it makes you happy—just this?" asked Cynthia wistfully, as the pathos of his maimed figure drove to her heart.

"Well, I reckon happiness is not so much in what comes as in the way you take it," he returned, smiling. "There was a time, you must remember, when I was the straightest shot of my day, and something of a lady-killer as well, if I do say it who shouldn't. I've done my part in a war and I'm not ashamed of it. I've taken the enemy's cannon under a fire hot enough to roast an ox, and I've sent more men to eternity than I like to think of; but I tell you honestly there's no battle-field under heaven worth an hour of this old bench. If I had my choice today, I'd rather see the flitting of those wrens than kill the biggest Yankee that ever lived. The time was when I didn't think so, but I know now that there's as much life out there in that old field as in the tightest-packed city street I ever saw—purer life, praise God, and sweeter to the taste. Why, look at this poplar leaf that blew across the road: I've studied the pattern of it for half an hour, and I've found out that such a wonder is worth going ten miles to see."

"Oh, I can't understand you," sighed Cynthia hopelessly. "I wish I could, but I can't—I was born different—so different."

"Bless your heart, honey, I was born different myself, and if I'd kept my leg and my arm I dare say I'd be strutting round on one and shaking the other in the face of God Almighty just as I used to do. A two-legged man is so busy getting about the world that he never has time to sit down and take a look around him. I tell you I see more in one hour as I am now than I saw in all the rest of my life when I was sound and whole. Why, I could sit here all day long and stare up at that blue sky, and then go to bed feeling that my twelve hours were full and brimming over. If I'd never seen anything in my life but that sky above the old pine, I should say at the end, 'Thank God for that one good look.' "[7]

[7]*The Deliverance* (New York: Doubleday, Page, 1904), pp. 105–8.

It may be noticed that Tucker is an observer rather than a physically active participant in the hard life of his postbellum time. For him who had once been very active physically, his maimed condition may have been all the more tormenting. Yet he had been able to adjust himself to his situation. It seems clear that Tucker has qualities of mind and heart in which he has been able to find support for his spirit, though physically broken and forced to live as a dependent upon his poverty-stricken family.

Ellen Glasgow endows Tucker's character with a number of the qualities which may be considered among the criteria for judging the presence of a civilized man. Tucker Corbin is not sentimental, but he does have sentiment—that is, honest feeling, emotions which he is not ashamed to acknowledge. He is devoid of "evasive idealism," yet he possesses positive ideals as to his relations to others. He is generous in sympathy, perception, and understanding, and he is kind. He possesses an innate dignity and a concern that the dignity of others be preserved. He has a keen sense of his own identity, but he is not morbidly sensitive. His sense of humor enables him to laugh amid his own misfortunes but to be no less sympathetic with his nieces, his overworked nephew, and his blind sister. Clearly, he is a proud man who is aware of his own worth, but his is not the foolish, weakening, destructive *hybris* of many of his contemporaries—indeed, of some members of his own family.

Ellen Glasgow's next civilized man, Marmaduke Littlepage of *They Stooped to Folly,* is, as with Tucker Corbin, a part of the "supporting cast" in the novel. He, too, had suffered physically as well as emotionally and had been forced, to some extent, into the role of observer. His situation enabled him to be more active than Tucker, and, as a painter, he could give visible form as an expression of his sense of beauty. Yet though he has been thwarted in his heart's desires, he is a man who possesses many of the qualities requisite for the civilized man.

It may seem rather strange that Ellen Glasgow introduced one of her civilized men into her ironic, sharply satiric treatment in comic fiction of the barbaric Victorian notion of "the ruined woman." Certainly, her three "ruined women"—poor Aunt Agatha, Mrs. Dalrymple, and Milly Burden—are portrayed with mingled sympathy and amusement. And Mary Victoria Littlepage, who knows all the answers except the right ones and is certain that she knows what is right for everyone else, is the target for some of the author's most superbly devastating portraiture. Of course, Mr. and Mrs. Littlepage, especially the latter, provide the central focus for this modern comedy of outmoded manners. Yet the book would be impoverished by the absence of Marmaduke, who observes with civilized mind and heart, and the keen sensitive awareness of an artist, the comedy as it is played out around him.

In her essay on *They Stooped to Folly*, Miss Glasgow contrasts Marmaduke to his brother, Virginius Littlepage. In the latter she saw that she had portrayed

the modern man who fears action, yet desires the things that only action can win . . . he is defeated not by superior numbers alone, but even more by an infirmity of the will. . . . His concluding episode with Mrs. Dalrymple reveals the individual human being as he has been moulded by inheritance, by tradition, by experience, and by the social forces through which his life is controlled.

In Marmaduke, on the contrary, we see the civilized man in despair of civilization, the artist in a society that classes art among the lesser utilities. Sensitive by nature, he wears, as a protective colouring, the buffoonery of truth. Though his point of view may throw an oblique light on the time, he does not, like Virginius, his brother, stand between the reader and the scene he observes. . . . Marmaduke's opinions, since he was handicapped by veracity, as well as by the vagabond heart of the artist, were inevitably tinged with the florid colours of his own personality. . . . Marmaduke, who had left one leg and the whole body of his idealism in the war zone [of World War I], had returned to Queenborough chiefly because, as a cripple and an indigent artist, there was nowhere else he could go. . . . Embittered romantic as he was, he had discovered that it was not only rational but logical to dislike human nature, and yet to like human beings.[8]

Marmaduke is not taken in by the evasions and the shams which substitute for reality among his contemporaries; he is, as he points out to Virginius, genuine, and he refuses to pretend to be something he is not. Marmaduke is no hero or saint; he is a very real human being who is subject to his own weaknesses and difficulties. Nor did his being an "embittered romantic" exclude Marmaduke,

[8]*A Certain Measure* (New York: Harcourt, Brace, 1943), pp. 238-41.

in Miss Glasgow's eyes, from the ranks of the civilized. For he had surmounted his bitterness; he had refused to surrender.

In *The Woman Within,* though not in a discussion of Marmaduke or this novel, Ellen Glasgow wrote a brief passage which, I believe, makes clearer why she considered Marmaduke Littlepage a civilized man. Here she said: "One might select realities, but one could not impose on Reality. Not if one were honest in one's interpretation, not if one possessed artistic integrity. For truth to art became in the end simple fidelity to one's own inner vision."[9] Whether Marmaduke in his paintings was able to demonstrate his fidelity to his "own inner vision" we have no way of knowing. None of his paintings has survived. But in his living, as delineated by Ellen Glasgow, Marmaduke Littlepage possessed personal integrity—fidelity to his "own inner vision" of himself and others—that sine qua non of Ellen Glasgow's civilized men: "the heart in the intellect."

I have said that Marmaduke was genuine and suggested this as, in part, a measure of his being considered civilized. A passage from a conversation between him and Virginius, his brother, may enlarge the meaning of that word *genuine* when applied to the maimed artist. Marmaduke and Virginius have been discussing the sad history of Aunt Agatha, immured for life for her youthful indiscretion. Virginius remarks:

"Even Mother, who had the tenderest heart in the world, never felt that Aunt Agatha had been treated too harshly. I confess that the idea never entered my mind until I married Victoria."

"Yes, I take off my hat to Victoria," Marmaduke replied generously. "If she always thinks the wrong thing, she never fails, except by accident, to do the right one. The truth is, though we seldom agree in our opinions, that Victoria and I are the only pair of genuine idealists left alive."

Mr. Littlepage smiled. "An unmatched pair, you must admit."

"Perhaps. Not so unmatched, however, as you might suppose. The point we have in common is that we are both genuine. We are neither of us so beautiful as Mary Victoria nor so intelligent as Louisa Goddard; but we are more real as far as we go, which isn't, I grant you, so far as it might be. Our only difference arises when Victoria fails to accept the greatest modern discovery that nothing

[9](New York: Harcourt, Brace, 1954), p. 125.

we do or say matters to the universe. She has never lost the primitive belief that the cosmos is her audience."

"Is there any reverence left in your nature, Marmaduke?"

"Very little. No genuine idealist who isn't as simpleminded as Victoria could reverence the conspiracy of evasion you optimists will call civilization. Only a materialist like Mary Victoria is capable of that kind of duplicity."

"Whatever you hold against Mary Victoria," Mr. Littlepage rejoined tartly, "you must admit that she is, with all her faults, an idealist."

"On the contrary," Marmaduke chuckled, "she is as materialistic as big business or organized Christianity. Have you forgotten the way she patronized the war as if it were her favorite charity?"[10]

The conversation ends shortly after, with Mr. Virginius Littlepage musing:

"I chose wealth, security, steadfast position, but Marmaduke gave all those things in exchange for liberation of spirit. He has been himself, however ignoble."[11]

A little later Virginius thinks, so Miss Glasgow reports:

Marmaduke, he saw with disapproving envy, had not compromised, had not waited for the opportune moment. He was shabby and untidy and disreputable, but he was also a free spirit. He had never been twisted into a conventional shape.[12]

General David Archbald of *The Sheltered Life,* the third of Miss Glasgow's civilized men, may be the most vividly and sympathetically drawn. As were Tucker Corbin and Marmaduke Littlepage, General Archbald had been a warrior. While I find no difficulty in equating the civilized condition with Tucker's and Marmaduke's having been soldiers, even though Ellen Glasgow so hated war, I do not find it easy to see David Archbald as a warrior—and not only a warrior, but a leader in war, a general. One may say that circumstances made it almost inevitable that Tucker and Marmaduke

[10]*They Stooped to Folly* (New York: Literary Guild, 1929), pp. 125-26.

[11]Ibid., p. 129.

[12]Ibid.

should fight in their wars. And one gathers that David Archbald had been drawn by old loyalties to fight for the Southern cause. As he is shown throughout the book to have been a man of ability, perhaps his commanding men at war should occasion no surprise, nor exclude General Archbald from the ranks of Ellen Glasgow's civilized men. I suspect that Ellen Glasgow, as well as her friend Dr. Douglas Southall Freeman, considered the commander of the Army of Northern Virginia a civilized man; and Robert E. Lee was a *professional* soldier.

General Archbald is the first of Miss Glasgow's civilized men to occupy a central position in the structure of the novel in which he appears. *The Sheltered Life* presents the lives of the Archbalds and the Birdsongs in Queenborough from a dual point of view: that of age, as seen through General Archbald, and that of childhood and youth, as seen through his granddaughter Jenny Blair Archbald.

The title of *The Sheltered Life* is bitterly ironic in that if anything is revealed in its pages it is that the lives of men and women, young and old, hold no shelter from those forces which inflict pain and sorrow. David Archbald, looking back from the vantage point of his eighty-three years, in those pages of her novel which the author named "The Deep Past," relives a life in which he could find no shelter from the presence of injustice, pain, and cruelty, in which loyalties to custom and tradition had not only made him a soldier, but, because circumstances had caused him and a young lady to be placed in a compromising situation, had led to his marriage to a woman whom he did not love. Perhaps in him one finds his sense of duty and loyalty to obligations undertaken defining, in part, his civilized character. Another of his dimensions is pity. So he muses in "The Deep Past":

No man needed protection less; but because he had lived a solitary male among women, he could never escape it, and because these women depended upon him, he had remained at their mercy. It was impossible to wound the feelings of women who owed him the bread they ate and the roof over their heads, and so long as he did not hurt their feelings, they would be stronger than he was. Always, from his earliest childhood, he mused, with a curious resentment against life, he had been the victim of pity. Of his own pity, not another's. Of that double-edged nerve of sympathy, like the aching nerve in a tooth, which throbbed at the sight of injustice or cruelty. One woman after another had enslaved his sympathy more than his passion, and never had she seemed to be the woman his passion demanded.[13]

Later he ponders over the times in which he now lives, in his old age, on the eve of the First World War:

Old General Archbald could not see that human nature was different from what it had been in his youth. To be sure, idealism, like patriotism, appeared to diminish with every material peace between conflicts; but he was near enough to the Spanish War, and indeed to the Civil War, to realize that the last battle has never been fought and the last empty word has never been spoken. Not that it mattered. All that he knew now was that he was too old to bother about life. He was too old to bother about cruelty, which he had seen all over the world, in every system invented by man; which he had seen in a velvet mask, in rags, and naked except for its own skin. . . . For one confirmed habit had not changed with the ages. Mankind was still calling human nature a system and trying vainly to put something else in its place.

But a world made, or even made over, by science was only a stark and colourless spectacle to old David Archbald. A thin-lipped world of facts without faith, of bones without flesh. . . .

But in the realm of ideas, where hope reigned, the prospect was brighter. There the crust of civilization, so thin and brittle over the world outside, was beginning to thicken. . . .

But he could not see that exact knowledge and precision of language had improved the quality of mankind. Well, the wonder in every age, he supposed, was not that most men were savage, but that a few men were civilized. Only a few in every age, and these few were the clowns in the parade. . . . (Miss Glasgow's ellipses).[14]

In the further development of "The Deep Past," Ellen Glasgow revealed how David Archbald had helped an escaping slave on his way to freedom and had endured the displeasure, not to say disgrace, meted out by society and his own family, who were loyal to the "peculiar institution"; how he had been, as it were, exiled to England and known a woman's love there; and how he had later married a woman he did not love and had lived the better part of a lifetime with her. "Well," he thinks, "the past was woven of

[13]*The Sheltered Life* (Garden City, N.Y.: Doubleday, Doran, 1932), pp. 134–35.

[14]Ibid., pp. 144–47.

contradictions. For eighty-three years he had lived two lives, and between these two different lives, which corresponded only in time, he could trace no connection. What he had wanted, he had never had; what he had wished to do, he had never done. . . ." (Miss Glasgow's ellipses).[15] And he ponders further: "He had been a good citizen, a successful lawyer, a faithful husband, an indulgent father; he had been, indeed, everything but himself."[16]

One may question whether David Archbald is, indeed, the civilized man of Ellen Glasgow's conception. Does he not see himself as thwarted throughout life, as having lived a life that was not his own? Is he, indeed, civilized? But Miss Glasgow suggests that he possessed a quality of heroic virtue belonging properly only to the civilized man who endures a life in which he follows the calls of inherited loyalties and duties, accepts obligations which, for him, go against the grain, and in the very process of becoming accepted as a worthy and successful citizen in Queenborough, a process which involves so much that is never of his own choosing, nevertheless remains true to his own inner being and does not lie to himself. General Archbald is a good man. And the goodness which is his, perhaps as with John Fincastle and Asa Timberlake, is the most important measure of his being civilized. His goodness has not been a spectacular display of heroism or virtue, but it has the keenness of a heroism existing beneath the seemingly uneventful surface of a life lived too much against the grain but without sham, malice, or bitterness. It may be that only those who possess such goodness are, in truth, civilized. David Archbald's portrait suggests so stern a restriction upon this society.

In a letter to Allen Tate dated September 22, 1932, Ellen Glasgow wrote: "By the Sheltered Life, I meant the whole civilization man has built to protect himself from reality. As you perceive, I was not concerned with the code of Virginia, but with the conventions of the world we call civilized. In General Archbald, the real protagonist, I was dealing with the fate of the civilized mind in a world where even the civilizations we make are uncivilized."[17] There may be further emphasis on her concern in *The*

---

[15]Ibid., p. 152.   [16]Ibid., p. 164.

[17]Blair Rouse, ed., *The Letters of Ellen Glasgow* (New York: Harcourt, Brace, 1958), p. 124. Hereinafter cited as *Letters*.

Sheltered Life in these statements in her essay on that novel in
A Certain Measure. Here she wrote: "Against this background of
futility was projected the contrasting character of General Archbald, a lover of wisdom, a humane and civilized soul, oppressed by
the burden of tragic remembrance. . . . the old man, left behind by
the years, is the central character of the book; and into his lonely
spirit I have put much of my ultimate feeling about life. He represents the tragedy, wherever it appears, of the civilized man in a
world that is not civilized." [18]

David Archbald had wished to be a poet in a time and place that
never tolerated poetry except in calfbound volumes bearing the
names of foreign authors. He was also a humanitarian in a society
that cultivated cruelty and insensitivity as a fine art and provided
cock-fighting for the lower orders and fox-hunting for the ladies
and gentlemen. A sheltered and sheltering gentleman, he lived in a
society in which women pretended to obey but actually gently
and inexorably dominated. As General Archbald in old age reflected upon his life, he was wise, yet not all wise; sadly weary, yet
not embittered. In the most consuming affections of his old age—
his love for Jenny Blair and for Eva Birdsong—General Archbald
was not able to escape the illusions of his class: he could not dispel
the myths of Jenny Blair's youthful innocence nor of Eva's imperishable beauty. Yet David Archbald was that rarest creature,
whether gentleman or commoner, the civilized man. Although
Ellen Glasgow created a number of such men, General Archbald
may offer her most perfect embodiment of this concept. Yet
General Archbald was never really sheltered. He was surely the
unsheltered civilized man in a hostile culture that thought itself
a civilization.

One usually sees John Fincastle of *Vein of Iron* in relation to the
others in the narrative: to his daughter, to his staunchly Calvinist
mother, and to his delicate, gentle, Tidewater Virginia wife. Less
often does the reader come close to John alone.

Another factor that may cause readers difficulty in imagining
John Fincastle is that he is the civilized man as philosopher. His

[18]Pp. 203-4.

drama is largely played out in the realm of the spirit and the
intellect, in his struggles in his inner thoughts with spiritual meanings and in his attempt to comprehend the nature of God and man
for himself and to put his understanding into words. To dramatize
the inward action of such spiritual and intellectual activity so that
it may be clearly realized in the imagination of the reader may be
an impossible task for any writer who is not both philosopher and
novelist and equally master of both thought and art. To depict a
philosopher as a character in a novel places an almost intolerable
burden on the novelist. If Miss Glasgow had dared to impart the
philosopher-character's philosophy in the pages of the novel, she
would have run the grave risk of transforming her novel into a
philosophical treatise, of having her character's thought assumed
to be her own, and of destroying the true focus of the book,
flattening the other characters and wrecking the narrative.

Ellen Glasgow avoids these dangers, for Ada Fincastle is the
central character in *Vein of Iron,* not John, her father. And Miss
Glasgow does not permit the reader to lose sight of this important
fact. Whether she had any inclination to expound John's philosophy or not, she refrains from doing so. Instead, she asserts that
he was a philosopher whose thought was heretical to the accepted
beliefs of his church, that he devoted years to writing the volumes
setting forth his philosophy, and that his work was read and understood for its value by only a few fellow spirits scattered about
the world. So the reader must accept John as philosopher on the
author's word. Of course, one may say that readers must make
such acceptances for all that occurs in any novel. Yet this is not
quite true, for the author could dramatize, present, show almost
everything else in her novel. She could only *assert* and suggest
John Fincastle's philosophy.

Notwithstanding the difficulties in seeing John Fincastle, he
appears as one who merits the accolade of "civilized." He surely
possesses Miss Glasgow's "heart in the intellect." Though he sees
clearly through the errors of thought and action among his neighbors, he can tolerate their blindness of mind and spirit and even
their intolerance toward him.

At least once, however, it seems to me that John Fincastle falls
short of civilized virtue. I am thinking of his actions when Ralph
McBride, whom Ada loves and expects to marry, is seduced into

a compromising situation by Janet Rowan. Custom insisted that the word of the girl must be believed. And John Fincastle joins in forcing Ralph into a blasphemous, loveless, marriage with the greedy, spiteful Janet. Only in John's sharing in this evil action does he seem less than courageous, less than wholly civilized. It does not appear to me that he follows the dictates of his conscience in this situation or shows the courage which he displays elsewhere in the novel.

Of John Fincastle, Ellen Glasgow wrote early in the pages of *Vein of Iron:*

It was true that the external world and all the part of his life that people called "real life"— . . . all the outward aspects of living seemed to him fragmentary, unreal, and fugitive. He had not willed this; he had struggled against the sense of exile that divided him from the thought of his time, from his dearest, his nearest. Nevertheless, it was there. His inner life alone, the secret life of the soul, was vital and intimate and secure.

. . . .

In the end he had been driven into obscurity, into poverty, into the strange kind of happiness that comes to the martyr and the drunkard. Why? Why? Who could answer? He might have been false to himself, and who would have suffered? But he had craved truth (yet who knows what is truth?) as another man might crave a drink or a drug. Was this endless seeking an inheritance from the past? Was it a survival of the westward thrust of the pioneer?[19]

Near the time of the publication of *Vein of Iron,* in 1935, Miss Glasgow wrote about her novel in a letter to Stark Young. She said of John Fincastle: "With John Fincastle, I treat of the fate, the isolation, of the scholar in America, of the thinker among the dynamos."[20] In comparable words she wrote to Bessie Zeban Jones: "For three years . . . I have lived night and day with these people. In John Fincastle (my favorite) I have written of the loneliness of the scholar in America. . . ."[21] And in another letter to a Miss Forbes, Ellen Glasgow said: "But John Fincastle was far more than a sceptical philosopher. For twenty years, in my early youth, my chief interest was the study of philosophy; and all that

[19](New York: Harcourt, Brace, 1935), pp. 50–51.

[20]*Letters,* p. 191.

[21]Ibid., p. 194.

I read and thought was embodied in my favorite character in *Vein of Iron.*"[22]

In her essay on *Vein of Iron,* which she published in *A Certain Measure,* Ellen Glasgow observed that fortitude was the chief of the elements that "composed the Presbyterian spirit and the Presbyterian theology," and she saw herself as studying "the vital principle of survival, which has enabled races and individuals to withstand the destructive forces of nature and civilization."[23] Here she seems to be using the word *civilization* to signify modern Western culture. Or one may read this as suggesting that her *civilized man* might have to be a person outside of, beyond, and in some respects *opposed to* what was generally called civilization.

Of John Fincastle she wrote in this essay, in words comparable to some of those already quoted from her letters: "In the later John Fincastle [there had been an earlier John], I was trying to portray the fate of the philosopher in an era of science, of the scholar in a world of mechanical inventions. His return to an earlier, spiritual age, and to the philosophy of Plotinus, is intellectually and historically accurate."[24]

Ellen Glasgow attempted to create in John Fincastle a philosopher-saint. But she could not demonstrate her character's philosophical stature; she could only imply his greatness. His spiritual purity and his attainment of something near the exaltation of the Eastern mystics are more effectively dramatized than his philosophical distinction.

John Fincastle is a civilized man. The leaders among the Scotch-Irish settlers had been their preachers; and these preachers had been scholars, even philosophers after their fashion, though rarely so unorthodox as John Fincastle. A philosopher in Shut-In Valley offered, therefore, no contradiction of probabilities.

Readers could think that Asa Timberlake of *In This Our Life* was a failure, a man defeated and overwhelmed by a frustrating and humiliating existence that could hardly be called a life. He is married to Lavinia, a pseudohypochondriac whom he no longer

[22]Ibid., p. 203.

[23]*A Certain Measure,* p. 169.

[24]Ibid., p. 171.

loves and who not only does not love him but simply uses him to insure her comfort while she waits for rich Uncle William Fitzroy to die and leave her a portion of his wealth. Miss Glasgow, in her time, created an interesting array of repulsive women, but Lavinia Timberlake surpasses most of them—except, perhaps, her daughter Stanley—in soft, selfish, greedy, petty meanness. I question whether Miss Glasgow should have written *Beyond Defeat,* the short sequel to *In This Our Life*. Yet I know that the writing and publication of that book was justified in at least one respect: Ellen Glasgow killed off Lavinia! Actually, Miss Glasgow wrote *Beyond Defeat* because she believed that her central meanings had not been made clear in the earlier novel, that Asa and his daughter Roy had not been understood. For Miss Glasgow believed that she had depicted Asa as one who had *not* been defeated by the disappointments and frustrations of his own life nor by the ugliness of the lives by which he was surrounded. Hurt? Humiliated? Yes. But Asa had never surrendered.

In the events of the novel, Asa is beset by the evil, meanness, weakness, and tragic waste in which Lavinia, their worthless daughter Stanley, and their rapacious old Uncle William Fitzroy are involved. But Asa refuses to succumb to the evil around him or to admit as truth the pretenses under which all the others, except Roy, his daughter, hide the ugliness of their lives.

When Stanley is involved in a hit-and-run automobile accident and tries to put the blame on Parry, the young Negro boy who has been taking care of her car, Asa sees through Stanley's lies, forces the truth from her, and sees that Parry is cleared of all blame and freed from jail. He cannot free Parry from the blight which Stanley's selfishness and utter weakness of character have cast over him. Yet Asa has done what he could; he is not depicted as a superman performing impossible deeds against impossible odds. But he does refuse to surrender to the evil and injustice around him, even when it involves his own daughter.

One problem for the reader of *In This Our Life* as well as for the author—and one which she may not fully have realized when she was writing the novel—is that Stanley steals the show. Ellen Glasgow did not intend this and did not admit that it had happened. Nevertheless, it is so. Stanley is—with apologies to my canine friends—a little bitch. She is irresponsible, greedy, selfish, utterly thoughtless of the rights and feelings of others. At least one of her sisters in evil weakness in Ellen Glasgow's fiction is Janet Rowan of *Vein of Iron,* but we never see Janet as closely and unpleasantly as we come to know Stanley. The latter believes there is nothing her pretty face and figure cannot get for her. She also believes that whatever she wants she should have, including her sister's fiancé. Stanley is as morally revolting as her mother, Lavinia; her mother, however, is dull, relatively inactive, and comparatively uninteresting except as an element in the horror that is Asa's life. But Stanley, as she steals Roy's fiancé, also tends to steal the interest of the reader. Perhaps it was inevitable that Miss Glasgow should make her seem more significant in the novel than she thought she was or intended her to appear. So it was not really surprising that the comparatively simpleminded film producers saw *In This Our Life* as a vehicle in which Bette Davis, as Stanley, could again play the part she continued to play following her performance in *Of Human Bondage,* complete with all the Davis histrionics. The film was worthless and a travesty of the novel Ellen Glasgow had written, but it is really not surprising that the filmmakers misread the book as they did.

Stanley is a weakly evil, immature child. Asa is a quiet, long-suffering, civilized gentleman imprisoned by circumstances in a snake pit inhabited by Stanley and Lavinia, the vulgar, rapacious Uncle William Fitzroy, and the two well-meaning but weak young men, the fiancés of Stanley and Roy. Seldom have moral weakness and selfishness been so powerfully revealed as destructive forces as in the pages of *In This Our Life.* Yet Asa Timberlake is that rarity among modern human beings: a good man, who has the strength of his goodness. His is the virtue of the civilized man who possesses compassion, pity, and the perceptive wisdom that enables him to pierce beneath the pretentious surfaces of most of his associates. Moreover, he has the quiet courage to defy his family and extract the truth from Stanley when she tries to shift her blame for a careless murder to the black servant. Asa does this even though he suffers great pain for what she has done and for what she is.

Asa's only relief from his life in the city involves defiance of Lavinia, Uncle William, and the "unco guid" in the Queenborough society. For he goes out on some Sundays to visit "Hunter's Fare" and to enjoy the soothing companionship of Kate Oliver, the widow of his friend Jack Oliver. "For twenty years and more," Ellen Glasgow wrote,

these Sabbath flights into the country and freedom had been the solitary pleasure, apart from Roy's infrequent companionship, in a life which, from its beginning, had been starved for delight. . . . Kate was the one human being with whom his hidden cave dweller had ever come out boldly under the open sky. His feeling for her was friendship, he knew, but it was friendship exalted to a major emotion. Whenever he thought of her, it was not as a possible lover but as a great companion. He had always, in the ancient language of chivalry, "respected" her. . . . In the last year, however, Asa had understood that he wanted more from Kate than these few Sunday afternoons at "Hunter's Fare." What he wanted was to spend his life with her and with the things they both loved—the fields and woods and streams and all the friendly animals on the farm.[25]

As we learn in *Beyond Defeat*, Asa is able eventually to achieve his wish; after Uncle William Fitzroy dies, Lavinia has the money for a nurse and can do without Asa, and he, in the face of the public opinion he scorns, leaves Lavinia and goes to live at "Hunter's Fare" and to work on the farm.

Asa Timberlake is a very special kind of civilized man: quiet, compassionate, enduring humiliation and despising sham, gentle, pitying the suffering of others, defying his family and all public opinion in Queenborough in seeking justice for Parry, and, later, seeking some measure of happiness at "Hunter's Fare" with Kate Oliver. Perhaps Asa is that rarest of civilized men: a truly good man who has some steel in his goodness. True virtue is far more difficult to depict vividly in the pages of fiction than is vice; hence, Ellen Glasgow may not entirely have succeeded in conveying Asa, the civilized good man, into the imaginations of some readers. Nevertheless, he is there in the pages of *In This Our Life* and *Beyond Defeat:* a civilized man in an uncivilized world, if one judges by the horrors of the Second World War as well as the cruelties imposed on Asa Timberlake.

Asa Timberlake is the unspectacular, apparently obscure individual who "possesses an inner strength by which to resist time

[25]*In This Our Life* (New York: Harcourt, Brace, 1941), p. 173.

and circumstance and so survive spiritually, although apparently defeated in the judgment of his world."[26] The depth and quality of a civilization depend upon the prevalence of such people and not upon the amoral materialism of such men as old William Fitzroy. There are tragic elements in the novel, especially in the lives of Asa, Roy, and Parry. But Parry is not a central figure, and Asa and Roy refuse to submit to circumstance. Miss Glasgow knew what she was doing with Asa and Roy, and her meaning should be clear to readers of *In This Our Life.* Perhaps she demanded a closer attention and perceptiveness from readers and critics than her novel received. Certainly she was pleased that in a review which she otherwise scorned, the anonymous reviewer *had* perceived that "tragedy is never in defeat but in surrender."[27]

I have suggested that a special quality of goodness may be a characteristic of the civilized. Roy Timberlake sought the goodness she may have unconsciously perceived in her father. As Miss Glasgow wrote to Van Wyck Brooks: "The whole theme was condensed into Roy's cry in the last paragraph. 'I want something to hold by! I want something good!' All through her confusion and blind groping she was moving toward that search for 'something good,' and all through the book I was writing with that cry in my mind."[28]

In a letter to Mrs. Bessie Zaban Jones, Miss Glasgow insisted that Stanley was a minor figure, that she had not seen the movie because the producers, as she realized from the advertisements, had "entirely missed the point of [her] novel."[29] And in another letter to Mrs. Jones, Miss Glasgow said: "In Asa, I was depicting, not a failure in life, but a man in whom character, not success, was an end in itself."[30] Though she does not use the word *civilized,* I submit that her words justify seeing Asa as such a man.

Writing to Van Wyck Brooks in March 1943, Ellen Glasgow underlined the significance the life of the intellect had for her, thus reminding one of the importance of the word *intellect* in her phrase "the heart in the intellect," by which she had characterized the essence of being civilized. She wrote to Mr. Brooks:

---

[26]Rouse, Introduction to *Letters,* p. 17.   [27]*Letters,* p. 282.

[28]*Letters,* p. 283.   [29]*Letters,* p. 302.   [30]*Letters,* p. 304.

Nothing in the war has appalled me more than the victory of the inventive mind over the intellect, which is, really, the victory of what we call "exact science" over philosophy. It may appear a small thing in a physical conflict, but a world in which all intellectual standards have fallen has turned into a nightmare. In order to conquer the German cruelty must we first become like Germans? Or do we feast upon horrors because cruelty is an ineradicable instinct in all humanity?[31]

This passage, read with the knowledge of subsequent events in the past thirty years and of America's deplorable performance in the affairs of the world in these three decades, becomes all the more poignant and bitter—and perceptive.

Later in 1943, in referring to a biography of James Henry Breasted, the great Egyptologist, in another letter to Mr. Brooks, Ellen Glasgow wrote sentences which, to me, suggest another facet of her ideas both of greatness and the civilized. Thus she wrote: "Superb as his work on Egypt was, and is, the man's fortitude, his greatness of character and his intellectual integrity, should stand as a monument to the old American dream. If what we call, or miscall, democracy can produce that quality of human being, then, surely, it is worth every sacrifice we have made."[32]

Further concern with what it meant to be civilized is revealed in a letter to Frank Morley which Miss Glasgow wrote late in 1943 concerning *Beyond Defeat:* "Asa and Kate, on the farm, rooted, not in a decaying tradition, but in nature and in simple goodness of life, represent the part of tradition that lives on, by adjustment, that does not repudiate the unknown and the untried."[33] In *A Certain Measure,* published in this same year, Miss Glasgow wrote: "My major theme is the conflict of human beings with human nature, of civilization with biology."[34] In another passage in this book, she wrote: "I have learned, from both the past and the present, that nations decay from within more often than they surrender to outward assault. . . . We have refused to acknowledge that the disintegration of character is the beginning, not the end, of defeat, or that this weakening moral fibre is first revealed in the

---

[31]*Letters,* p. 314.   [32]*Letters,* p. 328.   [33]*Letters,* p. 340.
[34]P. 250.

quick or slow decline of human relationships, and in the abrupt conversion to a triumphant materialism." [35]

Another passage in Ellen Glasgow's essay on *In This Our Life* is relevant: "Asa Timberlake mirrors the tragedy of a social system which lives, grows, and prospers by material standards alone." [36] And she quotes Henry David Thoreau's observation: " 'The mass of men lead lives of quiet desperation.' " "For this quiet desperation," she continued, "is the instinctive fortitude of the average man in his struggle with the forces of life, as well as with the brutal power of modern industrialism." [37] As may have been observed, Ellen Glasgow's attitude toward "fortitude" is somewhat ambiguous. Nevertheless, it is interesting to speculate as to what she might have to say about "triumphant materialism" and loss of honor in our times.

No saint, Asa Timberlake not only dislikes but despises Lavinia; he is the most thoroughly human and outwardly unheroic hero of all Ellen Glasgow's civilized men. A quiet, unobtrusive hero, Asa blends into the backgrounds of many scenes when the more noisy, shallow, or vicious individuals are making themselves seen and heard. Miss Glasgow reveals him to the observant reader; she may have failed to make him clear, for all his values, to the less perceptive.

He has endured the attrition of a mean existence without losing his humanity or his sense of humor; he has learned to observe the antics of his world with ironic amusement; and, in a sense, he has won a certain freedom of the spirit through irony rather than despair. He is still bound by his sense of responsibility, his heritage from his well-born mother and father. Hence he stays with Lavinia as long as she needs him. On the other hand, he is not blinded by any false notions of propriety. When he knows that his wife is independent and can have a nurse instead of him, he has no hesitation about going to "Hunter's Fare" for a few years of decency and happiness.

Asa's intended escape to "Hunter's Fare" should not be misunderstood, therefore, as an agrarian retreat from industrialism, for he does not condemn life; rather, he wishes to escape from a bad life and to have the kind of work he has always desired. More

[35]P. 252.   [36]Ibid., p. 253.   [37]Ibid.

than that, living on the farm with Kate Oliver will mean the companionship—even love of a sort—which he has missed through most of his existence. Asa's departure from the city is a very personal act and not a symbol of agrarianism.

Ellen Glasgow, writing just before the Second World War and during the first years of that conflict, evoked the atmosphere of those times. She suggested that for most human beings in the fourth decade of the twentieth century, human nature was too powerful to make possible the existence of the civilized person who is "genuine," who refuses shams, and who seeks a good life which is his own and not the ready-made set of reactions and inhibitions turned out by a money-dominated society in the name of a "way of life."

Asa Timberlake can be understood as belonging to a small minority of really civilized persons living in America in those times. It may not be an exaggeration to suggest that he and his fellows, women as well as men, would still be in a small minority in our world of the 1970s, so largely devoted to technological barbarism and computerized murder.

In her essay published in *I Believe,* edited by Clifton Fadiman and published in 1939, Ellen Glasgow recorded some views which have a bearing on her concept of the civilized. She asserted that she had long been a believing animal but that she could not believe in a God who "was omnipotent, but permitted pain to exist, and the Prince of Darkness to roam the earth in search of whom he might devour." Regarding the freedom of the will, she wrote: "I suppose I may call myself more or less of a pragmatist. Indefensible in theory, no doubt, that exalted error—if it be an error—appears necessary to the order of civilized man, and seems to justify, on higher grounds, its long record of service as a moral utility."[38]

She considered cruelty and intolerance arch-antagonists, but as she grew older, matters of religious creeds ceased to trouble her.[39] She had rejected her father's Calvinist God of Wrath but adored her mother's goodness of soul and her "vague religious instinct leaned toward a distant trust in some spirit, or divine essence,

[38](New York: Simon & Schuster), pp. 93-94.

[39]Ibid., p. 95.

which many poets and a few philosophers have called the Good."
While she rejected the Puritan idea of a special Providence "concerned with the intimate hopes and the special fate of mankind
alone," she did assume the existence of some consciousness superior
to that of mankind.[40]

Miss Glasgow believed "that a conscience may have evolved, by
and through biological necessity, in some men and women, but not
yet in mankind." And she thought there existed a minority that
rejected war but that "this dissenting minority can expect only the
painful fate of all civilized minorities wherever we find them. For
it is true that the most tragic figure in our modern society is not
the semi-barbarian; it is not even the sophisticated barbarian; it is
the truly civilized man who has been thrust back upon the level
of Neanderthal impulses."[41]

Though she believed in evolution, Ellen Glasgow did not assume
that evolution necessarily meant progress. Yet she did believe in
the existence of a few "ideas of sublime virtue, which are called
truth, justice, courage, loyalty, compassion . . . in a moral order . . .
not imposed by a supernatural decree, but throughout the ages . . .
slowly evolving from the mind of man."[42] Moreover, she thought
"that the approach to a fairer order lies, not without, but within;
and that the only way to make a civilized world is to begin and
end with the civilizing of man."[43]

She recognized the possibilities of a decline in what we have
called Western civilization, but she thought it "possible that,
whenever the threatened decline and fall of our culture overtakes
us in fact, those who are alive at the time will not know of the
catastrophe, and would not care if they did. It is more plausible,"
she wrote, "to assume that they will have something better to put
in its place, and that, following our example, they will continue
to miscall this something 'civilization.'"[44]

Ellen Glasgow asserted her belief in what she called "the now
discredited faculty of good taste, which means discrimination in
all things." And she thought that though there are many evils, "the
only sin is inhumanity." She also wrote: "I believe, too, that
benign laughter is the best tonic for life. If life is sad, it is also a

[40]Ibid., p. 96   [41]Ibid., pp. 105-7.   [42]Ibid., p. 107.   [43]Ibid., pp. 107-8.
[44]Ibid., p. 108.

laughing matter, and it has its moments of rapture."[45] Does the latter portion of this statement assure us of Ellen Glasgow's sense of humor: I am not so assured. I am certain that she was perhaps too well aware of the ironic elements in most human lives and that she had a sharp satiric rapier which she often wielded skillfully. But neither satire, irony, nor a talent for social comedy guarantee the presence of a sense of humor. The latter must include the ability to laugh at oneself, one's foibles, and even one's disasters. Ellen Glasgow had, to a high degree, a sense of the comic and the genius to embody *ironic* laughter in her comedy of manners. But I doubt that she actually had a sense of humor. However, I do believe that most of her civilized men possessed this sense of humor.

Finally, in her essay in *I Believe,* Ellen Glasgow asserted: "The true value of life can be measured only, as it borrows meaning, from the things that are valued above and beyond life."[46]

In June 1928, Clive Bell, a somewhat younger British contemporary of Ellen Glasgow and the brother-in-law of Virginia Woolf, published his *Civilization.* In it he attempts to come to grips with what it means to be civilized. I do not know if Miss Glasgow read this book; I have found no reference to it in her writings. But it may be interesting to compare this Bloomsbury aesthetician's ideas of the civilized with those of Ellen Glasgow.

Bell emphasizes as essential to the state of being civilized a "Sense of Values," which must develop from "examination and comparison of states of mind," and the "Enthronement of Reason," which grows out of the Critical Spirit.[47] This, in rather different philosophical terms, is not far from Ellen Glasgow's key phrase "the heart in the intellect." Bell developed these ideas further in words that may be pertinent to our comprehension of Miss Glasgow's civilized men.

A sense of values . . . is possessed only by those who are capable of sacrificing obvious and immediate goods to the more subtle and remote. People who deliberately sacrificed comfort to beauty— with no practical or superstitious end in view—would appear to me to possess a sense of values. To prefer a liberal to a technical

---

[45]Ibid., p. 109.   [46]Ibid., p. 110.

[47]Clive Bell, *Civilization* (West Drayton, Eng.: Penguin, 1947), p. 41. Hereinafter cited as Bell.

education, an education that teaches how to live rather than one that teaches how to gain, is another manifestation of this highly civilized sense. Reason is . . . enthroned when there is a prevalent opinion that everything requires, and must ultimately admit of, a rational explanation and justification.[48]

I am not at all sure that I agree with Clive Bell's rather stern delimitation of the meaning of *civilized* in his *Civilization*. And I should point out that Bell explains that not all members of what may be called a civilization will, necessarily, possess these essential characteristics: a Sense of Values and the Enthronement of Reason. Yet they must be sufficiently prevalent to set the tone of the culture. I believe that Ellen Glasgow could have agreed with this view. I doubt very much that the age in which we live can be said to be a true civilization when measured by these standards. We may be moving toward a state of civilization, carried forward ever so little by the presence of such people as Ellen Glasgow's civilized men, or by a Schweitzer, an Einstein, a Picasso, a Casals, a Bertrand Russell, a George Santayana, a Lewis Mumford, a Faulkner, or a Eudora Welty.

Clive Bell also wrote:

The savage who begins to criticize intellectually the customs and conventions of his tribe soon ceases to exist or ceases to be a savage: he has taken a long step towards civilization. So has he who begins, ever so dimly, to perceive that the true value of things is their value as means to states of mind. But so long as man remains natural and follows instinct he will not go far towards civilization. Civilization comes of reflection and education. Civilization is artificial.[49]

This pronouncement may shock, but reflection may lead to agreement with the truth it contains. I believe Ellen Glasgow would have agreed with this view. I do not recall that she ever expressed it in so bald a statement, but her civilized men have developed out of reflection and, usually, self-education. Often they are revealed in sharp contrasts to her savages who live by their natural and usually uncontrolled instincts. Witness General Archbald's grandfather in *The Sheltered Life*, a superstitious savage still existing in the bloody, hunting stage of culture, notwithstanding his

[48]Ibid., p. 42.   [49]Ibid., p. 44.

status as a "gentleman" in the society of his time and place. Or witness old William Fitzroy of *In This Our Life,* who exists largely in his greed for money, the gratification of his still lively sexual urges, and his delight in exercising his power in both. His interest in his niece, Stanley Timberlake, is far from avuncular, and she, who is entirely savage, wholly uncivilized, is instinctively aware of her uncle's urges and makes the most of them for her own advantage. Both are savages who think they are part of civilization. And so they are—the savage element that probably remains in the most completely civilized culture and is all the more dangerously cruel and hostile to truly civilized persons because it has been more or less released from the taboos with which, in some degree, the savage man surrounds and protects himself and his fellows.

A somewhat more explicit comparison of Ellen Glasgow's and Clive Bell's ideas of the natural and the civilized is suggested in Miss Glasgow's concern with the problems of the "conflict of human beings with human nature."[50] Clearly, she often saw her characters as human beings struggling against their "natural" animal instincts, which were, of course, still elements in their human nature. Her *civilized* human beings were no less human for being civilized, but one may risk the assumption that they had acquired a sense of values and enthroned reason: accomplishments unachieved and probably undreamed of by Janet Rowan and her father in *Vein of Iron* or by old Fletcher in *The Deliverance,* and most assuredly not by Cyrus Treadwell in *Virginia,* or by Uncle William or Stanley in *In This Our Life.* All these people are uncivilized savages who utterly lack the discrimination empowered by a sense of values and who live by their instincts rather than by reason.

It may be observed that among Ellen Glasgow's civilized people, only Marmaduke Littlepage is a creative artist, though John Fincastle's philosophy is surely creative. In this connection another of Clive Bell's observations is of interest: "The essential characteristic of a highly civilized society is not that it is creative, but that it is appreciative; savages create furiously."[51] I am not sure that I agree with Mr. Bell on this point, but I do believe that a case can be made for Ellen Glasgow's civilized people as appreciative. This

[50]*Letters,* p. 302.   [51]Bell, p. 49.

quality is emphasized in the portrayal of Tucker Corbin in *The Deliverance;* it is implicit in all her other civilized men.

I suspect that Western culture sadly lacks those two essentials specified by Clive Bell and embodied in Ellen Glasgow's civilized men: a Sense of Values, evinced in appreciation of what is truly valuable in the life of the mind and the spirit, and the Enthronement of Reason. Readers of Ellen Glasgow recall her doubts that her civilized men lived in a civilization. The events of recent decades offer little evidence that we have acquired the Sense of Values and have enthroned Reason in what we sometimes quaintly call "our way of life" and which we blithely assume constitutes civilization. Here and there are the good companions—Ellen Glasgow's civilized men. Otherwise, for the most part, we live without discrimination or reason—worshiping gadgets for comfort, assuming that technology is science, insensitive to beauty in Nature or Art, polluting our environment, and all too often blinded by an "evasive idealism" comparable to that of Virginia Pendleton's parents, in *Virginia,* who believed in taking a "True View" of things—their "True View" actually meaning closing their eyes and minds to what they did not wish to admit to sight or thought.

Many pages in Ellen Glasgow's novels and another passage in Bell's *Civilization* are relevant to what I have just denounced. Bell wrote: "Good manners are an amenity the value of which people with a sense of values will not under-estimate. But good manners come also of that reasonableness which is the other prime characteristic of civilization, since from reasonableness come open-mindedness, a willingness to listen to what others have to say, and a distaste for dictatorial methods."[52] In this passage Bell might be characterizing all of Ellen Glasgow's civilized men. One may add that true good manners—not pinchbeck imitations—are outward evidences of inward harmony of mind and spirit, of true tolerance of others and respect for their rights. As a sense of values implies taste, then taste implies discrimination in one's actions toward others as well as genuine self-respect. And the self-respect of a civilized person cannot exist where good manners and tolerance are absent.

[52] Ibid., p. 54.

In her life and in her art Ellen Glasgow evinced agreement with this statement in Clive Bell's book: "He who possesses a sense of values cannot be a Philistine; he will value art and thought and knowledge for their own sakes, not for their possible utility . . . [but] as direct means to good states of mind which alone are good as ends."[53] These words would be pertinent to understanding most of Miss Glasgow's civilized men and some of her women characters as well. It is relevant also to the novelist herself.

Another passage in Bell's essay seems even closer to Miss Glasgow's position: "A civilized man sympathizes with other civilized men no matter where they were born or to what race they belong and feels uneasy with brutes and Philistines though they be his blood relations living in the same parish."[54] Miss Glasgow seems to have had this experience throughout her life. She expresses it best, perhaps, in her portrayals of General Archbald and Asa Timberlake. Surely Asa lived an alienated existence from his family, all of whom, with the exception of Roy, were the rankest of Philistines; he found some measure of peace and sympathy with Kate Oliver, who, it seems likely, was a civilized woman.

Bell insisted:

One of the qualities that most clearly distinguish a civilized man from a savage is a sense of humour; and the sense of humour is in the last analysis nothing but a highly developed sense of values . . . of perceiving the ludicrousness of taking things too seriously and giving them an undue importance; and this power is enjoyed only by those who can tell ends from means. To attach to a means the importance due to an end is ridiculous; and because all human achievement falls something short of the ideal, to a thoroughly civilized person all human endeavour will appear at moments slightly comic. Nevertheless, the passionate pursuit of love, beauty, and truth will be laughed at loudly and for long only by fools who cannot understand the passion or appreciate its object.[55]

One may doubt that Ellen Glasgow or her civilized men would measure up to this quality of the sense of humor, as Clive Bell saw it. However, I suspect that Mr. Bell confused the comic and the humorous; they are not the same qualities, as I have indicated earlier.

---

[53]Ibid., p. 61.   [54]Ibid., p. 69.   [55]Ibid., p. 73.

Both Ellen Glasgow and Clive Bell believed that the civilized man possesses *tolerance;* Ellen Glasgow revealed this in her civilized men in every portrayal; Bell saw tolerance as the evidence of his "Enthronement of Reason." He wrote: "One sure basis of toleration is a clear intellectual perception that reason alone has the right to constrain liberty. Only reason can convince us of those three fundamental truths without a recognition of which there can be no effective liberty: that what we believe is not necessarily true; that what we like is not necessarily good; and that all questions are open."[56] Whether our tolerance or that of Ellen Glasgow would go this far, I am not too certain; yet I suspect that all her civilized characters might have subscribed to Bell's defining of tolerance most of their time and did exhibit such tolerance in their lives.

Bell saw many secondary—yet surely equally significant—qualities deriving from a Sense of Values and from Reason. Ellen Glasgow's civilized men share most of them: "a taste for truth and beauty, tolerance, intellectual honesty, fastidiousness, a sense of humour, good manners, curiosity, a dislike of vulgarity, brutality and over-emphasis, freedom from superstition and prudery, a fearless acceptance of the good things of life, a desire for complete self-expression and for a liberal education, a contempt for utilitarianism and philistinism, in two words—sweetness and light."[57] And Bell believed that "the individual mind is the fount and origin of civility."[58]

Miss Glasgow, I believe, would also have agreed with Bell's emphasis on the significance of the independence of mind of the individual person, the necessity of the preservation of individualism for the civilized. All her civilized men maintain their individuality of mind and spirit in the face of all the forces of barbarism and Philistinism in the nineteenth and twentieth centuries.

Were any of Ellen Glasgow's women civilized? In her earlier fiction they were "humors" characters, victims, or conventional "heroines" in the love story element of her books. Occasionally some women appear who might have been developed as "civilized" but were actually not so portrayed. Only Roy Timberlake of *In This Our*

---

[56]Ibid., pp. 78–79.   [57]Ibid., p. 104.   [58]Ibid., p. 105.

Life may be an approach by Ellen Glasgow to the portrayal of a civilized woman.

Susan Treadwell of *Virginia* and Corinna Page of *One Man in His Time* certainly have some of the qualities of the civilized person; but Susan is not sufficiently developed for the reader to be able to make a valid judgment, and Corinna Page has the misfortune to figure in an unsuccessful novel—unsuccessful as art—so that again the reader does not possess effective evidence. Edmonia Bredalbane of *The Romantic Comedians* is a delightful sophisticated woman in one of Miss Glasgow's masterpieces of social comedy, but her role seems to preclude the provision of evidence as to whether she was indeed civilized. Mrs. Littlepage of *They Stooped to Folly* may have been civilized, but Ellen Glasgow withheld the full evidence. Indeed, Victoria Littlepage is a tantalizing character in that one comes away from reading *They Stooped to Folly* wishing one could have known her better. Eva Birdsong of *The Sheltered Life* is the victim of the "Cult of the Southern Beauty." Ada Fincastle of *Vein of Iron* is an admirable brave woman, but apparently Ellen Glasgow saw her father, John, as the civilized member of that family.

What of Dorinda Oakley in *Barren Ground*? Surprisingly, perhaps, the evidence for seeing her as civilized is even less favorable than it is for some of the others I have named. The central quality in Dorinda is her fortitude in the face of disaster and discouragement; her fortitude, presumably, carries her through to material success on the farms and to a more or less satisfactory mode of life in her fifties. But fortitude in itself was not considered by Ellen Glasgow as a characteristic of her civilized person, nor did she always hold fortitude in such high regard as she appears to consider it in *Barren Ground*. In *A Certain Measure,* she wrote of Virginia Pendleton Treadwell's constancy: "Nothing but constancy was left to her, and constancy, when it has outlived its usefulness, is as barren as fortitude." [59] The title of the novel in which Dorinda appears is *Barren Ground;* there may be an interesting relation in the emphasis on Dorinda's "fortitude" and the "barren" of the title. Ellen Glasgow shows that a worthwhile life could be lived by Dorinda, with fortitude, but without joy, without delight.

[59] P. 92.

Dorinda's marriage to Nathan Pedlar is something less than kind, generous, or—civilized. One may question whether Dorinda's harsh exclusion of love or any evident happiness from her life has left her civilized.

Was Ellen Glasgow a "civilized" person? Many of her friends and readers would say that she was. Yet if one considers the explicit and implicit criteria explored here, one may entertain some doubts. Did she measure up to her own criteria as embodied in her fictional characters and as set forth in her nonfictional statements?

A letter that I received from Mrs. Marion Gause Canby, dated August 23, 1955, offers significant insights from a woman who had cherished the friendship of Ellen Glasgow. In this letter the wife of Dr. Henry Seidel Canby wrote of a visit with Miss Glasgow in Richmond near the end of the novelist's life and then of her reaction to reading *The Woman Within* when it was published in 1954. She had enjoyed her visit, but of *The Woman Within* she wrote:

Yet in reading *The Woman Within* (of which she spoke often that morning) I was amazed to see that the "vein of iron" which always sustains her books, had not been *her* personal support in times of sorrow. It seemed she had no *philosophic* acceptance of human tragedy to help her through, with its awareness of "scale," (Man against the stars, etc.). Each sorrow broke her heart all over again as though no one had ever died or met catastrophe before. Her lifelong research on the "vein of iron," or in clearer words, the tragedy of life on earth, didn't seem to apply to her. She was like a little girl in her grief over mother or sister, and I believe all this was the psychological explanation, anyhow, of her ill health. But perhaps this lack of what might be called a *good hardening* was after all one of the things that kept her so warm and free of personality, giving herself, always. And she never had to go against the grain. She was very actually emotionally and intellectually hungry, but her daily life was filled with devoted care and, being indulged, she indulged herself in sorrow—perhaps! I don't know— but somehow *The Woman Within* seemed to *me* in many ways a different person from the Ellen Glasgow I knew.[60]

I suggest that Miss Glasgow, in public, offered a mask of charm, but that in her autobiography the mask is absent, and she reveals

[60] *Letters,* p. 372.

her true self. Or it may with equal justice be argued that in her autobiography Miss Glasgow was forced to present, to a possible public, herself wearing yet another mask. I believe that in *The Woman Within* she presented herself and her life in forms she really believed to be true and that, in so doing, she revealed that vein, not of iron, but of sentimentality that was present throughout her life, even though consciously, as an artist, she avowed her hostility toward the sentimental.

The sentimental is also too often apparent in the endings of some of her novels. It is as though somehow she felt compelled to comfort herself and her readers with reassurances that the light of hope and a happiness of some sort might still lie beyond the pathos and void in a life she had clearly portrayed. So—in *Virginia* such hope is rather unconvincingly suggested in the news that Virginia's son is returning to her; in *The Miller of Old Church* an implausibly happy ending in marriage is contrived, even though two characters have to be conveniently done in; even in *Barren Ground* there is an inconclusive but suggested glow of something better beyond in Dorinda's life, even though the spirit and tone of that excellent novel run utterly counter to this ending, and Dorinda herself surely had cast out any shred of sentimentality or even sentiment from herself. In *The Romantic Comedians* and *They Stooped to Folly* the ring of comic laughter saves the author and the books from the sentimental. The ending of *In This Our Life* is inconclusive, and its sequel, *Beyond Defeat,* is possibly too symbolic on the one hand and too intent on reassuring the author and the reader on the other for it to be a successful ending for the account of the lives of Asa and Roy Timberlake. In *The Sheltered Life,* however, Ellen Glasgow did not shrink from the disaster toward which her novel moved. In the ending of this book there is no glowing sunset of hope, no promise of happiness tacked on to the dramatic portrayal of the danger and destructiveness of ignorance in Jenny Blair, weakness in George Birdsong, and the tragic fate of a life of pretense in Eva, forced on her by her role as a great beauty. In this great novel, probably Ellen Glasgow's finest work, the author admits no sentimental gesture and inexorably carries out her narrative and depicts its actions starkly, clearly, to the gunshot and George lying dead at Eva's feet. And to soft-minded readers who wanted to believe that George had shot himself, Miss

Glasgow refused that consolation and said plainly that Eva had killed him.

Ellen Glasgow did have a sentimental vein. This element and her self-pity are difficult to justify as civilized qualities in a person who otherwise might surely qualify as a civilized woman. Perhaps these elements in her own character worked against her development of a completely clear sense of the tragic. There are tragic elements and possibilities in *Barren Ground,* but whether the novel is indeed a tragic work is debatable. *The Sheltered Life* is, I believe, a tragedy of manners.

I have indicated most of the criteria by which Ellen Glasgow judged the quality of the civilized person. However, I also believe that in her portrayals of those she considered civilized, Ellen Glasgow revealed other qualities that belong in a summary of such criteria. These would be honesty with oneself and others, and, closely related, a keen sense of personal honor; a humane relation toward all living beings, which might be described as compassion; freedom from self-pity; sympathy; hatred of cruelty; a sense of justice; genuineness, or freedom from sham, including freedom from self-deception; freedom of spirit; love of beauty and the necessary sensitivity and perceptiveness to appreciate beauty wherever and however it may be found; kindness and generosity; genuine, honest feeling—emotion or sentiment—but never sentimentality; avoidance of "evasive idealism," yet possession of positive ideals given meaning in one's relations to others and to all life; concern for the dignity of others as well as awareness of one's own dignity, but without false notions of one's own self-importance; a keen sense of identity—knowing oneself, yet absence of any morbid sensitiveness; pride, but not false pride, nor the excessive pride the Greeks knew as *hybris;* a sense of inner, spiritual Reality; goodness; no fear of Truth when clearly recognized as Truth, but ever on guard against the False masquerading as Truth; and, finally, refusal to surrender to Evil and the False.

Ellen Glasgow as Feminist

Monique Parent Frazee

A LONE star among Southern gentlewomen to write progressive novels of manners, Ellen Glasgow has been commonly regarded as one in a long line of feminists. The recurrence of the term in her lifetime is sufficient proof that the label was not disagreeable to her. *Feminism,* she defined in 1914, as "a revolt from pretense of being . . . a struggle for the liberation of personality."[1] In 1950, without fundamental change, feminism was described by Josephine Jessup,[2] with particular reference to Ellen Glasgow, Edith Wharton, and Willa Cather, as the expression of woman's desire to be herself, that is, to measure attainment irrespective of sexual function; it concerned life under all its aspects; it went deeper than the mere demand for economic opportunity or political enfranchisement. Conveniently vague, this definition needs a reassessment in the light of the last thirty years' progress. Things and ideas have altered greatly since the Second World War, that is, since the death of Miss Glasgow. A diversity of movements have mobilized thousands of determined women with a variety of views, objectives, and emphases, as well as new means of action. They all converge, however, on one final goal: the liberation of woman, considered not as a concept but in terms of action and efficiency. Liberation means freedom, an issue, but also the methods and processes of achieving it: how to set women free from male bondage, a premise which seems unanimously accepted; how, for each woman, to free herself, body and soul. For the radical militant, it aims at little short of a total revolution of society, a reshaping of the world according to a new definition of sex and the cancellation of sex roles. To those reluctant to enter loudly and publicly the campaign for equal rights—be they physical, legal, or moral—fiction offered at least a

---

[1] "Feminism, a Definition," *Good Housekeeping,* 58 (May 1914), 683.

[2] *The Faith of Our Feminists* (New York: Richard K. Smith, 1950).

tamer battlefield. "There," as Christine Stansell aptly said, "an equally serious, and ultimately, perhaps, more significant battle for the emancipation of women was being fought."[3] Feminist novels were prompted by a deep sense of frustration in the face of the undisputed hegemony of the male on all fronts. Ellen Glasgow, rebellious in spirit but nonetheless conventional in conduct, bears more resemblance to Elizabeth Stuart Phelps, her American fore-runner, in her rejection of Calvinism and her father's authority, than to the two famous foreign "Georges": the highly daring George Eliot and George Sand, who both found in themselves sufficient energy and will to abandon home, family, religion, maiden names, to live for years with men not their husbands, and calmly—at least in appearance—to defy the world's hostility. In comparison, Ellen Glasgow, submissive to social dictum, appears to her biographers as a victim—less, however, of the Southern code of female behavior, less even of a conception of the overpowering male, than as a victim of herself, her half-lost illusions, her un-settled emotions, obscure desires, unconfessed dreams. The "woman within," weltering in self-pity, blatantly reveals that she never was truly "liberated." In private behavior, she knew no compromise; economic independence never opened the door to moral laxity. In contrast to this stern Calvinistic conduct belying her theories, her heroines give vent to more daring fantasy, and their adventures may give us ampler material for a fruitful confrontation with the tenets of women's liberation today.

I

At the level of concepts, the great issue of feminism seems to be the debate between Biology and Culture. All women agree with the evidence of fact: woman's role in almost all societies through-out the ages has been traditionally minor and subservient to man, from the lowest ranks of lip service to the most honored status of courtly love; the woman, as slave or idol, was assigned certain activities and barred from others, particularly those implying

[3]L. R. Edwards, M. Heath, and L. Baskin, eds., *Woman: An Issue* (Boston: Little, Brown & Co., 1972), p. 239.

power, authority, and final decision in the management of the world. Is the historical function of woman justified by her nature, or, as Ruth Gay phrases it: "What is biologically innate and what is learned in sexual differences?"[4] The question divides the calm observers and cheerful compliers on one hand from the discontented women on the other who make up Women's Lib. The former ascribe to biology the difference of sex roles: women are weaker, smaller, more emotional, sensitive, perceptive, and so on, because they are built so; sex roles are therefore determined by anatomy (shape and size of body), physiology (menstruation and child-bearing), and there is no arguing with nature about it. The active feminists refuse this theory; supported by anthropologists (though not all) and sociologists, they ascribe to culture, as being man-made, the responsibility for persuading women that they are inferior. The sex roles as they are defined today are the result of a conscious male conspiracy. Men and women are similar in physical and intellectual potentialities and therefore should enjoy equal rights. What echoes of this debate do we find adumbrated in Ellen Glasgow's mind and vision?

She endorsed Mary Wollstonecraft's argument that women's inferiority in intellect and achievement was only the result of men's tyranny, which allowed women no opportunity to develop themselves. "Let woman share the rights and she will emulate the virtues of men," said Mary Wollstonecraft in *The Vindication of the Rights of Women* (1792). Ellen Glasgow also applauded John Stuart Mill, of whom she declared herself to have been at eighteen "an eager student," "an ardent disciple."[5] We read in *On the Subjection of Women* (1869): "The legal subjection of one sex to another is wrong in itself, and now one of the chief hindrances to human improvement; it ought to be replaced by a principle of perfect equality." She read radical philosophers and sociologists. Her devotion to Darwin is too well known to need recall. Freud, she instinctively loathed but was prudent enough to dismiss quietly, since he was a leading light of her time and a direct influence on "the modern novel," which she hated. Anthropology, ecology,

---

[4] Ruth Gay, "The Literature of Feminism," *Dialogue,* 3 (1970), 45.

[5] *A Certain Measure* (New York: Harcourt, Brace, 1943), p. 57; *The Woman Within* (New York: Harcourt, Brace, 1954), p. 186.

sociology were hardly heard of at all in her circles, and she could not draw support from those then-young sciences. The true theoreticians of Women's Liberation had not appeared yet. The first master works were published after her death, pioneered by Mary Beard's *Woman as Force in History* (1946), Margaret Mead's *Male and Female* (1949), and Simone de Beauvoir's *The Second Sex* (1949). The enormous bevy of authors that would follow—Aileen Kraditor, Betty Friedan, Germaine Greer, Caroline Bird, Vivian Gornick, Barbara K. Moran, Kate Millett, and others—all came too late for Miss Glasgow. Nevertheless, the headlines and fundamental discussions in their books will give direction to our analysis.

Indeed, basic to all the feminist claims today is, in Gloria Levitas's words, the need for "a psychological conversion that is designed to free females from their belief that their function in life is to provide sexual satisfaction for males, or children for society. . . . women must be able to develop personalities and life styles in addition to—as well as in place of—motherhood."[6] To this Ellen Glasgow would have thoroughly subscribed, as we shall see, partly from the evidence of her life and personal conduct, partly through the illustrations provided by her heroines, whose experience vicariously mirrors her subconscious yearnings.

At first sight, Ellen Glasgow's intuitive vision of men and women is traditionally sexist. Those who surrounded her childhood, youth, and formative years generated this view, which no later experience was to eradicate. Her mother, sisters, and feminine friends whom she loved dearly she never looked upon as similar to men, but rather as of a different species, like herself: weaker physically, gentler, more sensitive, equal if not superior in intellect, definitely stronger in self-control, will power, and endurance, inheritors as they were of Southern female fortitude. The men in her life included her formidable father, rigid Calvinist, authoritarian patrician, the stern justiciar whose godlike image collapsed into a hypocritical caricature of virtue when his conjugal infidelity was revealed to his daughter. Suitors she found unsuitable, for reasons that will be examined later; suffice it to say that of them all, none responded to her ideal image of man. Finally, her two dearest masculine friends, her brother Frank and her brother-in-law Walter McCor-

---

[6]"The Anthropology of Women," *Dialogue,* 3 (1970), p. 36.

mack, both gentle, intelligent, sensitive men, committed suicide, evidencing a lack of fortitude which Ellen Glasgow would associate with the near totality of her heroes. Her conclusion inevitably was that man was neither Jupiter, as she had been taught to believe, nor Prometheus, as she would have liked to idealize him, but a paltry substitute whose pretense to power could only assert itself through tyranny. What did she make of the discovery? Did she offer a clue to the problem and a remedy for it?

II

One tenet of the women's movement is that reform must begin with a revised appraisal of the female body. Woman must rediscover her body as it is, not as an object of man's *bon plaisir;* she must investigate its potentialities instead of its limitations, its power instead of its weakness. In Ellen Glasgow's environment and fiction, this was unthinkable. The body, experienced as an object of shame and distress in terms of physiology, could afford no legitimate pleasure to a woman. At best, it became an instrument to adorn in order to please—restricted, in description, to the face (pretty features), hair (glossy), skin (white), no more. The naturalists would depict suggestive curves, which in her fiction only common people would allude to as a desirable "full figger." To mention physical attraction was vulgar, and she allowed this indulgence only to her alcoholics and profligates. Gentlemen robed their desires in sentimental and chaste terms. The body is then a torch, illumined by the inner light shining through the eyes, making a plain face look beautiful in a moment of intense emotion, namely, love. Laura Wilde in *The Wheel of Life,* Ellen Glasgow's closest alter ego, burning with spiritual fire, squirms under the lecherous looks of admiration from her carnal fiancé. Let us not invoke Victorian convention in this reserve. Between the wars, the novel had liberated the language of sex, but Ellen Glasgow still violently spurned "the lusty tone cultivated by Mr. Hemingway and his imitators,"[7] morons of literature rolling in the slime of their

---

[7]*A Certain Measure,* p. 179.

animality.[8] Let us find elsewhere the cause of this instinctive recoil from sex.

For poor Ellen, the body was ever a source of pain rather than enjoyment. Her frail health was dogged by two major ailments: deafness, a psychological as well as a physical handicap and a growing cause of misery, and headaches brought on by bad nerves. The body, therefore, was best when dormant and forgotten. Pain contributed to dull other sensations and physical impulses; hypersensitivity was at the cost of defective sensuality. In her lavish confessions, there is no indication of sexual yearnings or frustrations. Revealing is the vivid memory of an unfortunate episode at age eighteen with a New York literary adviser, which she strangely chose to relate in detail in *The Woman Within* several decades later; it explains her and her heroines' aversion for physical contact. "His hands were upon me who, even as a child, had hated to be pawed over, especially . . . pawed over by elderly uncles." From thereon, male lips would remain in her imagination "red and juicy," generative of "loathing . . . forever afterwards,"[9] as, without deep love, kisses were "nauseating" to Rachel in *The Descendant*.[10] Ellen Glasgow's heroines would not be tormented by the thorn in the flesh. Those who fall (and there is one in almost every novel) do so by mistake, out of negligence or ignorance, just to please the male partner, never to satisfy a personal urge. The author gives them plenty of sympathy and calls upon ours, as it is understood that these women can only be victims of men. Giving so much grist to the Women's Lib mill, she would most certainly not support their claim to pleasure in lovemaking and to separating sex from sentiment.

This leads us to the next issue: sex roles and behaviors. These can be diversely interpreted according to the type of society exemplified and the humor of the analyst. Morton Hunt, a rare male feminist—but is he really?—describes "woman . . . as a most useful

---

[8]Speech delivered at the dinner of the Friends of the Princeton Library, April 25, 1935, New York. Fragments were published in the *New York Times,* Apr. 26, 1935, and the talk was published as "Heroes and Monsters" in *Saturday Review,* 12 (May 4, 1935), 3-4.

[9]*The Woman Within,* pp. 96-97.

[10](New York: Harper & Bros., 1897), p. 73.

creature, good for carrying water, building the fire, preparing the food, making clothing, concocting herbal infusions and poultices, rearing the children, and, at night, though bone-weary from her labors, still available for the comfort of her mate and the relief of his natural tensions." [11] This obviously applies to the woman of "primitive societies": the squaw, the pioneer's female companion, and, I am told, the pre–Women's Lib American housewife of the twentieth century. Margaret Mead looks at a morally more advanced society when she lists "those roles which have historically belonged to women: to care for the young, nurse the sick, lay out the dead, attend women in childbirth, comfort the sorrowful, quiet unruliness and temper hotheadedness with gentleness and wisdom." [12] All in all, the natural vocation of woman seems to have been a peaceful devotion to her husband, children, and home—the acceptance of which, as we have seen, is part of a sexist view of women's roles.

Sexist by birth and training, Ellen Glasgow gradually learned to reject this biblical tradition. At first, like all other girls, like most women today, young and old, she believed that marriage was the normal status for the well-balanced woman who would lead a fuller life. She tried to conform; she was engaged three years to a gentle, soft-spoken, intellectual, poetlike minister but did not marry him. Much later she tried again, and harder, to adjust to a brilliant, bouncing, highly virile man, but failed likewise. Mr. Paradise and Henry Anderson were two opposite expressions of masculinity to her. The only man she acknowledged to have loved truly, the mysterious "Gerald," was a married man, a gentleman of duty, and therefore out of reach. There was no physical threat from him; he remained an abstraction. Denying man his rights to virility amounted to making him a disembodied demigod. Disappointed in finding men short of that power, Miss Glasgow, who had lived between the fear of not finding a husband and the greater fear of giving in to one, remained thus divided late in her mature life. This dilemma led her to despise the mate who could not subdue and win her.

---

[11]"A Male View of Female Evolution," *Diologue,* 3 (1970), 20.

[12]"Beyond the Household," *Dialogue,* 3 (1970), 3.

This torment would have been spared her had she known the present-day feminist theories. Women are fighting vehemently for the right to celibacy without sacrificing any of their social prestige and success. It seems a hard victory to win. Strange to say the unmarried women, emancipated or not, have not yet attained full social recognition. So true it is, in Miss Glasgow's facetious terms, that "the chasm between marriage and spinsterhood was as wide as the one between children and pickles." [13] She rebelled against the old prejudice against husbandless women. The long list of her spinsters—fallen and forever disgraced like "poor aunt Agatha" in *They Stooped to Folly;* painstakingly surviving in dignity like Miss Priscilla Batte, the schoolteacher in *Virginia;* or composedly radiant like Miss Amanda Lightfoot in *The Romantic Comedians,* who hid her distressed feelings behind an everlasting smile—not to mention the many unwed mothers of later novels—is a rollcall of suffering and frustration. The author protests against the theory dispensed by "generations of ancestors . . . that woman existed only to win love or to bestow it," and that man's "ideal woman was submissive and clinging. . . . meekness had always seemed to him [say man in general] the becoming mental and facial expression for the sex." [14] In the crude language of the unlettered, maternity "is the only thing a woman's fit for." A childless woman is no better than "a cow that wouldn't calve." [15] Again, the author thoroughly disagrees; coarse language associates with coarse naivete. Her refined artist, Rachel, engrossed with her painting, is not interested in "nursing hiccoughy babies." [16]

Neither was Miss Glasgow. Motherhood she never missed, asserted one of her closest friends. She looked upon it only as one experience she had not had. Her candid declaration of "the lack in me of the maternal instinct" (in *The Woman Within*) [17] must not be interpreted as a confession of counternature or a lack of femininity, but as a sincere recognition of a legitimate ambition to be

---

[13] *Virginia* (New York: Doubleday, Page, 1913), p. 148.

[14] *The Miller of Old Church* (New York: Doubleday, Page, 1911), pp. 79, 38.

[15] *The Deliverance* (New York: Doubleday, Page, 1904), p. 37.

[16] *The Descendant*, p. 68.

[17] P. 153.

herself and no more. Contraception, abortion, lesbianism—taboo subjects fifty years ago—are now topics openly discussed and publicly submitted for legalization, in the name of the right of women to choose for herself. Public opinion had (and still has) a long way to go to learn tolerance, to recognize that what is essential to the happiness and self-achievement of some women—marriage and maternity—may not be so for all. Ellen Glasgow was audacious in her time to hold that position, a pioneer in Women's Lib in her claim to the right to remain unattached, even though her arguments would betoken more frigidity than most liberated women would like to acknowledge. She clearly rejected sex and childbirth as "too violent"; she had always "disliked physical violence" and would "have found wholly inadequate the mere physical sensation which the youth of today seek so blithely." [18]

To the third part of traditional roles, housekeeping, Miss Glasgow did not give much thought. All such worries and trouble were left to the servants and, later, to her faithful companion, Miss Anne Virginia Bennett. Even so, the house chores she unilaterally condemned as "drudgery," especially obnoxious to the poor. Martha Burr in *Barren Ground* is one example among so many of the driven housekeeper, worn out by the daily routine of cooking, cleaning, mending, washing. There is no escape, no "other interests," no pleasure; there is just no time for it. Even in the best families, the housewife is trapped by the circular pattern of Kinder-Küche-Kirche(-Krap!), which the feminists denounce as imposture. In delicately Southern terms, James Branch Cabell recognizes this trap in *As I Remember It:* "As for the gentlewoman, what with the housekeeping [Küche], and their church [Kirche] and social duties, and the children [Kinder] too of course, why, but there you were! Books might be all very well in their place, but where was the time to read them in?" [19]

Virginia (1913), perhaps the first of Ellen Glasgow's greatest novels, offers the most unallayed exposure of this disastrous assignment of sex roles. Virginia Pendleton, the young heroine, at twenty "the feminine ideal of the ages," seems to have been born to give

[18]Ibid., p. 163.

[19]James Branch Cabell, *As I Remember It* (New York: Robert M. McBride, 1955), p. 140.

and receive love "in a community which offered few opportunities to women outside of the nursery or the kitchen [Kinder-Küche]. . . . Her education was founded upon the simple theory that the less a girl knew about life, the better prepared she would be to contend with it." Her acquired knowledge all came from "that bookcase which was filled with sugared falsehoods about life." She was doomed to stay ignorant, "and this ignorance of anything that could possibly be useful to her was supposed in some mysterious way to add to her value as a woman and to make her a more desirable companion to a man." This sums up the century-old declaration of dependence for woman, her vocation, her value depending entirely on her quality as a "desirable companion to a man." Virginia is a paragon of desirability. She marries the young man she loves, and loses him slowly, unconsciously, as Kinder and Küche devour all her attention. At thirty, she is already faded, no longer desirable. At forty-six, she is crushed to hear her own daughter deride the way of life of traditional women like herself. " 'They spent the rest of their lives in the storeroom or the kitchen slaving for the comfort of the men they could no longer amuse.' This so aptly described Virginia's own situation that . . . a wave of heartsickness swept over her." By that time her husband, a brilliant playwright, has abandoned her for a famous actress in New York. She finally grants him the divorce that he demands. Virginia, heartbroken, decidedly old and hopeless, comes back home "into the dreadful years, silent, grey, and endless." Vainly has she tried to vindicate her husband's conduct, under the cheap pretense that "men are different. One doesn't expect them to give up like women."[20]

"And why not? Why should women give up?" scream our feminists. Who can say they are wrong? The bitter destiny of Virginia is handled with subtle irony and unmixed determination. Ellen Glasgow had never created and never would re-create such a complete portrait of woman as slave and victim of man's selfishness. In *A Certain Measure* she declares: "Virginia was more than a woman; she was the embodiment of a forsaken ideal."[21] Other

[20] *Virginia*, pp. 5, 22, 145, 22, 430, 522, 430.
[21] P. 82.

heroines, early crushed in similar experiences, will not accept total failure so submissively. They will fight and meet with various degrees of success. To name but one, Gabriella, the forsaken wife of a worthless profligate, uses her "vein of iron" to recoup her balance, works for a living, and raises her two children. She changes her philosophy of life, refuses to be beaten; at thirty-eight she evades marriage with a sentimental eunuch and accepts a virile self-made man whose strong personality has captured her own. Here stops the tract for radical feminism, since the heroine, energetic and successful, has nonetheless to fall back upon the dominating male to recover her lost happiness.

Gabriella, however, takes a major step forward in the process of women's liberation when she becomes economically independent. The Southern code limited the professional openings for needy gentlewomen to two: teaching and nursing. The eleventh novel by Ellen Glasgow presents Gabriella's success as a hatmaker in New York. More fortunate than Lily Bart, the precious aristocratic belle of Edith Wharton's *The House of Mirth*, because she is stronger, more courageous and mature, Gabriella makes her way up in the trade line and finally owns her shop, whereas Lily, unable to sustain the effort, sinks and dies. Other heroines, successful artists (not to be confused with gentle ladies), make money through their talents. Rachel Gavin, painter, Mariana Musin, actress, become rich and famous but remain social outcasts in the Southern perspective. Ada Fincastle, forced by the hardships of the Depression to be a store assistant with a decreasing salary, lives in constant poverty. Eva Birdsong and Cora Archbald, in their "sheltered lives," would never think of a lucrative occupation. Dorinda Oakley, the brilliant exception, proves that a woman with brains can do better farming than ignorant and lazy men. Her study and experimentation transform her "barren ground" into productive pastures. Yet her economic success has such psychological motivation, namely, vengeance, that one can hardly see it as a feminist demonstration. No ambition to make money as such is ever evinced by our heroines: the problem does not seem to have existed for Ellen Glasgow, herself the unusual example of a self-supporting lady in the difficult path of literature. Although poverty was in daily evidence everywhere, it concerned men as well as women: "Society was to blame, . . . society was responsible."[22] She never puts the blame on men, the true leaders of this society.

In business, Miss Glasgow had a cold head and energetic efficiency. Literature is one thing, she used to say, the literary market another, and not a negligible one. She never was detached from the monetary rewards of her labor, and she obtained excellent contracts from her editors. You need a great deal of money to be able to despise it, she would philosophize. "Wealth could not buy happiness, but it could make unhappiness more comfortable."[23]

But on the whole, Ellen Glasgow's protest makes no reference to the poor working woman who toils long hours for a miserable salary, nor to the overworked housewife who comes home to a second phase of her day's drudgery, and not even to the lone woman with or without a family to support. And at the other end of the social scale, there is no concern either for the educated woman, no example of the university-trained woman with a legitimate ambition for recognition. To the last novel, we find no professional or career woman—doctor, lawyer, professor, writer— none with the responsibilities that tradition is wont to attribute to men, none even tempted to emulate men in the higher places; therefore, there is no rivalry. None of these heroines ever realizes even dimly that, in the feminists' terms, "for most of this country's history, women's place has been in the home, in the fields, in the factories, in the sweatshops, or any place except where power is."[24] This awareness is totally absent from Miss Glasgow's work and consciousness, and at this point she ceases to be useful to the cause of Women's Lib.

To mention power opens another dimension to our scrutiny, that of politics. A curious young lady in her twenties, Ellen Glasgow had been smuggled into the opera house in Roanoke to observe the proceedings of a Democratic state convention. She had "as a girl . . . found all this amusing and exciting," and later she used the episode in *The Romance of a Plain Man.* She remarks with juvenile pride that she was "a single feminine observer in an

---

[22]*The Woman Within*, p. 81.

[23]*In This Our Life* (New York: Harcourt, Brace, 1941), p. 152.

[24]*Woman: An Issue*, p. 17.

assemblage of more than a thousand men,"[25] but does not pause
to wonder with our feminists why, forever, "women have been
excluded from the decision-making levels of political parties, and
from all levels of government of American society."[26] No indig-
nation, no protest, no wish to participate, to lead, to wield power.
Her political activity was very limited in time and scope. When in
1909 she was approached by local women, all timid and fearful at
their audacity, she agreed reluctantly to join the Virginia League
for Women Suffrage. In London she marched with May Sinclair in
a suffrage parade. She repeated the experience in New York in
1911, but carefully omitted relating the unfortunate adventure.
Clad in white, her face overly rouged, she marched with her own
friends, including Mary Johnston. The crowd sneered and cried at
them: "Where are your trousers?" (and to her in particular) "Look
at this painted wall!" That was enough. She would never meddle
again with suffrage. She hated street parades and shouting mobs,
and feared the possibility of arrest. Her only suffragist heroine,
old aristocratic Miss Matoaca Bland (in *The Romance of a Plain
Man*) pays with her life for her participation in a suffragette manifestation in Richmond; death alone saves her from utter ridicule.
At bottom, Miss Glasgow lacked conviction. "If women wanted a
vote, I agreed they had a right to vote,"[27] she wrote, but she did
not believe that politics would fare the better for it. The few
articles she published later along this line have more to do with the
intellectual and moral emancipation of women than with specifically feminine political goals, such as divorce, responsiblity for and
guardianship of children, inheritance rights, legal facilities denied
to women, equal salaries, and so forth. Miss Glasgow failed to see
that the rights of women, like any serious public issue, cannot gain
recognition outside the channels of politics, whether or not one is
interested in political commitment. All feminists know today that
there can be no progress without legal ratification of the desired
provisions. Here again the novels are bare of such reference.

After this rather negative analysis of Ellen Glasgow's feminism,

---

[25]*A Certain Measure*, p. 62.

[26]*Woman: An Issue*, p. 17.

[27]*The Woman Within*, p. 187.

after pointing out her failure to take a position on very precise
issues such as sex, family, work and professional success, economic
promotion, and political responsiblity, it is time to assess the pith
and core of her feminism. To do this, we had best return to the
notions previously mentioned, the intellectual, moral, and emotional emancipation of woman, her aspiration to self-assertion and
her right to happiness according to her own free choice.

III

Miss Glasgow's consciousness of being a person entitled to her own
way of thinking began early, with her double rebellion, as we have
seen, against father and religion. Her first open act of emancipation
was her refusal to accompany him to church one Sunday. The next
step was an effort to decide on her own culture. At this point,
"I read what Father . . . feared and hated rather than what I,
myself, enjoyed. Right or wrong, I could not be moved. . . . Over
and over I repeated my variation of the modern creed: not 'my
life is my own!' as youth cries today, but 'my mind is my own!' "[28]
The absence of school training encouraged her drift from conformity. Her native curiosity assisted her in mastering the most arduous
material, philosophy, economy, literature. Other Southern women
had written books: sweet novels for young ladies, or history books
to the glory of the Confederacy. She completed her intellectual
liberation by writing exactly what she wanted to write, without
sparing her people, her times, the South, or the opinions of gentility. *The Descendant,* the most daring of all her novels in this
respect—situations, characters, happenings—marked her declaration
of independence. Intentions are clear: the newspaper edited by the
rebellious hero is called the *Iconoclast.* The hero himself is a social
outcast, a "bastard" whose birth forces him to leave his community, and he ends up in jail for murder. The heroine is an artist,
sure enough; no "nice girl" could accept concubinage with the
hero and retain the reader's sympathy. In this unconventional
couple, the woman is by far the stronger; however, she becomes

---

[28]Ibid., pp. 92-93.

for a while a victim of the male, since their cohabitation causes her talent to wither temporarily. Separation restores her to herself: woman triumphs if she is left alone. The tract is complete; it will not be presented again in this simplistic form.

The fundamental claim, however, blatant in this first novel, will reappear throughout the works to come: woman's desire to be herself, to exploit her potentialities, to lead her own life. If she is more often than not frustrated in this goal, it is because society offers more examples of women impeded by men's wills than the contrary. We have seen Virginia sinking under traditional sex roles, unmarried girls smothered by spinsterhood, widows dependent on the older generation for survival, abandoned women crushed by mundane disapproval. Children throw rocks at Ada, unmarried and pregnant; Dorinda runs away when she discovers her predicament. Yet both will rise up, fight, and win the battle against male domination. The weapon is courage, drawing on the old sources of Southern fortitude. But, in terms of feminism, there is a huge difference between the two heroines.

Dorinda is the archetype of the liberated woman. The daughter of an improvident farmer (the father here is the image of irresponsibility, poor, ignorant, incompetent, stubborn, totally unimaginative, his mind closed to progress), the innocent girl is seduced by her fiancé (the lover is weak, unsettled, alcoholic, cowardly, easily persuaded to marry another girl when threatened by the latter's brothers). After a welcome miscarriage and two years' absence from home (today she would have had an abortion), Dorinda returns to her barren land, makes it productive, achieves economic independence and financial prosperity. The male, rejected and unnecessary, is seen in a totally negative light. Dorinda could be any woman today, successful in any career. Her contempt for men never relents. She ends up contriving the ultimate humiliation of her seducer. In the guise of charity, she rescues his degenerate body from the poorhouse and buys his land, a superfluous addition to her own. Eventually, for economic convenience, she has married a kind, insipid eunuch with a ludicrous face; his death leaves her untouched. Dorinda, once the victim, has become the victor; but her triumph is only complete through her negation of man.

"Dorinda was free to grow, to change, to work out her own destiny," says the author.[29] So far, the feminist theory is satisfied. But then the story moves toward a dubious demonstration. Were Dorinda happy, all would be well; but she is not. To achieve success, she had to learn "to live without joy . . . to live gallantly, without delight."[30] In other words, she had to steel herself against the fundamental urges of woman toward happiness. Like Dreiser's Sister Carrie, who, at the zenith of her career, success, and economic independence, sighs over some wistful sense of loss, Dorinda, mature and rich, confesses that "success, achievement, victory over fate, all these things were nothing beside that imperishable illusion. Love was the only thing that made life desirable, and love was irrevocably lost to her."[31] A passing weakness or a revelation of the truth? She checks herself and concludes: "Though in a measure destiny had defeated her, for it had given her none of the gifts she had asked of it, still her failure was one of those defeats . . . which are victories."[32] Defeat—failure—victory—all one, what a confused philosophy is this? "None of the gifts she had asked": what were those mysterious gifts? Ada in *Vein of Iron* gives us a clue.

Ada's story begins in the same way. She is pregnant and abandoned by her fiancé. However, she keeps her baby, raises him through shame and love, and later marries her seducer. They remain poor—his nervous instability and the Depression assure that. Sickness and poverty are ever present; yet her fortitude endures, and her final cry of feminine triumph is "O Ralph, we have been happy together." "Yes," he answers reluctantly, because it has been all her doing, not his, "we've had a poor life . . . but we've been happy together."[33] Ada has had "the gifts of life" which Dorinda denied herself. She has retained her femininity by keeping her heart alive, at whatever cost. Stronger than her partner, she props his softness with her energy, tempers his bitterness with her affection; she is his moral support, and finds joy in this feminine

---

[29]*A Certain Measure*, p. 155.

[30]Ibid., pp. 154–55.

[31]*Barren Ground* (Garden City, N.Y.: Grosset & Dunlap, 1925), p. 446.

[32]Ibid., p. 447.

[33]*Vein of Iron* (New York: Harcourt, Brace, 1935), p. 462.

role. Here is the catch, the vicious circle of destiny. Love being the
only thing that makes life worthwhile to a woman, and man the
only partner to give and receive love, whenever man is found
wanting, woman is doomed to unhappiness. But is happiness a
right? Virginia thought so, "unquestionably,"[34] feeling, with Milly
Burden, Jenny Blair, Roy, Stanley, and others, that "craving for
happiness" deep in their nature. But in *They Stooped to Folly,* it
is an old man who replies with restrictive pessimism: "Remember,
my child, that happiness is not a right but a blessing."[35]

Let us recapitulate the fate of woman in the hands of Ellen
Glasgow. Virginia cherished her role of slave and perished in
despair. Gabriella rebelled and flourished, but ultimately slipped
back into matrimony. Dorinda fought and conquered, but in the
process killed her heart and all chance of happiness. More flexible,
Ada submitted to her emotional demands and ultimately found
happiness. Which of these four women reflects most the feministic
spirit of the author?

Raised like Virginia and faithful to that line of conduct, free,
independent, and prosperous like Dorinda, Ellen Glasgow appears
as an intellectual counterpart of the latter. Proud and tortured,
"the woman within" retraces the same emotional struggle; she
seems to have paid the same price in her desperate search for
serenity. Perhaps she found peace—happiness never. But in the
light of recent progress in Women's Lib, we may venture this suggestion: today, Ellen Glasgow would *not* publish *The Woman
Within.* She would not flaunt her victimization. She would not
assume the part of melodramatic endurance. She probably would
turn to more sensible and positive means of psychological liberation. Times have changed; new solutions, new outlets have opened
that were taboo then. Divorce was still considered a catastrophe
for women. We have mentioned lesbianism before: let us hasten to
say that, in all of Ellen Glasgow's writings, there is not the slightest
indication, even remotely subconscious, in situations, characters,
imagery, commentary, or terminology, that a republic of women
would be a desirable thing. There is not one of her heroines (prac-
tically all victims of men) who did not obscurely wish that males

[34]*Virginia,* p. 33.

[35](Garden City, N.Y.: Doubleday, Doran, 1929), p. 114.

be greater so as to be more adequate mates. Contempt for men never bars women from wanting them. Then why aren't they greatest? Why are they all so uniformly mediocre, second-rate, if not scoundrels?

In that pale gallery of unimpressive men, very few are masculine enough to be rich and influential—and those who are, are tough, scornful, cruel, insensitive, like Cyrus Treadwell; most are economic failures; the lovers are weak, selfish, spineless, alcoholic. Shall we speak of a prejudice, a bias against manhood? Let us open the very first novel, *The Descendant;* the first men to appear who, we shall learn later, have good hearts and common sense, are thus depicted: a minister of the church is "small" (no comment), "ill-omened" (without any subsequent evidence of this), "chinless" (a sign of degeneracy), "ignorant" (Michael, the pig boy, will soon outwit his master's theology). The farmer who employs Michael is "a negative character" (although good and virtuous), "since to be wicked necessitates action."[36] We may ponder on this qualifier, persistent throughout the novels as applied to men: *negative.*

Negative, the oncoming farmers of the same breed such as Burr and Oakley; the rare intellectuals, such as Michael Akershem, Anthony Algarcife, Ralph McBride, who cannot control their intelligence and impulses; negative, the nice young gentlemen, such as Dudley Webb, Roger Adams, Arthur Peyton, David Blackburn, John Benham, Craig Fleming; even more so, the weaklings lost in alcohol and vice, Will Fletcher, Arnold Kemper, Jonathan Gay, Oliver Treadwell, Jason Greylock, Martin Welding, George Birdsong. The few men of character, their foils, Nick Burr, Ben Starr, Abel Revercomb, Gideon Vetch, and the reformed ones, Dan Montjoy, Daniel Ordway, Christopher Blake, fail to come out for want of proper characterization.

Such is not the case, however, for a handful of older men who (with the brilliant exception of Gamaliel Honeywell, the sexagenarian "romantic comedian") escape the damning, as if age alone would confer on men dignity and psychological depth. Shall we ask Miss Glasgow whether this is due to wisdom acquired by experience or to the decline of virility? Take for example John Fincastle, the gentle philosopher, and Asa Timberlake, two of her

[36]*The Descendant,* pp. 4, 20, 11.

finest male characterizations. Both suffer and endure, but fail to achieve the stature of minor episodic characters who die a heroic death. John Fincastle writes books of subversive philosophy that will never be published, keeps his family in poverty, gives them the example of passive fortitude in the face of adversity, and finally starves to death. He does not fight; he can never confront his human responsibilities. Lost in his dreams, he elicits pity, not admiration. Asa Timberlake, unredeemed by any intellectual achievement, is even more a failure. Unable as he is to satisfy his wife, to raise and support his daughters morally, he represents a male version of the exploited woman, of the hopeless wife, enduring the odds of life and finding relief only in his final flight from home. Few books are as devoid of happiness as *In This Our Life.* Strange to say, Asa was Miss Glasgow's favorite hero, her epitome of manhood. Isn't it significant? She tried to persuade us that his endurance had secured him moral victory: "That Asa should be regarded as my idea of failure by so many . . . readers [including me] proves . . . that we are in danger of forgetting that character is an end in itself."[37] Poignantly illustrated in Faulkner's *Wild Palms,* the demonstration here is pale and unconvincing. There is a creative way of enduring, an ultimate victory in suffering accepted *for* a purpose; but Asa does not know for what, or what else he could do. Unlike Prometheus or Sisyphus, he buys no future of liberty for anybody, and his final freedom is acquired at the price of desertion, not redemption. So in the end these two also remain insignificant and negative. They are the typical production of female creativity, revealing an innate difficulty in achieving greatness in male characterization. Here we face a bias common to most women novelists, even more flagrant with feminists, this more or less conscious determination to belittle man in order to magnify woman. This is all the more regrettable as the purpose defeats itself and the demonstration comes to nought. The more mediocre the male partners, the less convincing becomes the superiority of women to dominate or defeat them.

We may wonder how these superwomen (Dorinda for example) would react to true men. But, like the radical feminists, Miss Glasgow tends to deny the existence of the species and views the

---

[37]*A Certain Measure,* p. 253.

superior man as a figment of female imagination and credulity. We shall not open the debate at this stage, but we may ask: what do women gain in conquering such poor terrain? We may tentatively conclude that hers is a shortcoming in creative art more than a flaw in feminism. Probably Ellen Glasgow thought obscurely with Anaïs Nin that, notwithstanding the defective quality of men, perhaps because of it, women should take the responsibility for their lives, and, by doing so, would "feel less helpless than when we put the blame on society or man. . . . To take destiny into our own hands is more inspiring than expecting others to direct our destiny for us."[38] Her indictment of men's passivity is meant to stimulate women's as well:

This passivity can be converted to creative will. . . . To become man, or like man, is no solution. There is far too much imitation of man in the Women's Movement. That is merely a displacement of power. . . . The women who truly identify with their oppressor, as the cliché goes, are the women who are acting like men, masculinizing themselves, not those who seek to convert or transform man. There is no liberation of one group at the expense of another. Liberation can only come totally and in unison.[39]

This statement, made in 1972 by an older woman of letters, pictures much of what Miss Glasgow's feminism was and might be today. Yes to the emancipation of woman's intelligence, spirit, self-accomplishment, self-responsibility. No to her masculinization, no to the cancellation of her femininity. Woman's liberation should not be won at the expense of her past privileges or personal values. It is safe to believe that Miss Glasgow would forgo none of the Southern traditional manners: courtesy, chivalry, social graces, "a yellow rose on the breakfast tray," the right of women to be beautiful and attractive. Even if beauty comes second to character, all her favorite heroines have interesting features, "a beauty less of flesh than of spirit."[40] Moral beauty, artistic beauty, demands

---

[38]*Woman: An Issue,* p. 25.

[39]Ibid., p. 28.

[40]"The Difference," in *The Shadowy Third* (Garden City, N.Y.: Doubleday, Page, 1923), p. 227. Also, *The Builders* (Garden City, N.Y.: Doubleday, Page, 1919), p. 115, and Betty Ambler (*The Battle-Ground*), Gabriella (*Life and Gabriella*), Caroline Meade (*The Builders*), Laura Wilde (*The Wheel of Life*), Milly (*The Ancient Law*), Ada (*Vein of Iron*).

self-discipline and taste. "The whole truth must embrace the in-
terior world as well as external appearances."[41] She would no
doubt reject the "external appearances" of many women liberators
today: the cult of homeliness, the coarse loud voices, the angry
tones, the unwashed bodies, the ugly clothes, the masculine gait,
the unisex haircut, slovenliness, promiscuity, aggressive separate-
ness. These things she would deplore as ungainly masks to deeper
truths, with the risk of doing disservice to the cause of true
feminism. Radicalism stands at the opposite of measure and good
taste. Radicalism has to work for immediate efficiency, with hits
and blows and violence in order to burst open recalcitrant doors.
Ellen Glasgow hated violence; she chose more subdued means of
action: moderate, disciplined, gentle; yet, under her velvet glove,
one feels the iron hand of conviction, the cutting edge of her wit
and satire. These were not the least of her weapons, particularly in
dethroning the male idol in a man-made world, from the *Iconoclast*
of her youthful years to "the romantic comedians" of her sunset
laughter. This major aspect of her talent was left deliberately untouched in the present paper, because revolutionists cannot afford
humor; comedy is an insult to the seriousness of their purpose. But
Miss Glasgow would sacrifice to no restrictive militantism. Strong,
with unfathomable mental reserves of "blood and irony,"[42] she
was able to plead aptly for the cause of feminism and lose nothing
of her femininity. In the final analysis, in behavior as in writing,
Ellen Glasgow stood for aesthetics and placed her loyalty first and
last in literature as "experience illuminated . . . an interpretation
of life."[43]

[41]*A Certain Measure*, p. 28.

[42]Ibid., p. 28.

[43]Ibid., pp. 14–15.

An Essay in Bibliography

An Essay in Bibliography

Edgar E. MacDonald

I. *Bibliography*

THE first extensive checklist of Ellen Glasgow's works was William H. Egly's "Bibliography of Ellen Anderson Gholson Glasgow" (*Bulletin of Bibliography*, Sept.-Dec. 1940), which was revised and expanded by W. D. Quesenbery, Jr., in his "Ellen Glasgow: A Critical Bibliography" (*Bulletin of Bibliography*, May-Aug. 1959, and Sept.-Dec. 1959). These lists have, however, been superseded by the book-length bibliography from the University Press of Virginia.

Ellen Glasgow, A Bibliography, by William W. Kelly, and edited by Oliver Steele (Charlottesville, Va., 1964), was designed to fill the need for a comprehensive critical, analytical and enumerative bibliography. Published by The Bibliographical Society of Virginia, this work is divided into three major sections: (1) "Writings of Ellen Glasgow and Book Reviews," containing Books and Reviews, Collected Editions, Stories in Periodicals, and Contributions to Books; (2) "Ellen Glasgow Biography and Criticism," containing Biographical Portraits, Honors, and Sketches, Biographical and Critical Material in Periodicals, and Dissertations Completed on Ellen Glasgow; and (3) "Manuscripts in the Ellen Glasgow Collection" containing Checklist of Letters to Ellen Glasgow, Chronology of Letters to Ellen Glasgow, Catalogue of Ellen Glasgow Manuscripts, Notebooks, Biography, Poems, Miscellaneous Manuscripts and Letters, Letters, Genealogy, and Fiction. The book concludes with a twenty-seven-page index. Professor Kelly's Introduction is perceptive in its review of Ellen Glasgow's literary fortunes, and his description of the manuscripts in the Alderman Library Ellen Glasgow Collection at the University of Virginia is of solid value to the student. The collector of Glasgow, however, will be disappointed in Section A of Part I, "Writings of Ellen Glasgow and Book Reviews," especially in light of the editor's assertion that "the notes are sufficient to identify any copy of an Ellen Glasgow book printed to date." A random application of the descriptive criteria in this bibliography reveals many discrepancies or what appear to be variants from the norms. The editor does not list an 1899 edition of *The Descendant* nor a 1903 edition of *The Battle-Ground*, and one suspects he may have overlooked other editions. Mr. Steele relies heavily on plate damage as revealed by the Hinman Collator to distinguish among various impressions. While a valuable aid, type damage is too subject to a number of causes for it to constitute exclusive "proof" of a run.[1] Measurements are eschewed, except for gutters, and rarely are we given details of bindings.[2] Endpapers, featured in later Glasgow novels, are not commented on. In his Preface, Steele professes an attempt "to list all the impressions of Ellen Glasgow's books" but advises that "the descriptions are not fully analytical."[3] He assures us, however, that "the notes are the result of a thorough bibliographical analysis." Given that statement, we must assume that he elected not to report the complete results of that analysis.[4] The frequency of "copy seen rebound" and even "no copy seen" can only mean that the bibliographer has not consulted "the required large number of copies for examination" that Fredson Bowers advises.[5] Keeping in mind the admonition, once again by Bowers, that "one must recognize that the complex methods of modern printing and sale do not lend themselves readily to classification," one can still express disappointment that the enlightenment promised by the bibliographer was not forthcoming. These criticisms aside, the *Bibliography* is attractive as a book, it contains a large amount of information necessary for a detailed study of Glasgow, and even

[1] Fredson Bowers in *Principles of Bibliographical Description* (Princeton: Princeton University Press, 1949) gives various reasons for flaws in print on pp. 369, 372, 385.

[2] Bowers observes that bindings, while collateral to the printed sheets, are a part of publishing history, "and a bibiographer can ignore this historical fact only at his peril" (p. 411).

[3] A lengthier listing of discrepancies is given in this reviewer's "Ellen Glasgow: An Essay in Bibliography," *Resources for American Literary Study,* 2 (Autumn 1972), 132-33.

[4] The first requirement that Bowers lists for a modern bibliography is a "full description of the book as a material object" (p. 367).

[5] Steele never indicates the location of his test copies, a point stressed by Bowers, p. 362.

the disappointed collector will find it useful if used with discretion. With an expanded interest in Glasgow studies, it is hoped that a new edition of this work will be forthcoming.

Frederick P. W. McDowell supplied an Ellen Glasgow checklist in *A Bibliographical Guide to the Study of Southern Literature* (Baton Rouge, La., 1969) of limited value, doubtless owing to editorial restrictions. It might have served as a supplement to the Kelly *Bibliography,* but this it does in no significant way. The *Annual PMLA Bibliography* remains the best continuing supplement for Glasgow students.

II. *Editions*

Except for *A Certain Measure,* first editions of Ellen Glasgow's works are described in Merle D. Johnson's *American First Editions,* fourth edition revised and enlarged by Jacob Blanck (New York, 1942). First and later editions are also listed in the Kelly *Bibliography,* but there the reservations detailed in the previous section should be noted. *The Old Dominion Edition of the Works of Ellen Glasgow* (Garden City, N.Y., 1929–33) and *The Virginia Edition of the Works of Ellen Glasgow* (New York, 1938) were neither complete, the first containing eight novels and excluding eight as well as the stories and poems, and the latter including twelve novels and excluding six earlier novels as well as the stories and poems.

Certain Glasgow titles remain in print; in addition, certain of her writings have appeared in print for the first time during the last decade. In the former category are *The Voice of the People, The Battle-Ground, Barren Ground, Vein of Iron, In This Our Life, The Freeman and Other Poems,* and *A Certain Measure.* Most of these titles are in paperback, with an attractive *Vein of Iron* from Harbrace and a lurid *In This Our Life* from Avon. New Glasgow publications embrace a variety of matter; letters will be considered in Section III.

A previously unpublished short story by Ellen Glasgow, "The Professional Instinct," has been edited by William W. Kelly (*Western Humanities Review,* Autumn 1962). It is a parable of a woman who would willingly sacrifice all her attainments and security for an egotistical male unworthy of her sacrifice. Richard K. Meeker later included it in his collection of Ellen Glasgow stories and sees it as a reflection of Miss Glasgow's relationship with Henry Anderson; this reader rather sees it as Miss Glasgow and almost any male.

Ellen Glasgow appears in charming guise in" 'Literary Realism or Nominalism' by Ellen Glasgow: An Unpublished Essay," edited by Luther Y. Gore (*American Literature,* Mar. 1962). Light in tone, deft in phrase, the essay is presented as an imaginary conversation, a dialogue discussing writers and writing, treating less ponderously the realism-romantic debate that Cabell and others jousted in during the 1920s:

We have no literary criticism, merely reviews of fashions; we are primarily concerned with neither philosophy nor method, but with the tasteful display of either fancy dress or homespun. Our one permanent interest is in externals; and the first demand we make of our novelists is that they shall follow what the authors of "fashion notes" in the daily press describe as "the prevailing style."

In *The Collected Stories of Ellen Glasgow* (Baton Rouge, La., 1963), Richard K. Meeker brought together the eleven short stories published during her life and the one published posthumously. In a graceful introduction he situates them in her development as a writer, categorizes them neatly, and comments on their relationship with the novels. He rather convinces us that although she held the genre in small esteem, she displayed considerable talent in their composition, and that they should not be neglected in a total assessment.

In 1966, Luther Y. Gore's doctoral dissertation, the editing and annotating of Ellen Glasgow's last work, *Beyond Defeat,* was published (Charlottesville, Va.), a mistake on several counts. The work of a dying woman well beyond her literary prime, this inconsequential epilogue could have no interest whatsoever for a general reader and indeed would misrepresent Miss Glasgow for that reader in a cruel way. For those scholars interested in her work as a totality, there are the manuscripts of *Beyond Defeat* at the University of Virginia, there is Mr. Gore's dissertation, there is an analysis of this work in Joan Foster Santas's *Ellen Glasgow's American Dream* (considered in Section V. 2), and there was the extended treatment given to this material in the Kelly *Bibliography.* In Section B, Part III, of the latter, over fifty pages are given to the three drafts of this work with all the significant changes that Ellen

Glasgow made in each. Indeed, the Editor's Preface calls attention to the preferential treatment that *Beyond Defeat* receives. In his Introduction, Mr. Gore states that "the decision not to publish *Beyond Defeat* was probably well taken on Ellen Glasgow's part," yet he makes no direct case for his publishing the work. His commentaries on her methods of composition are cogent, but none of his observations justifies the appearance of this work in print.

Glasgow scholars deplore the fact that at the present writing several of her major novels are not in print. The irony of her peripheral work being made available instead of her masterpiece, *The Sheltered Life,* would not have been lost on Miss Glasgow. Secondhand copies of her novels are bringing ever higher prices, so that one can only hope that an enterprising publisher will soon make her best novels stock items. Also, as Frederick McDowell suggests, a collection of her essays, such as the one mentioned above, would make a welcome volume.

III. *Manuscripts and Letters*

The Kelly *Bibliography* gives a detailed listing of manuscripts in the Ellen Glasgow Papers at the University of Virginia but ignores holdings in other libraries. *American Literary Manuscripts* (Austin, Tex., 1960) lists a number of libraries with Glasgow material, in particular Harvard, the New York Public, the University of North Carolina, and Princeton. Harvard, as the repository of the papers of Walter Hines Page and Howard Mumford Jones, holds letters that span the half century of Ellen Glasgow's career. The University of Virginia, as the holder of the papers of a number of Glasgow correspondents, has perhaps the largest collection of Glasgow letters. E. Stanly Godbold lists these related manuscript holdings in his Selected Bibliography, in *Ellen Glasgow and the Woman Within* (see Section IV). Owing to James Branch Cabell's system of filing letters from correspondents in presentation copies of their works, the James Branch Cabell Library at Virginia Commonwealth University has recently acquired a number of notes, postcards, and letters from Ellen Glasgow along with his library. Significant Glasgow letters still remain in private hands; most of these in time, doubtless, will be deposited in libraries.

Letters of Ellen Glasgow (New York, 1958), a genteel selection edited by Blair Rouse, neither amazed with their profundity of thought nor impressed with their generosity of observation. Included in this volume are the letters of one who held her person and her work in proper esteem, bowing to neither popular opinion nor critical indifference. Supplementing these letters, others have since been published.

James B. Colvert edited "Agent and Author: Ellen Glasgow's Letters to Paul Revere Reynolds" (*Studies in Bibliography,* 1961). These letters underline her concern for a "discriminating audience," her desire to be published in England, her predilection for the novel over the short story, and her small regard for serialization.

Ellen Glasgow also appears in charming form in *Five Letters from Ellen Glasgow concerning Censorship* (Richmond, Va., 1962). This elegant pamphlet has an Introductory Note by Louis D. Rubin, Jr., and the letters present Miss Glasgow assessing *Elmer Gantry* negatively as literature but defending its right to appear on library shelves, expressing distaste for Charles Wertenbaker's *Boojum,* but overall affirming her conviction "that there should be no moral censorship of literature."

In "Ellen Glasgow's Letters to the Saxtons" (*American Literature,* May 1963), Douglas Day presents and comments on five letters to Eugene F. and Martha Saxton in which, among other details of minor interest, Miss Glasgow touches on her duties as a judge in The Harper Prize Novel Competition in 1933: "I wish somebody would write a novel on the idea that there is as much life in sitting still with one's own soul as there is in speeding to nowhere. . . . Do you know anybody brave enough to write such a book?" One will occasionally come across a letter of Ellen Glasgow's published in the letters of another writer, such as Gertrude Stein or Upton Sinclair. She corresponded with a large number of people, usually expressing herself strongly on whatever topic that engaged her at the moment. In the light of the wealth of Glasgow letters at the University of Virginia alone, a new selection would be welcome in published form, one that would give a more rounded portrait of the writer with less concern for a genteel image.

IV. *Biography*

The New York Times Index and the Kelly bibliography record the numerous interviews given by Ellen Glasgow and the impressions of her contemporaries. Her many letters also give us insight into the personality of the woman, but the truly objective portraits did not appear until after her death.

When her autobiography, *The Woman Within* (New York, 1954), appeared posthumously, it provoked a wide spectrum of reactions. Her literary executors had waited for the death of Henry Anderson before revealing Ellen Glasgow's unflattering and inaccurate account of their engagement. The book was hailed as "Ellen Glasgow's 'Honest' Autobiography," although James Branch Cabell wrote that he distrusted "the entire book throughout as a factual record." Ellen Glasgow may have intended the work to be a truthful recounting of her life as she experienced it, but she was accustomed to writing novels. More than for most writers, her emotional life and her career were the same. Seeing people and events through a "filter," she gives accounts that are not always in accord with the facts as recorded in letters and the observations of others. In the major studies of Ellen Glasgow, Monique Parent early cast a dubious eye on certain details as given in *The Woman Within;* other Glasgow scholars continue to accept it as factual biography. Ellen Glasgow's translation of incidents into intense feeling will have to be delicately balanced by anyone attempting to evaluate the woman or her work.

In "Speaks with Candor of a Great Lady," a chapter in *As I Remember It* (New York, 1955), James Branch Cabell makes the well-substantiated claim that he knew Ellen Glasgow for the last twenty years of her life better than anyone else. In particular, he recounts his role in her designation as a "social historian" and his revisions of *In This Our Life.* His portrait of her late years is deftly sketched, blending irony and admiration in his account of their relationship.

In 1962, two studies of Glasgow appeared: Blair Rouse's *Ellen Glasgow* (New York) and Monique Parent's monumental, 574-page *Ellen Glasgow: Romancière* (Paris). The former will be considered in Section V. 2, but, owing to the exhaustive biographical research that went into the latter, it is reviewed here. Monique Parent, a

Parisienne by birth and education, undertook her research on Ellen Glasgow for the French *doctorat d'état*. She made many trips to Virginia, where she interviewed those who had known, seen, or, in some cases, heard of Ellen Glasgow, in particular Miss Glasgow's sister Rebe Tutwiler, her long-time companion Anne Virginia Bennett, her life-long friend Roberta Wellford, her literary executrix Irita Van Doren, and, or course, James Branch Cabell. Mlle Parent made many friends in Virginia, and she was accorded an insight into the mores and personality of its people, which she interpreted with finesse; she had an instinctive feeling for the environment that formed the woman and writer that Ellen Glasgow became.

Mlle Parent divided her work into the classic three parts of French literary analysis, "The Environment," "The Woman," and "The Work." The first part is a comprehensive view of the South and its history, which she felt necessary for her French readers but which also has value for American students studying Ellen Glasgow in depth.[6] Her second part, "The Woman," is of greater value, for Mlle Parent first gives us a deftly realized exterior portrait, such as others have only approached, and then goes on to penetrate the masks for a character analysis that is intimately revealing yet still generous. The third part, dealing with the novels, is sound but does not surpass the critical evaluations of McDowell or Rouse. While her threefold approach inevitably leads to some overlapping, a general fault with many French theses, the resulting depth of her work compensates for minor flaws. This work was received with its highest accolade by the faculty of the Sorbonne in 1960 and was published in 1962. William W. Kelly, in his *Ellen Glasgow: A Bibliography*, sees it as "probably the most exhaustive and comprehensive discussion of Miss Glasgow's life and career yet published." Professor McDowell's reaction to this work in *A Bibliographical Guide to the Study of Southern Literature* is critical: "The complex of social, ethical, philosophical, and religious

---

[6]Richard P. Adams, reviewing this work for *Etudes Anglaises* (1963), thinks otherwise: "In her comments on the historical background and social milieu of Ellen Glasgow's work, Miss Parent is less happy." The reviewer then proceeds to criticize Glasgow's interpretation of the South; she was "too polite to tell the truth." When the reviewer gets back to Parent, he admires her "lively and sympathetic, yet detached and judicious exposition of Ellen Glasgow's life and character."

values out of which Ellen Glasgow wrote require sharper definition than they have received from Monique Parent." But it is peculiarly in these areas that she excels. For depth, breadth, balance, and psychological insight, hers is the best portrait of Ellen Glasgow to date.

The latest biography to appear is *Ellen Glasgow and the Woman Within* (Baton Rouge, La., 1972), by E. Stanly Godbold, Jr. In it Professor Godbold makes a noble attempt to reveal Ellen Glasgow as a personage, and doubtless his truthfulness concerning many aspects of her life will come as a surprise to those who have been nourished on the public image she cultivated and projected during her lifetime. While it may be "the first full biography" of Ellen Glasgow, as the dust wrapper asserts, it is far from being the "definitive account of her life" that is further proclaimed. Her early formative years are not covered in depth, and indeed J. R. Raper gives a more detailed analysis of these years in his *Without Shelter* (see Section V. 2). Mr. Godbold is the first to rely heavily on the notes which Marjorie Kinnan Rawlings made for her projected biography, but he seems unaware that some of Mrs. Rawlings's sources were less than candid and some may have actually withheld information of vital interest for a biographer. Faced with equivocal "evidence," Mrs. Rawlings herself relinquished the objective of an intimate biography of Ellen Glasgow. Although Mr. Godbold relies on the Rawlings Papers extensively, he ignores, at least in any acknowledgment, the serious biographical research done by Monique Parent in her *Ellen Glasgow: Romancière*. In his personal interviews with Richmond "friends of Miss Glasgow," in several notable instances he accepts and quotes information supplied by a person who had no social or literary contact with Ellen Glasgow whatsoever. In treating Ellen Glasgow's affair with "Gerald B.," Godbold wavers between well-founded caution—"How much of her imagination went into the writing of the chapter is impossible to say"—and incautious assertion—"Gerald died in 1905." As Mr. Godbold moves toward Ellen Glasgow's later years with their copious documentation and fresher memories, his portrait takes on veracity. Chapter 11, "Historical Revelations," seems rather an insertion, perhaps lifted from an earlier paper, but it sums up with cogency her role as a social historian. Like every other assessment of Ellen Glasgow as a writer, *Ellen Glasgow and*

the Woman Within leaves the reader vaguely uncomfortable about
her place in American letters. Perhaps a total assessment of all her
novels is unfair to her as a writer; it obscures rather than enlightens,
especially if the reading proposes to analyze her psyche. As for the
woman, Mr. Godbold gives us Ellen Glasgow the eccentric, very
true in many respects but certainly not the final delineation.

V. *Criticism*

1. Critical Reception during Her Life

The best of the contemporary assessments of Miss Glasgow's works
have been assimilated in the full-length studies which are listed
below in Section V. 2, "Books," none of which actually appeared
in her lifetime. All these materials have been admirably annotated
by McDowell and Rouse, and the reader is referred to the following
section for a discussion of these works. Rouse's resume in Chapter
10 of his *Ellen Glasgow* is a model of concise critical reporting.

For the most part, Ellen Glasgow's novels enjoyed a favorable
critical reception during her literary career. She early announced
her serious intent as an artist, and her shortcomings as a writer,
even her lapses into dullness, were generally overlooked out of
respect for her ethical ideals. She cultivated critics who reviewed
favorably and indeed directed their attention to those aspects of
her work that she wished underlined for the less observant. This is
not to imply that the criticism of James Southall Wilson, Howard
Mumford Jones, James Branch Cabell, and others classified as admiring friends is not worth the scholar's attention today; however
these acolytes all wrote with the realization that the surfacely
Olympian, interiorly intense woman of whom they wrote would
pass judgment on their work. Carl Van Doren, Stuart Pratt Sherman, Carl Van Vechten, Henry Seidel Canby, and J. Donald Adams
were also among the illustrious who commented on her work in
terms highly acceptable to the author. But Ellen Glasgow was an
astute scholar as well as an instructor; her friendly reviewers helped
her to define her aims, and her abilities grew as her own percep-
tions of art and life expanded. She wrote that she had read almost
every treatise on writing that was available, and her library, as
catalogued by her nephew, Carrington Cabell Tutwiler, Jr., *Ellen*

Glasgow's Library (Charlottesville, Va., 1968), a descriptive pamphlet of thirty-one pages, and *A Catalogue of the Library of Ellen Glasgow* (Charlottesville, Va., 1969), a book of 287 pages, attest to her wide reading of the major Western novelists.

Having read the criticism of others during a lifetime, she absorbed, assimilated, "recollected," and in time became her own best spokeswoman for the work she had "intended" to write. *A Certain Measure,* her last work to appear in her lifetime, is Ellen Glasgow at her best. Wise, witty, sometimes factual, she discourses with ease on literature in general and her works in particular. Growing out of earlier prefaces to her novels, prefaces in which critical opinion had helped her to codify her thoughts concerning literary techniques (in a formula suggested by Cabell), this work considers both objectively and subjectively her novels in terms of objectives and fulfillment, always generously. As Cabell observed, these essays read well, and there is evidence that some of the urbanity is his. Edgar E. MacDonald, in "The Glasgow-Cabell Entente" (*American Literature,* Mar. 1969), and E. Stanly Godbold, Jr., in *Ellen Glasgow and the Woman Within,* see his hand in their composition; Cabell intended a heavy irony in his review of *A Certain Measure* when he wrote pointedly: "It is, in brief, all Ellen Glasgow." But the true irony is that it remains a book about Ellen Glasgow by Ellen Glasgow. Despite her neuroses and biases, she was a perceptive critic, and herein she carefully chose her best efforts to amplify in comment. *A Certain Measure* remains an interesting, even valuable commentary on her work.

William W. Kelly's Ph.D. dissertation (Duke, 1957), "Struggle for Recognition: A Study of the Literary Reputation of Ellen Glasgow," has proved of value for scholars interested in the contemporary criticism of her work. In the review of critical articles in periodicals below, the emphasis will be, for the most part, on the more objective criticism following the death of Ellen Glasgow in 1945.

2. Books

Frederick P. W. McDowell's *Ellen Glasgow and the Ironic Art of Fiction* (Madison, Wis., 1960) was the first book-length study of

Glasgow to appear. Chapter 1, "The Artist and Her Time," is adequate in recounting the basic facts of Glasgow's career; it conveys
however, no intimacy of feeling for the writer or her environment.
Reservations must be made about his belief that Ellen Glasgow
came to admire her father's "unselfishness" and his uncritical acceptance of *The Woman Within* as factual biography, in particular
her account of the "Gerald B." affair.[7] The bulk of McDowell's
book is devoted to an analysis of the Glasgow opus, her theory
and practice, and his presentation is accurate and solid. His bibliography sums up in an exemplary manner the major Glasgow
criticism to that time. Blair Rouse terms this work an "excellent"
critical study (*Ellen Glasgow*, 1962); C. Hugh Holman sees it as
"not too perceptive or critically discerning a treatment" (*Three
Modes of Southern Fiction*, 1966 [see Section V.3]).

Two years later, two new studies of Glasgow were published:
Monique Parent's *Ellen Glasgow: Romancière* (discussed in Section
IV) and Blair Rouse's *Ellen Glasgow* in Twayne's U.S. Authors
Series (New York, 1962). Professor Rouse had earlier edited the
Letters of Ellen Glasgow (New York, 1958); he had an interest in
Glasgow of long standing, having been accorded a personal interview with her in 1941. While the compact format of the Twayne
Series doubtless imposed restrictions on Mr. Rouse, his is a more
than adequate overview and is in some respects superior to other
titles in that series. At the same time it is somewhat pedestrian in
observation, and his championship of Miss Glasgow understandably
has him citing her more favorable critics. Wholly commendable is
his Bibliography, wherein he gives concise evaluations of previous
Glasgow scholarship. This work, available in paper as well as hard
covers, is of special value in the classroom, giving the student the
essential details for a rounded understanding of the social critic
and novelist.

Louis Auchincloss's *Ellen Glasgow* (Minneapolis, 1964), No. 33
in the University of Minnesota Pamphlets on American Writers,
brings us the insight of a critic who is himself a novelist. Into a

---

[7]By the time Professor McDowell came to compile his Bibliography for *A
Bibliographical Guide to the Study of Southern Literature* (Baton Rouge: Louisiana
State University Press, 1969) some nine years later, he appeared more cautious: "Ellen
Glasgow remains a controversial figure in Richmond; and the difficulties alone in documenting and interpreting her autobiography, *The Woman Within,* are great" (p. 204).

brief forty pages he instills a remarkably clear and balanced assessment of Ellen Glasgow, written in an urbane style that pleases as it informs. This study was incorporated into Mr. Auchincloss's *Pioneers and Caretakers* (Minneapolis, 1965). Like the Rouse work, this pamphlet too is a handy aid for the classroom student.

Joan Foster Santas's *Ellen Glasgow's American Dream* (Charlottesville, Va., 1965) is a dissertation perpetrated in print. A rehash of every pronouncement Glasgow ever made about writing, as well as a rewarming of almost every observation made about her by others, its breezy prolixity successfully buries Mrs. Santas's "thesis." This type of work is the antithesis of Mlle Parent's painstaking research.

In *Without Shelter* (Baton Rouge, La., 1971), also an outgrowth of a dissertation, J. R. Raper analyzes Ellen Glasgow's early fiction with the object of illustrating the Darwinian influences. In addition he takes issue with Joan Santas, Blair Rouse, and Barbara Giles's "Character and Fate: The Novels of Ellen Glasgow" (*Mainstream*, Sept. 1956) on points of interpretation, and attempts to expand in more specific detail certain biographical episodes that bear on Ellen Glasgow's work. While this aspect of his study is not perfectly realized, it moves in the direction of greatest need in Glasgow studies, a psychological understanding of the woman who turned weakness into strength in her struggle for comprehension and self-realization. Professor Raper's critical analyses of the novels are wholly admirable; his Bibliography is a catch-all of miscellanea.

Marion K. Richards's thesis, *Ellen Glasgow's Development as a Novelist* (The Hague, 1971), is one of the latest book-length studies to appear in print, although it was written ten years ago. Mrs. Richards's approach is to examine the novels through *Barren Ground* in the light of the revelations in *A Certain Measure* and *The Woman Within*. This approach might have had some validity fifteen years ago, but now this work is simply an out-of-date thesis. Also, Mrs. Richards's Bibliography is the most anemic of all those in the studies reviewed above, since it was not updated after completion as a dissertation. Although she has read the novels perceptively, her easy acceptance of critic Glasgow commenting on the writer appears naive. References to Mary Johnston as Mrs. Johnston shock the reader. Summing up all Glasgow's earlier work (Betrayal Theme, Setting, Symbolism, Style, Structure) as reflected in *Barren Ground* is a tidy thesis device, but it cannot be justified as an extramural contribution to Glasgow scholarship. The studies which precede this late arrival excel *Ellen Glasgow's Development as a Novelist* too comprehensively for anyone to find this limited work of any significant value. The most recent book-length study of Glasgow, *Ellen Glasgow and the Woman Within,* by E. Stanly Godbold, Jr., is considered in Section IV.

3. Chapters and Commentaries in Books

As an avowed and accepted interpreter of a time and place, Ellen Glasgow continues to enjoy consideration in the general surveys of American social thought and the American novel. Remarkably enough, she has elicited rather kind appraisals from the more acidulous critics, such as Kazin and Geismar, and has been cavalierly derided by the usually kinder omnipotents.

Alfred Kazin, a social critic scornful of the twenties, castigated the sophisticates of the "James Branch Cabell School" in *On Native Grounds* (New York, 1942; rev. ed., Garden City, N.Y., 1956; reprinted in *Literature in America,* edited by Philip Rahv, New York, 1957). On the other hand, he wrote glowingly of Ellen Glasgow, comparing her *Sheltered Life* with Chekhov's *Cherry Orchard:*

When she discovered about 1913, the year she published *Virginia,* that the comedy of manners was her work, she made it serve what the very best comedies of manners have always served: as an index to the qualities of a civilization, and as a subtle guide to its covert tragedy. From one point of view, of course, her talent was only the highest expression of the society she lampooned; but her attacks on Southern complacency were never complacent in themselves. She belonged to a tradition and lived out her career in it; and her understanding seemed all the more moving because she was so deeply and immovably a participant in the world she scorned.

In a briefer but equally kind consideration, Henry Steele Commager in *The American Mind* (New Haven, Conn., 1950) underlined Glasgow's growing disenchantment with the New South and its material values as well as the irony of her finding strength in a past she had rejected.

In *The Faith of Our Feminists: A Study in the Novels of Edith Wharton, Ellen Glasgow, Willa Cather* (New York, 1950), Josephine Lurie Jessup gives us a perfectly innocuous if pedestrian review of the Glasgow opus. She advises us that Ellen Glasgow's "mission was to magnify woman." She admits, rather charmingly, that *Virginia* contradicts her thesis.

Frederick J. Hoffman in *The Modern Novel in America, 1900-1950* (Chicago, 1951; rev. ed., New York, 1956) elected to treat only Glasgow's later novels. He admired her social comedies, her subtle uses of viewpoint, but found her irony at times intrusive—characters became puppets for her commentaries. On the other hand, Dorinda in *Barren Ground* was too much the "model of heroic womanhood." *Vein of Iron* was impregnated with "too much contrived pathos." Thus the reader is prevented from viewing the characters of the comedies seriously and on the other hand is told that he cannot view the characters of the fortitude novels seriously enough.

Majl Ewing in "The Civilized Uses of Irony: Ellen Glasgow," *English Studies in Honor of James Southall Wilson* (Charlottesville, Va., 1951) sees Ellen Glasgow's gift for irony springing from her awareness of the absurdities attendant on male-female sexual relationships, and detects this gift as early as *The Wheel of Life* (1906). In this work Ellen Glasgow "has discovered the life force—biological attraction—which henceforth makes so much of the comedy and tragedy of her novels." Her gift flowered in the three comedies of the city. Ewing speculates, as have others, on the possible influence of Cabell on its first major appearance in *The Romantic Comedians.*

N. Elizabeth Monroe contributed "Ellen Glasgow: Ironist of Manners," to *Fifty Years of the American Novel: A Christian Appraisal,* edited by Harold C. Gardiner (New York, 1951), a revision of her article first published in *America* (Apr. 1951). She touches on the neglect accorded Ellen Glasgow at that date but concludes: "A writer with so much to say and so conscious of the means to saying it need not worry about neglect." While generally laudatory in tone, Miss Monroe reproaches Ellen Glasgow for presenting "too many frustrated people, too many despairing moods, too many gallant poses." Recalling the subtitle of this survey, she adds that "religion is always treated skeptically and ironically, as though the novelist herself saw religion only as part of an outworn code." Miss Monroe had earlier written a long critical appraisal, "Contemplation of Manners in Ellen Glasgow," *The Novel and Society: A Critical Study of the Modern Novel* (Chapel Hill, N.C., 1941), which Ellen Glasgow is said to have found imperceptive. Perhaps Miss Glasgow did not care for such assertions as: "She has never turned her art inward on the processes of her own thought and feeling." On the whole, though, it was a needed review of Glasgow's total work at the time, and much of what Miss Monroe had to say remains valid today.

Van Wyck Brooks saw Ellen Glasgow as more than a regionalist in *The Confident Years: 1885–1915* (New York, 1952): "In her reaffirmation of reality and life against what used to be called the dead hand of tradition, Ellen Glasgow was a part of the world movement of her time—just as her Virginia scene was, in fact, a wider scene, the all-American scene of two generations." Brooks also presented brief critical and personal sketches in *Our Literary Heritage: A Pictorial History of the Writer in America* (New York, 1956) and *From the Shadow of the Mountain: My Post-Meridian Years* (New York, 1951).

Edward Wagenknecht devotes a generous chapter, "Ellen Glasgow: Triumph and Despair," to the writer in his *Cavalcade of the American Novel* (New York, 1952). Ever a kind reviewer, it is his usual warm appreciation, taking the pronouncements of the author under consideration at face value. Blair Rouse sees Wagenknecht's critique as a "somewhat inaccurate account of her career," but other than its acceptance of Glasgow as a reliable critic of Glasgow the writer, a course many scholars readily follow, it is a relatively accurate and comprehensive overview of her work. Wagenknecht sees her characters as "better Stoics than Christians," although they, like their creator, never quite abandon a mystic vision of a final unity.

Maxwell Geismar also devotes a generous chapter to Glasgow in *Rebels and Ancestors: The American Novel, 1890–1915* (Cambridge, Mass., 1953), underscoring the fact that her best work appeared after she was fifty: "In this late blooming Indian summer she broke through the double armor of culture and temperament." Geismar generally writes approvingly of Glasgow, but along with other sociologically attuned critics he expresses dismay that her

"Colonels" and "darkies" speak the clichés of stereotypes, implying that in these instances she ceases to be the realist. As an interesting and privileged critic, Geismar indulges in mild audacities that mildly titillate the professorial drudge; he compares *The Wheel of Life* (1906) with *The Great Gatsby*. He makes that early work sound better than most readers seem to remember it; but then we are reassured when he adds that "the moralistic tone of the conclusion is probably the main reason why *The Wheel of Life* has been an unduly neglected work." And then he sees *The Miller of Old Church*, which some of us seem to remember as having some charm, as an inferior work. What one would be tempted to term plot-rehashes in another critic's commentary become with Geismar a matter of debate so that in the end he gives us a probing, enlightening analysis. He underlines more clearly than any other Glasgow critic how the growth of moral discernment in her characters paralleled her personal emotional dilemmas and their resolution, a growth marked by the mixed tone of her work, "both elegiac and ironic." In finally escaping "from the constrictive sexuality at the center of her own emotions . . . she was able, in her last period of work, to break through the armor of the southern legend itself."

In contrast to these on-the-whole favorable commentaries, John Edward Hardy in "Ellen Glasgow," *Southern Renascence*, edited by Louis D. Rubin, Jr., and Robert D. Jacobs (Baltimore, 1953), is negative, condescending, gratuitously snide, and gloriously unprophetic. The essay has some interest as a classic example of the critic being superior to the artist and to other critics in lauding a minor work over other novels, in this instance *The Miller of Old Church*. He states that "Ellen Glasgow . . . is in *no way* essentially a realist. She is . . . essentially a sentimentalist." He does "not advocate a Glasgow critical revival," advice prodigiously ignored in the intervening twenty years by a large number of perceptive critics, including one of his editors.

The South in American Literature, 1607-1900 (Durham, N.C., 1954), by Jay B. Hubbell, gives us a brief review of the Glasgow opus. Professor Hubbell traces her development as a novelist and suggests a heterogeneous collection of influences—James, Howells, Cable, Cabell. In his "Ellen Glasgow: Artist and Social Historian," in *South and Southwest: Literary Essays and Reminiscences*, by

Jay B. Hubbell (Durham, N.C., 1965), he is discursive and charmingly anecdotal, recounting his long acquaintance with Glasgow's work and his personal association with the woman. He sees her as a pioneer, more representative of a place than Faulkner. He defends her claim to having conceived a "history of Virginian manners" quite early, as opposed to Cabell's revelation that it was his conception rather late in her career. Professor Hubbell states, "I do not think Cabell's memory on these points accurate. . . . Ellen Glasgow was quite aware of what she was doing." Another personal reminiscence is given us by Isaac F. Marcosson in *Before I Forget* (New York, 1959). Associated with Walter Hines Page in the Doubleday, Page Company, Mr. Marcosson sketches a long (since 1900), admiring, literary friendship with Ellen Glasgow, revealing the totally committed devotion a contemporary could feel for the writer and the woman.

In "Ellen Glasgow and the Southern Literary Tradition," *Virginia in History and Tradition,* edited by R. C. Simonini, Jr. (Farmville, Va., 1958), C. Hugh Holman comments on those writers who, judged by an older Southern literary tradition, were excluded from the classification of Southern writer, notably Poe, Glasgow, Wolfe, Faulkner. In an easy style, broadly allusive, he convinces the reader that, rather than being outside, these writers are most representative of a tradition of Southern literary art. Glasgow shares with them

a sense of evil, a pessimism about man's potential, a tragic sense of life, a deep-rooted sense of the interplay of past and present, a peculiar sensitivity to time as a complex element in narrative art, a sense of place as a dramatic dimension, and a thorough-going belief in the intrinsic value of art as an end in itself, with an attendant Aristotelian concern with forms and techniques.

In *Three Modes of Southern Fiction* (Athens, Ga., 1966), Holman gives a further analysis of Ellen Glasgow's work in relation to that of Faulkner and Wolfe. His broad scholarly background brings clarity to diversity, especially in his opening and closing chapters wherein he melds history and geography in defining the complex nuances of *southern*. In the chapter devoted specifically to Glasgow, "The Novelist of Manners as Social Critic," Holman observes that the novel of manners in the tradition of Jane Austen presents the testing of "men and women by accepted standards of conduct in a sharply arrested moment in history." Ellen Glasgow's comedies of manners differ in that "her characters are tested not by their conformity to a meaningful code but by their futile rebellion against a dead one." Ellen Glasgow's attitude toward her culture was ultimately ambivalent: "Not to love it was, for Miss Glasgow at least, impossible; and yet to fail to subject it to ironic analysis would be to succumb to its worst failings." The clarity and urbanity of Professor Holman's style raises the scholarly essay to an art form. This essay was later included in Holman's *The Roots of Southern Writing* (Athens, Ga., 1972).

Louis D. Rubin, Jr., observes Miss Glasgow with his left eye, slightly jaundiced, while beaming with his right upon James Branch Cabell in *No Place on Earth* (Austin, Tex., 1959). Rubin makes no claim to having exhaustively reread all the works of either author, but he has read selectively in depth and gives us insights not found elsewhere. His approach to Miss Glasgow, however, seems rather severe and results in the type of commentary where Gideon Vetch of *One Man in His Time* (1922), a minor novel in the Glasgow canon, is compared with Willie Stark in *All the King's Men,* Warren's masterpiece. Although Rubin challenges, with reason, Ellen Glasgow's claims to literary prescience in projecting her social history, he accepts Cabell's claims to Olympian forethought in planning an epic cycle, although the latter was from the beginning of his career suspected of being a falsifier of a large order. On the positive side, Rubin's analysis points up the common problem of many Glasgow heroines of marrying beneath them or of not marrying at all. He admires her awareness of the implications in the confrontations of members of the First Families of Virginia with people of lower status; consequently he prefers her comedies to her novels of "high seriousness." His final word for Ellen Glasgow is *transitional.*

Three years after *No Place on Earth* appeared, Louis Rubin covered the same material in an address given before the Friends of the Richmond Public Library, published by that group in 1966 under the title *Richmond as a Literary Capital.* His thesis is the same, that Glasgow's and Cabell's Richmond was a strange translation of the Richmond of mundane experience. Here he again favors the comedies; however, in a more mellow mood he stresses the idea that there were *two* Ellen Glasgows, related to be sure.

This assessment judges her "a very heroic woman, not only for what she did, but for what she tried to do." The ideas he expostulates in the above are presented again in "Two in Richmond," first in *South: Modern Southern Literature in Its Cultural Setting* (New York, 1961) and later in *The Curious Death of the Novel* (Baton Rouge, La., 1967).

Willard Thorp in *American Writing in the Twentieth Century* (Cambridge, Mass., 1960), like Louis Rubin, favors the comedies and regrets that Miss Glasgow discovered her "vein of high comedy" late in life, owing, perhaps, to her early adherence to the "realism preached by W. D. Howells and his disciples." H. Wayne Morgan terms his essays in *Writers in Transition* (New York, 1963) "old-fashioned appreciations," and his "Ellen Glasgow: The Qualities of Endurance" does not belie that genial classification nor does it exclude reasonable balance. As his chapter title indicates, he writes of Miss Glasgow's efforts to define human fortitude; in her work we feel the stresses inherent in the "shift from agrarian to industrial America." John R. Welsh's essay, "Egdon Heath Revisited: Ellen Glasgow's *Barren Ground*," in *Reality and Myth* (Nashville, Tenn., 1964), develops the expected comparison of *The Return of the Native* with *Barren Ground,* in particular the analogies of characters (especially rustics), symbol (heather-broomsedge), theme (environment versus human will), and circumstance (sexual attraction versus common sense). Both novels are tributes to the human spirit of survival in adverse environments ("the world").

Warner Berthoff in his brief and gloomy assessment of Ellen Glasgow in *The Ferment of Realism* (New York, 1965) informs us that "the buried vein of authenticity in Ellen Glasgow's work is almost entirely subjective and emotional." Then he flatly states that "as social history and social criticism her novels are well-bred fantasy." Howard Mumford Jones in *Jeffersonianism and the American Novel* (New York, 1966) sees three ladies in particular, Wharton, Cather, and Glasgow, bridging the gap between the writers of "the golden age" of the later nineteenth century and their successors who abandoned the premises of the "natural aristocracy." Robert E. Spiller refreshingly treats Ellen Glasgow as a novelist rather than as a historian in his *The Cycle of American Literature* (New York, 1967), seeing her efforts as a writer bent on achieving "something like Hawthorne's truth to the human heart." In her slow but determined advancement in ability, he sees her succeeding where others have failed. "With a flexible style, capable of almost tragic intensity or comic irony at will, she was able to interpret, out of her own understanding of herself, the shift in values which had so completely altered the society of which she was a part."

A segment of a doctoral dissertation, "The Decline of the Southern Gentleman Ideal: Indian Summer," by Kenneth M. England (Vanderbilt, 1957), was published by Georgia State College as one of its *School of Arts and Sciences Research Papers*, no. 15, Apr. 1967. In this segment, Professor England exhaustively analyzes the character of Asa Timberlake of *In This Our Life*. Asa's code is based on an idealized concept of a beautiful self-sacrificing mother who is symbolic of Mother South. While Asa is in the pattern of the Southern gentleman, his noble actions seem peculiarly lacking in conviction; but we are assured "he possesses character and maintains it, and that is in itself a triumph even though he represents ideals that no longer prevail."

William Leigh Godshalk contributed a preface and copious notes for a new edition of *The Voice of the People* (New Haven, 1972). He reviews the sociology for which the work has been abundantly praised but goes on to suggest that its merits in this area have overshadowed its artistic values. He credits Miss Glasgow for her skillful development of the theme of isolation and a style which has "historical density." In characterization, he sees the novel's heroine as "the central figure, standing between the opposed forces of Nick and Dudley, polar characters contrasting in their actions, their physical and mental attributes, and their political ideals." Professor Godshalk especially admires the symbolism of the novel, and as for the constantly shifting point of view, he sees it as a device to achieve ironic effect. "Though the overall impression is dark and autumnal, the artistry is impeccable, and *The Voice of the People* is a much better novel than many critics have been willing to admit."

4. Recent Articles in Periodicals

The current diversity of interest in Ellen Glasgow is especially apparent in the variety of periodicals, in particular the smaller, that are presenting articles on every aspect of her work. She is accorded handsome recognition in the communist publication *Mainstream* (Barbara Giles, "Character and Fate: The Novels of Ellen Glasgow," Sept. 1956), as well as the Catholic weekly *America* (Nellie Elizabeth Monroe, "Ellen Glasgow: Ironist of Manners," Apr. 1951). The controversy surrounding the inception of Glasgow's social history has elicited a continuing discussion in periodicals as well as books. The first article treating the subject in depth, reviewing the evidence from early to late, is Daniel W. Patterson's "Ellen Glasgow's Plan for a Social History of Virginia" (*Modern Fiction Studies,* Winter 1959–60). This reasonable presentation of Cabell versus Glasgow as the "planner" provoked a rather ill tempered rereading of the evidence by Oliver L. Steele in "Ellen Glasgow, Social History, and the 'Virginia Edition' " (*Modern Fiction Studies,* Summer 1961). Mr. Steele is the author of several articles on plate damage and impressions of Glasgow novels and the editor of the Kelly *Bibliography*; he also presented a memoir from a Glasgow notebook, "Gertrude Stein and Ellen Glasgow: Memoir of a Meeting" (*American Literature,* Mar. 1961). Edgar E. MacDonald in "The Glasgow-Cabell Entente" (*American Literature,* Mar. 1969) cites letters and notes that support Cabell's claims to first seeing the Glasgow opus as a planned history. The formula for prefaces which resulted in *A Certain Measure* was his, he supplied the title for that work, and his hand is evident elsewhere. The continuing discussion is due in part to the phrasing of Ellen Glasgow's intentions in her early letters; whatever her early intent may have been, a body of work that constitutes a social history resulted.

Frederick P. W. McDowell, author of the first book-length study of Glasgow, earlier gave us an overview of her work in "Ellen Glasgow and the Art of the Novel" (*Philological Quarterly,* July 1951), an analysis of her literary techniques as enunciated in *A Certain Measure,* and their application to her novels. In " 'The Old Pagan Scorn of Everlasting Mercy'—Ellen Glasgow's *The Deliverance*" (*Twentieth Century Literature,* Jan. 1959), McDowell points up the vitality of her earlier novels. He analyzes the symbolic values of the characters in that novel and, more specifically, Christopher Blake's revenge motivation and its consequences. Professor McDowell sees *The Deliverance* as "more significant as a psychological than as a sociological study," the character of Guy Carraway serving as "Miss Glasgow's disinterested Jamesean spectator." He concludes that the matured sense of form which unites social scene and characters, the larger motivating forces as well as the emotional, and "her realization of the close relationship between the tragic and the comic in human affairs all indicate the stature of this novel." In "Theme and Artistry in Ellen Glasgow's *The Sheltered Life*" (*Texas Studies in Literature and Language,* Winter 1960), McDowell in a masterly analysis, a definitive exposition, presents the case that *The Sheltered Life* is not only Glasgow's best novel but one of the artistic achievements of her time. A digressive confession intrudes here: in Richmond, where Ellen Glasgow's personality still loomed large, it was difficult for us to concede she had a critical intelligence. The scholarly proofs presented by such "foreigners" as Professor McDowell came as shocks. Didn't our Ellen have them all fooled? Or were we the ones who were fooled?

Allen W. Becker's studies for his dissertation, "Ellen Glasgow: Her Novels and Their Place in the Development of Southern Fiction" (Johns Hopkins, 1956), resulted in three articles in scholarly publications. In "Ellen Glasgow's Social History" (*Texas Studies in English,* 1957), he discusses six of her earlier novels as a chronological series intended to document the impact of the New South upon the Old. In *Voice, Battle, Deliverance, Romance, Virginia,* and *Life and Gabriella,* Ellen Glasgow employed a technique of allowing a character to epitomize a segment of Southern society, but the results are marred by sentiment, auctorial intrusion, and distortion of the character for the sake of her thesis. These novels are the *esquisses* for the more successful treatment of the same material in *Barren Ground, Sheltered Life,* and *Vein of Iron.* Becker contributed the central section, "The Period 1865–1925," of a three-part article, "Agrarianism as a Theme in Southern Literature" (*Georgia Review,* Summer 1957). Here he situates Glasgow between Thomas Nelson Page and James Branch Cabell, terming *Barren Ground* "the most openly agrarian work of the period under consideration." Dorinda Oakley attempts "to recapture her soul by marrying it to the land." Glasgow, however, became disillusioned with the industrialization she welcomed in her earlier novels. The agrarian South, which her first hero left in *The Descendant,* is symbolically returned to by her last hero in *Beyond Defeat.* In

"Ellen Glasgow and the Southern Literary Tradition" (*Modern Fiction Studies,* Winter 1959), Professor Becker asserts that she "brought to Southern letters the first conscious literary realism," her most radical innovation lying in her rejection of the aristocratic basis of society. Yet Miss Glasgow did not totally abandon the romantic love story, the noble Southern woman, nor the rhetorical style of earlier writers. Her later novels, "in their new outlook on industrialism, in their regionalism, and in their use of the family as a symbol, display the central concerns and viewpoints in the fiction of the Southern revival." Some scholars might take exception to Professor Becker's assertion that interest in Glasgow's novels "lies in their 'history,' for none are literary successes."

Newton Baird in "Leadership in Ideal Proportions: Ellen Glasgow's *The Voice of the People*" (*Talisman,* Winter-Spring 1956-57) treats that novel to a detailed analysis, in particular the character of Nicholas Burr, the honest country boy, morally and politically victorious over a decadent aristocracy. Sentimentality is the one weakness "of a quite brilliant author," one who "was able to construct in this novel an intricate triangular relationship of courage, integrity and betrayal. Within the triangle is the dominant theme of the author's entire body of work: the destructive or uncivilized element in human nature as opposed to moral intelligence." Robert Holland, in "Miss Glasgow's 'Prufrock' " (*American Quarterly,* Winter 1957), postulates that in her chronicles of Virginia, Ellen Glasgow viewed World War I as "the ridge which separates, in a general way, the struggles of order from the death of order: beyond this ridge loom confusion and loss of will." Bracketing the contemporary wasteland are *The Sheltered Life* and *In This Our Life,* with *They Stooped to Folly* lying, in point of time treated, between. Holland makes an extended comparison of Virginius Curle Littlepage of the latter novel with Eliot's Prufrock. Glasgow's "modern" hero is impotent because "will and desire are at secret odds, so that desire is constantly thwarted by will. Reflecting the fragmented state of modern consciousness, the personal spirit of Mr. Littlepage is torn between two worlds and two cultural claims." Holland's final paragraph, a scholium "in which the words *success* and *failure* have the same pair of referents," will benumb all but the resolute logician.

Joan Curlee's "Ellen Glasgow's South" (*Ball State Teachers*

College Forum, Winter 1961–62) is a brief overall review of Glasgow's work with the emphasis on her interpretation of the South, Old and New. Dr. Curlee relies heavily on *A Certain Measure* and cites older critical opinions. R. H. Dillard in "The Writer's Best Solace: Textual Revisions in Ellen Glasgow's *The Past*" (*Studies in Bibliography,* 1966) assures us that Ellen Glasgow was the conscientious reviser she claimed to be. "The Past," the work Mr. Dillard considered, is her short story, not to be confused with "The Deep Past," the central section of *The Sheltered Life.* William F. Heald sees a number of Ellen Glasgow's "vividly realized minor characters" as grotesques. His "Ellen Glasgow and the Grotesque" (*Mississippi Quarterly,* Winter 1964–65) thus associates her with a host of latter-day European and Southern writers. This focusing on the incongruities of characters grows out of an author's "realization that man is both sublime and ridiculous, that man's life is both laughable and terrifying." Too bad, concludes Mr. Heald, that Ellen Glasgow's feeling for *bienséance* made her shrink from presenting "the violent and the extreme" in her larger portraits. K. A. Heineman, in "Ellen Glasgow: The Death of the Chivalrous Tradition" (*Forum,* 1967), postulates that Glasgow's upholding of the rights of women and the dignity of the common man helped to break the spell of the chivalrous tradition. Robert Hudspeth reexamines the contrasting points of view, youth and age, as a thematic device in "Point of View in Ellen Glasgow's *The Sheltered Life*" (*Thoth,* Spring 1963). Edgar E. MacDonald's "Glasgow and James: On the Techniques of the Novel" (*Stylus* [Randolph-Macon College], Fall 1965) redefines Glasgow's *romantic-realistic* position in relation to other writers and places her close to Henry James in literary philosophy. A number of analogous passages from *A Certain Measure* and *The Art of the Novel* are juxtaposed. Nancy Minter McCollum skims over several analogous points in "Glasgow's and Cabell's Comedies of Virginia" (*Georgia Review,* Summer 1964). Both authors wrote "of the prolonged worship of the chivalric tradition during the late nineteenth century and early twentieth century in Virginia," Glasgow sprinkling salt, Cabell sugar. They share an "inherited sense of delicacy." While Glasgow's optimism is restricted, Cabell's gaiety is only the surface of his pessimism. Styles differ greatly, Cabell's "mannered, high-flown, irreverent, flamboyant, iconoclastic," Glasgow's "logical, restrained, catholic.

Yet the end result for both is poetic prose of a pure and controlled nature." J. J. Murphy's theme in "Marriage and Desire in Ellen Glasgow's *They Stooped to Folly*" (*Descant* [Texas Christian], Fall 1965) is that in this work Ellen Glasgow embraced the Victorian concept of mutual responsibility in marriage. Victorian?

Blair Rouse, the most dedicated of all Glasgow scholars, has devoted some thirty-five years to championing her work and defending her honor against critical onslaughts. His earlier commentaries are incorporated in his *Ellen Glasgow*, reviewed above, in Section V. 2, but two recent articles attest to his continuing zeal. In "Ellen Glasgow: The Novelist in America" (*The Cabellian*, Autumn 1971), he takes us on a leisurely consideration of the role of the professional novelist in America from Cooper to Faulkner and treats more particularly Ellen Glasgow's search for "an intelligent recognition from critics and readers whom she could respect." The true artist is one who treats "experience" as "an illumination of life," and this was ever Glasgow's goal. In "Ellen Glasgow: Manners and Art" (*The Cabellian*, Spring 1972), Rouse reviews the most serious critical objections to her work, acknowledging that her faults as a novelist—oversimplification, a reliance on Victorian serial techniques, a stubborn adherence to intuition for characterization—do indeed exist. Then he asks: "What, on the other hand, were her achievements?" The answer: "In her nineteen novels Ellen Glasgow created complex patterns which enable one to understand more clearly the meaning of life during the past century." Rouse proceeds to develop the positive characteristics inherent in her work and concludes that "Ellen Glasgow, like other American and European novelists of our time, faced the problem of writing fiction that would be serious and intelligent as well as affirmative in statement yet would be neither oversimplified nor ambiguous." Ironically, as her champion points our perceptively, she occasionally "found her answer in the affirmation of a tragic character—in tragic meanings."

5. Graduate Studies

Interest in Ellen Glasgow on the graduate level continues to grow, reflecting, in part, the increased emphasis on Southern literature in American literary studies. Even more, the titles of recent dissertations suggest that in a world of fluctuating values the questing student has turned instinctively to a writer whose career embodied a life-long, tortured search for sustaining values. The Kelly Bibliography lists sixteen dissertations, the earliest by Blair Rouse (1942). At least three doctoral studies preceded, and some twenty-one more have been completed since the Kelly listing.

Brie, Friedrich. "Ellen Glasgow." Universität Freiburg, 1931.

Harrison, Marion Clifford. "Social Types in Southern Prose Fiction." Michigan, 1931.

Mayo, Betsy Burke. "The Virginia Woman of the New South as Shown in the Novels of Ellen Glasgow." Southern Methodist University, 1941.

Rouse, H. Blair. "Studies in the Works of Ellen Glasgow." Illinois, 1942.

Cater, Althea. "Social Attitudes in Five Contemporary Southern Novelists: Erskine Caldwell, William Faulkner, Ellen Glasgow, Caroline Gordon, and T. S. Stribling." Michigan, 1946.

Jessup, Josephine L. "The Fate of Our Feminists: Edith Wharton, Ellen Glasgow, and Willa Cather." Vanderbilt, 1948.

Haarmann, Eva Marie. "Die Charakterisierung in Ellen Glasgow's 'Novels of the Country and Novels of the City'" [title as given by Kelly]; "Die Soziale und Politische Geschichte Virginians in den Romanen der Ellen Glasgow" [title as given by Parent], Vienna, 1951.

Kreider, Thomas M. "Ellen Glasgow: Southern Opponent to the Philistine." Cincinnati, 1952.

Nilon, Charles. "The Treatment of Negro Characters by Representative American Novelists: Cooper, Melville, Tourgee, Glasgow, Faulkner." Wisconsin, 1952.

Thomas, J. Josef. "Ellen Glasgow: Ein Beitrag zum Studium des Traditionalismus in der amerikanischen erzählenden Literatur des 20. Jahrhunderts." Cologne, 1952.

Wehmeier, Helga. "Die Widerspiegelung und Entwicklung erd ökonomischen und geistigen Struktur des amerikanischen Staates Virginia von 1850 bis 1930 in den Romanen von Ellen Glasgow." Berlin, Humbolt, 1952.

Meyer, Edgar. "The Art of Ellen Glasgow." Denver, 1955.

Becker, Allen. "Ellen Glasgow: Her Novels and Their Place in the Development of Southern Fiction." Johns Hopkins, 1956.

Briney, Martha M. "Ellen Glasgow: Social Critic." Michigan State, 1956.

Hierth, Harrison. "Ellen Glasgow's Ideal of the Lady with Some Contrasts in Sidney Lanier, George W. Cable, and Mark Twain." Wisconsin, 1956.

Kelly, William W. "Struggle for Recognition: A Study of the Literary Reputation of Ellen Glasgow." Duke, 1957.

Moake, Frank B. "The Problems of Characterization in the Novels of Ellen Glasgow." Illinois, 1957.

Patterson, Daniel W. "Ellen Glasgow's Use of Virginia History." North Carolina, 1959.

Edwards, Herbert W. "A Study of Values in Selected Published Prose of Ellen Glasgow." New York University, 1960.

Parent, Monique. "Ellen Glasgow: Romancière." Paris, 1960.

Richards, Marion Kazmann. "The Development of Ellen Glasgow as a Novelist." Columbia, 1961.

Santas, Joan Foster. "Ellen Glasgow's American Dream." Cornell, 1963.

White, James Edward, Jr. "Symbols in the Novels of Ellen Glasgow," Boston U., 1964.

Gore, Luther Y. "Ellen Glasgow's *Beyond Defeat,* A Critical Edition: Volume One, Editor's Introduction; Volume Two, The Text of *Beyond Defeat*." Virginia, 1964.

Bressler, Maybelle Jean. "A Critical Study of the Published Novels of Ellen Glasgow." Nebraska, 1965.

Dillard, R. H. W. "Pragmatic Realism: A Biography of Ellen Glasgow's Novels." Virginia, 1965.

Raper, Julius R., Jr. "Ellen Glasgow and Darwinism, 1873–1906." Northwestern, 1966.

Mendoza, Helen N. "The Past in Ellen Glasgow." Minnesota, 1966.

Bates, Richard D. "Changing View: A Study of Ellen Glasgow's Fluctuating Social Philosophy." South Carolina, 1966.

Dunn, Norma E. "Ellen Glasgow's Search for Truth." Pennsylvania, 1968.

Gatlin, Judith T. "Ellen Glasgow's Artistry." Iowa, 1969.

Sharma, O. P. "Feminist Image in the Novels of Ellen Glasgow: The Early Phase." *Research Bulletin* (Arts), Punjab U., Chandigarh, 1969.

Murphy, Denis Michael. "Vein of Ambivalence: Structure, Stylistic, and Personal Dualisms in Ellen Glasgow's Major Novels." Princeton, 1969.

Kish, Dorothy. "'An Immortal Part, In This Place'—Setting in Ellen Glasgow's Novels." Pittsburgh, 1970.

Godbold, Edward Stanly, Jr. "Ellen Glasgow and the Woman Within." Duke, 1970.

Hewitt, Rosalie. "Aristocracy and the Modern American Novel of Manners: Edith Wharton, F. Scott Fitzgerald, Ellen Glasgow and James Gould Cozzens." Purdue, 1970.

Hughes, Nina Edwards. "Ellen Glasgow and the 'Literature of Place.'" Columbia, 1970.

Beckham, Beverly Spears. "The Satire of Ellen Glasgow." Georgia, 1972.

Scura, Dorothy McInnis. "Ellen Glasgow and James Branch Cabell: The Record of a Literary Friendship." North Carolina, 1973.

Allsup, Judith L. "Feminism in the Novels of Ellen Glasgow." Southern Illinois, 1973.

6. Summary Observations

After gorging at the banquet of Glasgow criticism, this reader still hungers for the definitive statements concerning the woman, the social historian, the novelist. The complexity of the woman, a willful artistic ego in conflict with her environment, has been dealt with, but not yet in terms that reveal the person behind the persona. At one extreme in the studies, she is the wax mannequin smiling stoically beyond the uncomprehending bourgeoisie; at the other, she is the garishly dressed, overpainted neurotic who provokes stares from the proletariat. Her role as social historian, as J. Donald Adams suggested rather early, has probably been overemphasized. She wrote of her time and place, truthfully no doubt, for the past was part of the present in Virginia, but her theme was rather of the human heart circumscribed by existential concepts. There is no escaping the fact, however, that she assured the current interest in her career in announcing that she had early conceived of "a social history of Virginia" in the *comédie humaine* tradition, thereby becoming, as R. C. Wood observed, "a favorite of American literary historians forever looking for historical patterns, and of regionalists whose middling tendency [is] to isolate the local nature at the expense of the human" (review of *The Letters of Ellen Glasgow,* in Randolph-Macon College *Bulletin*, Sept. 1958). As a novelist, she built her books in an isolation that appears the norm for literary genius in America, but that she adhered to a classic English concept, a Hardy "tradition," is undeniable. *Barren Ground* and *The Sheltered Life* recount the inevitable defeat of the romantic in a material world as well as the inevitable seduction of the realist by romantic ideals. But, again to quote Professor Wood, "The formalist critics who dominate the serious journals today cannot get past her inconsistencies of tone, her pages of sentiment, her structural mistakes." Perhaps, as J. R. Raper suggests, when American criticism gives over its preoccupation with the fiction of sensation and returns to an appreciation of novels of vision, Ellen Glasgow's gifts as a novelist will rise in esteem.

VI. *A Biographical Appendix*

In some biographical references and on many cards in the card index files of most libraries, one finds Ellen Glasgow's birth year still given as 1874. *Who Was Who* gives that date, doubtless following the data given in previous editions of *Who's Who*. Most scholars, however, record her birth date as April 22, 1873, following her lead in *The Woman Within:*

There has always been a confusion, or simple inaccuracy concerning the hour and date of my birth. All through my childhood Mother celebrated my birthday on the 22nd of April. I still accept her authority, though I discovered a few years ago, when we consulted the old family Bible, which is now in the possession of my sister,

Rebe Tutwiler, that Father had recorded the unhappy event as occurring on April 21st. As I came into the world precisely at four o'clock in the morning, by the testimony of all concerned, I suppose Father had considered it was still night, while Mother, a more sanguine spirit, who welcomed ten children with joy, had dreamed of the more confident morning.

But we made still another discovery in this Bible adventure. It appeared, by the record in faded ink, that I was born, not in 1874, as I had always assumed, but in 1873. Many years ago, in filling in a slip for *Who's Who*, my sister Cary must have, inadvertently, counted back from January, instead of April. As long as she lived with me, she looked after all records, business or literary, and so much time had passed when Rebe and I chanced, by accident, upon the mistake that the attempt to track down so slight an inaccuracy appeared trivial. But, after this, I did not give the date of birth, except when I needed it for passports, or for business records, where I gave it as April 22, 1873. For I still believe that Mother was right and that I came in the morning. Not that it matters (pp. 5-6).

Both city and state vital records list the births of Ellen Glasgow's brothers and sisters but perversely do not have hers recorded. Her death certificate, filled out by her nurse-companion, Anne Virginia Bennett, gives her dates as April 22, 1874–November 21, 1945. Her tombstone in Hollywood Cemetery also records these years. The 1880 federal census, however, for the household of F. T. Glasgow, East Cary Street, Richmond, lists her age as seven, making her born in 1873. Although census records are not always accurate, the ages of the other Glasgow children in the 1880 Census are given precisely as recorded elsewhere; there is no valid reason to believe that an error might have been made solely in her case. Ellen Glasgow was clearly born in 1873, as she most probably knew all along.

Another biographical matter concerning Miss Glasgow centers on the elusive "Gerald B." Several of the book-length studies devoted to her speculate on the identity of "Gerald B.," the lover who figures in *The Woman Within*. Most often a physician is suspected, following the hint given by Dr. Joseph Collins, New York physician and amateur critic. Rather remarkably, no one has speculated about a literary man; although Ellen Glasgow consulted a number of medical men in New York during her early visits, she also met socially a number of literary personages.

Burton Rascoe, essentially a newspaper reporter, albeit a literary one, wrote James Branch Cabell a long letter upon reading Cabell's just-published *As I Remember It* in 1955. Desiring to review it, he informed Cabell, he had telephoned Irita Van Doren, book-editor at that time of the New York *Herald-Tribune* and one of Ellen Glasgow's literary executors. After writing enthusiastically of *As I Remember It*, he continued:

My distaste for the *Herald-Tribune* has been as acute as my distaste for the *Times, Post* and *Saturday Review* for a very long time and my relations with Irita, which, though cordial enough on the rare occasions I have seen her in these fifteen years, have been nonexistent. But I shoved pride, suffering from several rebuffs, into my pocket and phoned her. She said she had already assigned the book for review but volunteered her own opinion of the book. She said the portions about "Percie" (although I did not know she was on such intimate terms with Mrs. Cabell as to use that name, which was unknown to me until I encountered it in *As I Remembered It*) but that she "could strangle James with my bare hands for what he did to Ellen" [*sic*].

I said I thought the chapter on Miss Glasgow was an affectionate and admiring tribute and that you had not told anything about her peculiarities of temperament (such as her biting criticism of all other living novelists) that I had not experienced from Miss Glasgow's own lips. But Irita (as I have long called her) insisted that you had depicted Miss Glasgow as "a mean and terrible bitch." To which I could only reply that I did not think that such was your intention and that it was not what I got out of the portrait.

Which reminds me that, for an inveterate habit of trying not to hear any tales or rumors about the private lives of persons I have known, liked or admired, and of, having heard something, refraining from repeating it to others, I now put to paper something that Irita told me about "Ellen" which I have never before repeated to anybody, not even to Hazel—namely, that Ellen loathed and abominated her father because she learned after she was grown up that she had a Negro half-sister and that her father had, far from keeping knowledge of his Negro mistress from her mother, had taunted her with the fact.

Irita told this unguardedly to a group in the Herald-Tribune offices, which included Isabel Paterson, two stenographers, Belle Rosenbaum and myself. I just dropped in, so I do not know what all she had revealed about the private life of Miss Glasgow before I came in; but she went on to tell that Ellen had been deeply in love with Hewitt Howland, editor for her publisher, Bobbs-Merrill, and had been Howland's mistress, since Howland was married and not free to marry her. I had known Howland and Mrs. Howland in Chicago and later in New York and I had never known anything about this matter from anybody hitherto. If Irita is so anxious to preserve the memory of Miss Glasgow as wholly free of any fault or human error, why should she so freely disclose information about Miss Glasgow which she could only have gotten from very confidential sources?

. . . How did Irita happen to be chosen by Miss Glasgow to be Miss Glasgow's literary executor and (seemingly) the only heir to any proprietary interest in Miss Glasgow's fame? Irita has no literary judgment whatever. To the best of my knowledge, she never wrote anything about Miss Glasgow or ever bothered to read any of her books. That is, until about the time of the publication of Miss Glasgow's autobiographical book, which Irita now tells me she edited in manuscript.

Rascoe then went on to reminisce about his meetings with Ellen Glasgow in an uncomplimentary way and finally returned to the question asked earlier:

But how and why did Irita come so prominently into the Glasgow picture? I ask *why* because I have never known Irita to do anything, show any courtesy, make any effort to be nice, without a definite and careful fore-calculation as to just what extent it would be of material benefit to her in money, prestige, or power. Frankly, I can't see what she figured to get out of being Miss Glasgow's literary executor, because it involves a tedious amount of work with no rewards that I can imagine.[8]

Rascoe was in error in referring to Bobbs-Merrill as Ellen Glasgow's publisher, but he appears factual otherwise. Hewitt Hanson Howland was born in Indianapolis, October 8, 1863, and was therefore ten years older than Ellen Glasgow. He became an advisory editor for the Bobbs-Merrill Company in 1900, about the time that Ellen Glasgow met "Gerald B." In a book of quotations which Ellen Glasgow cherished, the initials "H. H." appear along with autographs of her mother and two of her sisters.[9] Hewitt Howland married Manie Cobb, sister of Irvin S. Cobb. In 1932,

---

[8]This letter is in the Cabell Collection and is cited with the kind permission of Edmund Berkeley, Jr., Curator of Manuscripts, University of Virginia Library.

[9]Carrington Cabell Tutwiler, Jr., *A Catalogue of the Library of Ellen Glasgow* (Charlottesville: University of Virginia Press, 1967), p. 18.285.

after reading *The Sheltered Life* "at one sitting," Manie Howland
wrote Ellen Glasgow a laudatory letter. She closed with

I can't tell you how enormously I admire you. I loved you from
the minute I met you. Since I know how genuinely you abhor all
cruelty and unnecessary suffering it gives a new meaning to what
you write and makes me ever more your grateful

Manie Howland[10]

Hewitt Howland's career as an editor and friend to numerous
writers was a distinguished one. He died May 10, 1944, leaving no
heirs.

During her reign as the Lady of Shalott in an island called
Richmond, Ellen Glasgow was ambivalent in her attitudes: she
both did and did not want to be rescued from her four gray walls.
There are even Richmonders (*anno Domini* 1974) who suggest
that, despite the lady's passionate revelations and those letters in
the University of Virginia Library, she died inviolate. Throughout
her life she sought someone to repose her trust in, someone
stronger than herself. But God and man did not measure up to
her standards of either justice or fidelity. She fulfilled herself in
her work, and in *The Sheltered Life* she shaped her loneliness, her
intelligence and compassion, into a timeless offering for all who
hunger for meaningful lives.

[10]This letter is filed under the name *Marie* Howland in the Glasgow Papers, but the
signature is clearly *Manie*. It is cited with the kind permission of Edmund Berkeley, Jr.,
Curator of Manuscripts, University of Virginia.

Index

Index

Adams, Henry, 7
Adams, J. Donald, 109, 200, 219
Adams, Richard P., 198
Aiken, Conrad, 48, 52
Aldrich, Thomas Bailey, 77
Allen, James Lane, 48, 76
Allsup, Judith L., 219
Anderson, Henry, 108, 173, 194, 197
Anderson, James, 32
Anderson, Sherwood, 12, 47, 53, 54, 55, 56, 59, 60, 62, 63
Anthony, Katharine, 53
Arnavon, Cyrille, 14
Arnold, Matthew, 21
Atherton, Gertrude, 13
Auchincloss, Louis, 104, 113, 123, 202–3
Austen, Jane, 18, 19, 208

Baird, Newton, 214
Balch, Emily Clark, 46, 47, 49, 53, 54, 55, 59–60
Balzac, Honoré de, 12, 67, 71
Barr, Stringfellow, 47, 51, 54, 60
Baskin, L., 168
Bates, Richard D., 218
Beard, Mary, 170
Beatty, Richmond Croom, 14
Beauvoir, Simone de, 170
Becker, Allen W., 213-14, 218
Becker, Carl, 7
Beckham, Beverly Spears, 219
Bell, Clive, 157-62
Bennett, Anne Virginia, 32, 175, 198, 221
Berkeley, Edmund, Jr., 223, 224
Berthoff, Warner, 210
Bird, Caroline, 170
Bishop, John Peale, 53, 54
Blake, William, 17
Blanck, Jacob, 193
Blotner, Joseph, 52

Bondurant, Agnes M., 26
Bowers, Fredson, 192
Bowie, Elizabeth Branch, 37
Bowie, Walter Russell, 39
Boyd, James, 48, 52, 53, 54, 60
Bradford, Roark, 51
Branch, Christopher, 39
Branch, James Read, 35, 41
Branch, John Patteson, 39
Branch, Martha Louise Patteson, 36
Branch, Thomas, 35, 39, 42
Breasted, James Henry, 153
Bressler, Maybelle Jean, 218
Brickell, Herschel, 48, 49, 53
Brie, Friedrich, 217
Briney, Martha M., 218
Brooks, Van Wyck, 14, 152-53, 206
Browning, Robert, 8
Bryan, William Jennings, 9–10, 74–75
Burt, Katherine Newlin, 52
Burt, Struthers, 52-53
Byron, George Gordon, Lord, 8, 13

Cabell, Anne Harris Branch, 27, 36–37, 39, 40–42
Cabell, Ballard Hartwell, 42-43
Cabell, James Branch, 2, 4, 11, 25-45, 46, 48, 49, 50, 51, 52, 53–54, 55–56, 57, 63, 64, 67, 109, 175, 195, 197, 198, 200, 201, 204, 205, 207, 208, 209, 212, 213, 215, 219, 222
Cabell, Margaret Freeman, 44, 47
Cabell, Maude Morgan, 3
Cabell, Priscilla Bradley, 42–43, 222
Cabell, Robert Gamble, Jr., 36–37, 39, 40
Cabell, Robert G., III, 3
Cable, George Washington, 28, 207, 218
Caine, Hall, 8, 76
Caldwell, Erskine, 2, 4, 15, 217
Calverton, V. F., 10
Campbell, Killis, 9

Canby, Henry Seidel, 14–15, 164, 200
Canby, Marion Gause, 164
Caperton, Helena LeFroy, 29
Carlyle, Thomas, 109
Casals, Pablo, 158
Cater, Althea, 217
Cather, Willa, 3, 13, 44, 50, 167, 210, 217
Chapman, Mary, 52–53
Chapman, Stanton, 52–53
Chase, Richard, 28
Chaucer, Geoffrey, 114
Chekhov, Anton, 204
Clark, Emily. *See* Balch, Emily Clark
Clark, Kenneth, 132–33
Cobb, Irvin S., 51, 223
Collins, Joseph, 221
Collins, Wilkie, 78
Colum, Padraic, 44
Colvert, James B., 196
Commager, Henry Steele, 204
Comstock, Anthony, 75
Conrad, Joseph, 77
Cooke, John Esten, 1, 26, 44
Cooper, James Fenimore, 18, 28, 216, 217
Copenhaver, Eleanor, 47
Copenhaver, Laura Lou, 47, 55
Corelli, Marie, 75
Cowley, Malcolm, 1, 12
Cozzens, James Gould, 219
Craddock, Charles Egbert, 48
Cunliffe, Marcus, 14
Curlee, Joan, 214–15

D'Annunzio, Gabriele, 75
Darrow, Clarence, 10
Darwin, Charles, 20, 108, 169
Davidson, Donald, 46, 47, 52, 54, 55, 59, 60–61
Davidson, Mrs. Donald, 47
Davis, Bette, 150
Davis, Richard Harding, 76
Day, Douglas, 196
Dickens, Charles, 8, 17, 18, 19–20, 26
Dillard, R. H. W., 215, 218
Dodd, William E., 53, 55
Dostoevsky, Feodor Mikhailovich, 20, 60
Dreiser, Theodore, 16, 44, 83, 182
Duke, Carrie Coleman, 31–32

Duke, James Buchanan, 54
Dumas, Alexandre, 72
du Maurier, George, 71
Dunn, Norma E., 219

Edward VII, 30
Edwards, Herbert W., 218
Edwards, L. R., 168
Egly, William H., 191
Einstein, Albert, 158
Eliot, George, 17, 78, 168
Eliot, T. S., 121–22, 214
Elizabeth I, 117
Emerson, Ralph Waldo, 11, 17
England, Kenneth M., 211
Ewing, Majl, 13–14, 205

Fadiman, Clifton, 155
Faulkner, William, 1, 2, 4, 12, 14, 17, 20, 44, 46, 52, 54, 62–63, 106, 158, 185, 208, 216, 217
Fielding, Henry, 17
Fiske, John, 76–77
Fitzgerald, F. Scott, 68, 219
Flaubert, Gustave, 11
Fletcher, John Gould, 56
Fletcher, Mrs. John Gould, 47
Forbes, Miss, 147
Frazee, Monique Parent, 197–99, 202, 218
Frederic, Harold, 74
Frederick, William, 47
Freeman, Douglas Southall, 142
Freud, Sigmund, 169
Friedan, Betty, 170
Fuller, Margaret, 9

Gandhi, Indira, 8
Gardiner, Harold, 205
Gatlin, Judith T., 219
Gay, Ruth, 169
Geismar, Maxwell, 16, 204, 206–7
George, Henry, 108
Gibbon, Edward, 7
Gileo, Barbara, 203, 212
Gissing, George, 71
Gitlin, Paul, 47
Glasgow, Arthur, 29
Glasgow, Ellen: works—*The Ancient Law*, 186; *Barren Ground*, 7, 11, 13, 14,

Glasgow, Ellen (*cont.*)

29, 67, 81, 82, 84, 109-11, 113, 119, 121, 134, 163-64, 165, 166, 175, 182, 193, 203, 204, 205, 210, 213, 220; *The Battle-Ground,* 27, 33, 78, 82-83, 186, 192, 193, 214; *Beyond Defeat,* 67, 149, 151, 165, 194-95, 213, 218; *The Builders,* 33, 109, 134, 186; *A Certain Measure,* 12, 32, 33, 70, 81, 111, 116, 120, 136, 139, 145, 148, 153-54, 163, 171, 176, 179, 182, 185, 187, 193, 201, 203, 212, 215; *The Deliverance,* 26, 33, 79, 82-90, 134, 135-38, 159, 160, 174, 212-13; *The Descendant,* 1, 2, 11, 12, 67, 68-81, 172, 174, 180, 184, 192, 213; *The Freeman and Other Poems,* 193; *In This Our Life,* 1, 2, 33, 67, 79, 81, 84, 111, 123, 134, 148-55, 159, 162-63, 165, 178, 185, 193, 197, 211, 214; *Life and Gabriella,* 33-34, 67, 77, 83, 109, 186, 213; *The Miller of Old Church,* 26, 78, 82-84, 90-97, 165, 174, 207; *One Man in His Time,* 14, 28, 33, 109, 163, 209; *Phases of an Inferior Planet,* 11, 20, 67, 68, 69, 71, 73-74, 75, 77-81; *The Romance of a Plain Man,* 33, 83, 91, 105, 178, 179, 213; *The Romantic Comedians,* 28, 33, 67, 82, 84, 98, 108-28, 163, 165, 174, 205; *The Shadowy Third,* 67, 186; *The Sheltered Life,* 20, 30-31, 33, 53, 67, 70, 78, 81, 82, 84, 107, 108-28, 134, 136, 141-45, 158-59, 163, 165-66, 195, 204, 213, 214, 215, 220, 224; *They Stooped to Folly,* 28, 33, 67, 79, 81, 82, 84, 98, 107, 108-28, 134, 138-41, 163, 165, 174, 183, 214, 216; *Vein of Iron,* 33, 67, 84, 111, 134, 136, 145-48, 150, 159, 163, 182-83, 186, 193, 205, 213; *Virginia,* 11, 27, 82-84, 97-107, 135, 159, 160, 163, 165, 174, 175-76, 204, 205, 213; *The Voice of the People,* 26, 28, 33, 67, 82, 84, 91, 134-35, 193, 211, 213, 214; *The Wheel of Life,* 67, 68, 171, 186, 205, 207; *The Woman Within,* 29, 108, 109, 110, 140, 164-65, 172, 174, 178, 179, 183, 197, 202, 203, 220-21

Glasgow, F. T., 221
Glasgow, Frank, 170
Glenn, Garrard W., 47, 48
Glenn, Mrs. Garrard W., 48
Glenn, Isa, 47, 48, 49-50, 53
Godbold, E. Stanley, Jr., 195, 199-200, 201, 204, 219
Godshalk, William Leigh, 211
Goethe, Johann Wolfgang von, 19, 20
Gordon, Caroline, 52, 217
Gore, Luther Y., 194-95, 218
Gornick, Vivian, 170
Gray, Thomas, 15
Green, Paul, 48, 50, 52, 54-55, 61, 63, 64
Greer, Germaine, 170

Haarmann, Eva Marie, 217
Hahn, Emily, 11
Halberstam, David, 7
Hardy, John Edward, 15-16, 207
Hardy, Thomas, 14, 15, 71, 78, 90, 220
Harraden, Beatrice, 76
Harrison, Marion Clifford, 217
Hawthorne, Nathaniel, 19, 20
Heald, William F., 215
Heath, M., 168
Hegel, Georg Wilhelm Friedrich, 20
Heineman, K. A., 215
Hemingway, Ernest, 68
Henderson, Archibald, 46, 47, 50, 52, 62, 64
Henderson, Mrs. Archibald, 47
Herodotus, 7
Hewitt, Rosalie, 219
Heyward, Dorothy, 52
Heyward, Du Bose, 46, 47, 48, 50, 52, 60, 62, 64
Hicks, Granville, 13
Hierth, Harrison, 218
Hoffman, Frederick J., 205
Holland, Robert, 122, 214
Holman, C. Hugh, 4, 202, 208-9
Howells, William Dean, 207, 210
Howland, Hewitt Hanson, 222-24
Howland, Manie Cobb, 223-24
Hubbell, Jay B., 207-9

Hudspeth, Robert, 215
Hughes, Nina Edwards, 219
Hugo, Victor, 71
Hunt, Morton, 172-73
Huntington, Ellsworth, 132

Ibsen, Henrik, 72-73, 78

Jacobs, Robert D., 14, 15, 207
James, Henry, 25-26, 43-44, 77, 78, 123, 207, 215
James, William, 77
Jefferson, Thomas, 7, 9, 60, 61
Jessup, Josephine Lurie, 167, 205, 217
Johnson, Merle D., 193
Johnston, Annie Fellows, 76
Johnston, Mary, 15, 31, 46, 53, 179, 203
Jones, Bessie Zeban, 147, 152
Jones, Howard Mumford, 47, 48, 49, 56-57, 195, 200, 210

Kazin, Alfred, 10, 204
Keats, John, 17
Kelly, William W., 3, 75, 191-93, 194, 195, 197, 198, 201, 212, 217, 218
Kerr, Walter, 127
Kipling, Rudyard, 76
Kish, Dorothy, 219
Knapp, Samuel, 8, 10
Kraditor, Aileen, 170
Kreider, Thomas M., 217

Landor, Walter Savage, 8, 17
Lanier, Sidney, 218
Lee, Lawrence, 53
Lee, Robert E., 142
Levitas, Gloria, 170
Lewis, R. W. B., 9
Lewisohn, Ludwig, 10, 13
Lubbock, Percy, 78
Lynen, John F., 12
Lytle, Andrew Nelson, 53

Macauley, Thomas Babington, 7-8
McCollum, Nancy Minter, 215-16
McCormack, Walter, 170-71
McCullers, Carson, 1
MacDonald, Edgar E., 3, 37, 201, 212, 215

McDowell, Frederick P. W., 63, 193, 195, 198, 200, 201-2, 212-13
McKinley, William, 10, 74
Macy, John, 9, 11
Malraux, André, 20
Marcosson, Isaac F., 208
Marshall, John, 9
Masefield, John, 8
Matthiessen, F. O., 9
Maupassant, Guy de, 12, 75
Mayo, Betsy Burke, 217
Mead, Margaret, 170, 173
Meeker, Richard, 193-94
Melville, Herman, 9, 13, 217
Mencken, H. L., 47, 48, 51-52
Mencken, Sara Haardt, 52
Mendoze, Helen N., 218
Meredith, George, 18, 81
Meyer, Edgar, 218
Mill, John Stuart, 20, 169
Millett, Kate, 170
Moake, Frank B., 218
Moncure, Gabriella Brooke, 38
Moncure, George V., 35
Monroe, Nellie Elizabeth, 205-6, 212
Montague, Margaret Prescott, 51
Moran, Barbara K., 170
Morgan, H. Wayne, 210
Morley, Frank, 153
Morris, Wright, 12
Morrison, Theodore, 114
Mumford, Lewis, 158
Mumford, Mary Branch, 31, 39
Munson, Gorham B., 11
Murphy, Denis Michael, 219
Murphy, J. J., 216
Myers, E. T. D., 37

Nietzsche, Friedrich Wilhelm, 108
Nilon, Charles, 217
Nin, Anaïs, 186

Page, Thomas Nelson, 1, 44, 48, 213
Page, Walter Hines, 195, 208
Paradise, Frank, 193
Parent, Monique. *See* Frazee, Monique Parent
Parkman, Francis, 7
Parrington, Vernon L., 10, 11
Parry, Albert, 11

Paterson, Isabel, 222
Patterson, Daniel W., 212, 218
Patteson, Dr., 36
Peterkin, Julia, 51
Phelps, Elizabeth Stuart, 168
Phillips, U. B., 53
Picasso, Pablo, 158
Pinckney, Josephine, 46, 47, 52, 61-62
Poe, Edgar Allan, 9, 99, 208
Poirier, Richard, 12
Pratt, Agnes Rothery, 53
Prior, Mrs. Granville T., 64
Puccini, Giacomo, 71

Quesenbery, W. D., Jr., 191

Rahv, Philip, 204
Raimond, C. E., 76
Ransom, John Crowe, 50
Raper, Julius R., Jr., 90, 199, 203, 218, 220
Rascoe, Burton, 51, 222-23
Rawlings, Marjorie Kinnan, 199
Reese, Lizette Woodworth, 51
Reynolds, Paul Revere, 196
Rice, Alice Hegan, 46, 52
Rice, Cale Young, 52, 54
Richards, Marion Kazmann, 203-4, 218
Richardson, Samuel, 12, 17
Richmond, George H., 75
Ritchie, Thomas, 26-27
Robbins, Elizabeth, 76
Roberts, Elizabeth Madox, 51
Rosenbaum, Belle, 222
Rouse, Blair, 68, 108, 144, 152, 196, 197, 198, 200, 202, 203, 206, 216, 217
Royce, Josiah, 76
Rubin, Louis D., Jr., 14, 15, 112-13, 196, 207, 209-10
Russell, Bertrand, 158

Sand, George, 168
Santas, Joan Foster, 194, 203, 218
Santayana, George, 158
Sass, Herbert Ravenal, 51
Saxton, Eugene F., 196
Saxton, Martha, 196
Schopenhauer, Arthur, 19, 72, 108
Schweitzer, Albert, 158

Scott, Frederic R., 37
Scott, Frederic William, 37, 38
Scott, John Walker, 36, 37, 39
Scott, Sarah Frances Branch, 37
Scura, Dorothy McInnis, 219
Seymour-Smith, Martin, 114-15
Shakespeare, William, 19
Sharma, O. P., 219
Shaw, George Bernard, 62, 77, 106
Sheldon, Charles M., 76
Sherman, Stuart Pratt, 200
Sienkiewicz, Henryk, 76
Simonini, R. C., Jr., 208
Sinclair, May, 179
Sinclair, Upton, 196
Smith, C. Alphonso, 11
Smith, Sydney, 10
Sophocles, 18, 20
Spalding, Bishop, 77
Spencer, Herbert, 18, 20, 72
Spiller, Robert E., 9, 14, 210-11
Stallings, Laurence, 49
Stallings, Helen Poteat (Mrs. Laurence Stallings), 53
Stansell, Christine, 168
Steele, Oliver L., 191-93, 212
Stein, Gertrude, 196, 212
Stovall, Floyd, 13
Strauss, Richard, 127
Stribling, T. S., 51, 217

Tacitus, Cornelius, 7
Tate, Allen, 47, 52, 54, 55, 59, 60, 61, 63, 120, 122, 144
Taylor, Walter Fuller, 13
Tennyson, Alfred Lord, 75
Thackeray, William Makepeace, 8, 17, 26, 113
Thomas, J. Josef, 217
Thoreau, Henry David, 154
Thorp, Willard, 210
Toomer, Jean, 11
Tourgée, Albian W., 217
Trent, William Porterfield, 9
Trilling, Lionel, 10
Trine, Ralph Waldo, 76
Trollope, Anthony, 8
Troubetzkoy, Amélie Rives, 47, 53, 60
Troubetzkoy, Pierre, 47, 60
Turgenev, Ivan Sergeevich, 19

Tuttleton, James W., 16
Tutwiler, Cabell C., 35
Tutwiler, Carrington Cabell, Jr., 200–201, 223
Tutwiler, Rebe Glasgow, 35, 198, 220–21
Twain, Mark, 218
Tyler, Moses Coit, 8

Updike, John, 16

Valentine, Lila Meade, 31
Van Doren, Carl, 200
Van Doren, Irita, 53, 198, 222–23
Van Vechten, Carl, 200
Voltaire, 7

Wagenknecht, Edward, 206
Warren, Robert Penn, 4, 44, 209
Warton, Thomas, 8
Washington, George, 9
Wehmeier, Helga, 217
Wellford, Roberta, 198
Welsh, John R., 14, 210

Welty, Eudora, 1, 4, 158
Wendell, Barrett, 8–9, 10, 13
Wertenbaker, Charles, 196
West, Ray B., 12
Wharton, Edith, 13, 28, 167, 177, 210, 217, 219
White, James Edward, Jr., 218
Wilde, Oscar, 72, 73
Wilson, Augusta J. Evans, 17
Wilson, Edmund, 11–12
Wilson, James Southall, 13, 46, 47, 49, 50–51, 52, 53, 55, 56, 59, 60, 61, 62, 63, 64, 200, 205
Wilson, Woodrow, 10
Wolfe, Thomas, 2, 4, 12, 47, 50, 51, 56, 64, 113, 208
Wollstonecraft, Mary, 169
Wood, R. C., 220
Woodward, C. Vann, 4
Woolf, Virginia, 157
Wordsworth, William, 8

Young, Stark, 48, 50, 51, 59, 64, 147

Zola, Émile, 12, 18